Exclusionary Violence

Social History, Popular Culture, and Politics in Germany
Geoff Eley, Series Editor

(continued on last page)

Exclusionary Violence

Antisemitic Riots in Modern
German History

Edited by
Christhard Hoffmann,
Werner Bergmann, and
Helmut Walser Smith

Ann Arbor
THE UNIVERSITY OF MICHIGAN PRESS

Copyright © by the University of Michigan 2002
All rights reserved
Published in the United States of America by
The University of Michigan Press
Manufactured in the United States of America
⊗ Printed on acid-free paper

2005   2004   2003   2002   4   3   2   1

A CIP catalog record for this book is available from the British Library.

Library of Congress Cataloging-in-Publication Data

Exclusionary violence : antisemitic riots in modern German history / edited
    by Christhard Hoffmann, Werner Bergmann, and Helmut Walser Smith.
      p.   cm. — (Social history, popular culture, and politics in
    Germany)
      Includes bibliographical references (p.   ) and index.
      ISBN 0-472-09796-2 (cloth : alk. paper) — ISBN 0-472-06796-6
    (pbk. : alk. paper)
      1. Antisemitism—Germany.   2. Germany—Ethnic relations.
    3. Jews—Persecutions—Germany.   I. Hoffmann, Christhard, 1952–
    II. Bergmann, Werner, 1950–   III. Smith, Helmut Walser, 1962–   IV. Series.

    DS146.G4   E93   2002
    305.892'4043'09034—dc21   2001005532

Contents

Preface

This project began in September 1997 as a session of the twenty-first annual conference of the German Studies Association in Washington, D.C. Organized by Christhard Hoffmann, then DAAD Visiting Professor at the History Department of the University of California, Berkeley, the session brought together German and American scholars specializing in the history of antisemitic violence in modern Germany. Since then, the essays have been significantly revised, and new contributions have been added. The result is the first comprehensive work on antisemitic violence in modern Germany.

The majority of the authors either are or have been affiliated with the Zentrum für Antisemitismusforschung (Center for Research on Antisemitism) of the Technical University of Berlin. The Center has supported a great deal of the research for this volume, especially as part of the pioneering research project Antisemitism in German Popular Culture, 1815–1850, directed by Herbert A. Strauss, and as part of its ongoing research concentrations on the sociological theory of pogroms. We wish to thank the Center for providing the funds for the translation of those articles originally written in German. Miriamne Fields translated most of these contributions, and Christine Kulke (University of California, Berkeley) and Dirk Moses (University of Sydney) translated or edited individual articles. We would also like to thank Elisabeth Lindner of the Center's staff, who proofread parts of the manuscript and arranged for the illustrations.

We would like to express our gratitude to Geoff Eley for considering the manuscript as part of the Michigan series Social History, Popular Culture, and Politics in Germany and to the two anonymous readers at the University of Michigan Press for their helpful suggestions. Finally, we thank Liz Suhay of the University of Michigan Press for her work and encouragement, and Nancy Trotic for her careful copyediting, which significantly improved the final manuscript.

Introduction

Werner Bergmann, Christhard Hoffmann,
and Helmut Walser Smith

Pogrom is a Russian word that means "devastation." It also evokes anti-semitic violence—wanton, unorganized, and archaic. Historians of the modern period have come to associate this kind of violence with Russia, where, especially at the end of the long nineteenth century, bloody pogroms in Elizavetgrad in 1881, Kishinev in 1903, and the Pale of Settlement in 1905–6 cost untold lives and inaugurated great waves of Jewish exodus. In modern Germany, by contrast, this kind of violence seemed not as endemic. It had, however, been part and parcel of life in medieval Germany, a time when bloody anti-Jewish riots routinely punctuated a persecutory landscape. Accusations of ritual murder, charges of desecration of the Host, insinuations of poisoned wells causing the Black Death—all of this led to periodic and severe violence against Jews.[1] Being exclusionary, this violence significantly transformed the relation between groups that had previously coexisted. As in Russia in the nineteenth and early twentieth centuries, in medieval German cities and states violence led to the mass expulsion and exodus of Jews.

On the surface, modern Germany looked very different. In the course of the nineteenth century, Jewish emancipation occurred: gradual, imperfect, with fits and starts, but it occurred. So, too, did a reaction. A place tolerant in some ways, nineteenth-century Germany also emerged as the locus classicus of modern antisemitism. Based on racial theory rather than religious doctrine, this was the genus of antisemitism that—via a twisted road—led to the gas chambers and crematoriums of Auschwitz.

---

1. For an overview, see Mordechai Breuer, "The Jewish Middle Ages," in *German Jewish History in Modern Times,* edited by Michael A. Meyer (New York, 1996), 7–78.

To trace this twisted road, historians of modern Germany have largely focused on the trajectory of antisemitic ideas, connecting the extreme antisemitism of the Second Reich to the racist fantasies of the Third. Whether this extreme antisemitism existed on the fringe of society or enjoyed wide societal support remains an open question.[2] Yet historians of both dispositions draw a line connecting the antisemitic ideas of the nineteenth century to the genocidal violence of the twentieth century. But if the ideas were kith and kin, the resulting violence was not. Unlike the Russian pogroms, or the medieval riots, the Holocaust was methodical and organized. It aimed at the destruction of an entire people. It was driven by a powerful state. And it bore the mark of the modern.

The dichotomies drawn in this account are illuminating, but they are also too stark. Russia was not without a nationalist-inspired antisemitism, nor was it free from modern racism; and nineteenth-century Germany was not without significant violence. And as in the medieval period, this violence erupted with rhythmic regularity. Antisemitic violence of considerable moment occurred in Germany in 1819, 1830, 1848–49, 1881, and 1900. Not just the incidence of antisemitic violence, but also its place in a larger European history claims our attention. "In sum the pogroms in southern Russia in the early 1880s were the Hep! Hep! riots of Germany in 1819 writ very large," writes David Vital in his recently published *A People Apart: The Jews in Europe, 1789–1939.*[3] Like the Russian pogroms of the 1880s, the German riots of 1819 were modern riots, sparked not by the recrudescence of age-old antagonisms but rather by economic distress and by popular reactions to changing relations between Christians and Jews. Moreover, they were not local; the Hep Hep riots of 1819 constituted the first set of nationwide antisemitic riots since the Middle Ages. In this way, too, Germany proved a laboratory of a much more menacing modernity.

Germany, however, was not alone. Anti-Jewish riots also occurred in periods of political conflict and crisis in the Italian states during the course of Jewish emancipation and in the throes of the Revolution of 1848, in France at the time of the Dreyfus Affair, in Bohemia following an accusation of ritual murder in the town of Polná in 1899, in South Wales in 1911 following labor unrest in mines and railroads, in Poland in Lvov in 1929

---

2. On the history of antisemitism, the best short introduction is still Helmut Berding, *Moderner Antisemitismus in Deutschland* (Frankfurt/Main, 1988). For an excellent survey of recent literature, see Till van Rahden, "Ideologie und Gewalt: Neuerscheinungen über den Antisemitismus in der deutschen Geschichte des 19. und fruehen 20. Jahrhunderts," *Neue Politische Literatur* 41 (1996): 11–29. On questions of continuity, see the insightful, though by now nearly dated, remarks in Shulamit Volkov, "Kontinuität und Diskontinuität im deutschen Antisemitismus," *Vierteljahrshefte für Zeitgeschichte* 33 (1985): 221–43.

3. David Vital, *A People Apart: The Jews in Europe, 1789–1939* (New York, 1999), 188.

and in Kielce in 1946.[4] Beyond these incidents, there is also the wider context of religious antagonism culminating in violence, such as occurred, and continues to occur, between Protestants and Catholics in Northern Ireland, between Jews and Muslims in Algeria and Tunisia, and between Hindus and Muslims in India. There is, in addition, an overlapping context of ethnic violence. In the United States alone, there were numerous riots against Chinese immigrants in the nineteenth century: the Los Angeles Massacre of 1871, the Rock Springs Massacre in Wyoming in 1885, and the Seattle and Tacoma riots and expulsions of the same year.[5] In the first half of the twentieth century, a series of riots targeted African Americans: in Atlanta in 1906; in Springfield, Illinois, in 1908; in East St. Louis in 1917; and in Detroit in 1943.[6] These instances of violence are only some of the more prominent and well-researched cases. Needless to say, the phenomenon of religious and ethnic violence continues to mark and mar our world.

Many paths led to our exceptionally violent modernity, some less obvious. By narrating "exclusionary violence" as archaic, as situated in darker ages and in more backward countries, historians have overlooked its significance to the development of modern antisemitism in Germany

---

4. On Italy, see Lionella Neppi Modona Viterbo and Sonia Oberdorfer, "1799: Un Pogrom in Toscana," *La Rassegna Mensile di Israel* 53, no. 3 (1987): 341–59; Jean-Pierre Filippini, "Difesa della Patria e odio degli ebrei: Il Tumulto del 9 Luglio 1800 a Livorno," *Ricerce Storico,* 1992, 303–36; and Salvatore Foa, "Il '48 e gli Ebrei d'Acqui," *Il Vessillo Israelitico* 61 (1913): 243–51. On France, see Stephen Wilson, "The Antisemitic Riots of 1898 in France," *Historical Journal* 16 (1973): 789–806. On Wales, see Geoffrey Alderman, "The Anti-Jewish Riots of August 1911 in South Wales," *Welsh History Review* 6 (1972): 190–200; and Tony Kushner, "Anti-semitism and Austerity: The August 1947 Riots in Britain," in *Racial Violence in Britain, 1840–1950,* edited by Panikos Panayi (Leicester, 1993), 149–68. On Poland, see Antony Polonsky, "A Failed Pogrom: The Demonstration in Lwów, June 1929," in *The Jews of Poland between Two World Wars,* edited by Israel Gutman et al. (Hanover, 1989), 109–25; and Stanislaw Meducki, "The Pogrom in Kielce on 4 July 1946," *Polin* 9 (1996): 158–69.

5. On anti-Chinese riots, see Roger Daniels, ed., *Anti-Chinese Violence in North America* (New York, 1978).

6. On riots against African Americans, see Charles Crowe, "Racial Massacre in Atlanta, September 22, 1906," *Journal of Negro History* 54 (1969): 150–73; Elliott Rudwick, *Race Riot at East St. Louis, July 2, 1917* (Urbana, Ill., 1964); Dominic J. Capeci and Martha Wilkerson, *Layered Violence: The Detroit Riot of 1943* (Jackson, Miss., 1991); and Roberta Senechal de la Roche, *The Sociogenesis of a Race Riot: Springfield, Illinois, in 1908* (Urbana, Ill., 1990). By comparison, anti-Jewish riots seem to be a relatively minor phenomenon in the United States, though antisemitism is not. With respect to anti-Jewish violence by National Socialists of German descent in the United States on November 9 and 10, 1938, see Cornelia Wilhelm, *Bewegung oder Verein? Nationalsozialistische Volkstumspolitik in den USA* (Stuttgart, 1998). Note the relative absence of antisemitic collective violence in the United States as reflected in Leonard Dinnerstein, *Anti-semitism in America* (Oxford, 1994).

and Europe (as well as the reasons for its continued presence in the contemporary world). They have, for one thing, underestimated the degree to which modern violence in Germany foreshadowed the more famous pogroms of the east, which, as I. Michael Aronson reminds us, "were almost unknown in Russia prior to 1881."[7] They have also obscured the way in which pogroms of the late nineteenth century were a more general phenomenon of central and eastern Europe, Germany included. And they have rendered less clear both the importance of exclusionary violence to the rise of modern antisemitism in Germany, and the place of antisemitic violence (as opposed to antisemitic ideology) in the prehistory of the Holocaust.[8] Collective acts of exclusionary violence—pogroms, to use the Russian word—were not dead-end streets of archaic protest. Rather, they led eventually to new kinds of destruction.

To understand this violence, we consider it from different disciplinary perspectives. From the standpoint of ethnologically inspired microhistory, we consider its meaning (section I). From the vantage of comparative sociology, we locate its societal underpinnings and situate it within the wider phenomenon of collective violence (section II). And as historians, we put forward a periodization and offer a historiographical context (section III).

I

"Men do harm," Machiavelli wrote in *The Prince,* "either because they fear you or because they hate you."[9] The effort to understand either fear or hate, or combinations of both, underlies attempts to understand modern antisemitism and the violence it sometimes engenders. In their more sophisticated variations, theories of social strain, which focus on fear, have suggested that when society is out of kilter, threatened groups react by projecting their aggression against a minority, in this case the Jews. In German history, Hans Rosenberg offered the boldest explanation for the societal underpinnings of fear funneling into antisemitism. He argued that the rise of modern antisemitism occurred in the context of the Great Depression of 1873–96, which decreased agricultural profits, depressed

---

7. I. Michael Aronson, "The Anti-Jewish Pogroms in Russia in 1881," in *Pogroms: Anti-Jewish Violence in Modern Russian History,* edited by John D. Klier and Shlomo Lambroza (Cambridge, 1992), 44. For more detail, see Aronson, *Troubled Waters: The Origins of the 1881 Anti-Jewish Pogroms in Russia* (Pittsburgh, 1990).

8. There are important exceptions, however. See Rainer Erb and Werner Bergmann, *Die Nachtseite der Judenemanzipation: Der Widerstand gegen die Integration der Juden in Deutschland, 1780–1860* (Berlin, 1989); and Dirk Walter, *Antisemitische Kriminalität und Gewalt: Judenfeindschaft in der Weimarer Republik* (Bonn, 1999).

9. Niccolo Machiavelli, *The Prince,* trans. George Bull (New York, 1961), 61, cited by Edward Muir, *Mad Blood Stirring: Vendetta in Renaissance Italy* (Baltimore, 1998), xix.

prices and wages, brought about layoffs and business foreclosures, and undermined the position of independent farmers and artisans, who now feared falling into the ranks of laborers. Anxious, they focused their fear on the Jews.[10]

Rosenberg's sweeping and powerful interpretation focused on the connection between social crisis and new forms of antisemitism, not on violence as such. Yet Rosenberg assumed rather than demonstrated the mechanism between societal strain and the reaction to it.[11] Historians have since called for more precision in this respect. Dirk Blasius, for example, has demanded that historians "correlate the so-called 'Jewish question' with the overall development of modern, capitalist societies."[12] But correlations are only part of the problem. The real challenge, as Clifford Geertz once argued, is to demonstrate "how the trick is really done."[13] For unless one is a behaviorist subscribing to the notion that stimulus A leads inexorably to reaction B, the problem of how strain leads to fear culminating in aggression resulting in violence remains unsolved. And it remains unsolved because insufficient attention is paid to the actual situations in which violence occurs and the actual vocabularies of hatred that are employed.[14] Consequently, we learn little about how social strain leads to an emotion such as fear and a sentiment such as hate, and how hate leads to words that maim or actions that injure or kill.[15]

A second tradition of research into the history of antisemitic violence plots violence as the manifest expression of an underlying, unchanging hatred, Christians of Jews. Norman Cohn, in his influential *Warrant for Genocide,* puts the case succinctly:

---

10. Hans Rosenberg, *Grosse Depression und Bismarckzeit: Wirtschaftsablauf, Gesellschaft und Politik in Mitteleuropa* (Berlin, 1967), 88–117.

11. See especially Geoff Eley, "Hans Rosenberg and the Great Depression of 1873–1896: Politics and Economics in Recent German Historiography, 1960–1980," in idem, *From Unification to Nazism: Reinterpreting the German Past* (Winchester, Mass., 1986), 23–41; and James F. Harris, *The People Speak! Anti-semitism and Emancipation in Nineteenth-Century Bavaria* (Ann Arbor, 1994), 220–21. For this criticism with respect to strain theories generally, see Clifford Geertz, "Ideology as a Cultural System," in idem, *The Interpretation of Cultures* (New York, 1973), 207.

12. Dirk Blasius, " 'Judenfrage' und Gesellschaftsgeschichte," *Neue politische Literatur* 23 (1978): 17.

13. Geertz, "Ideology as a Cultural System," 207.

14. Eley, "Hans Rosenberg and the Great Depression," 33. See also Till van Rahden, "Words and Actions: Rethinking the Social History of German Antisemitism, Breslau, 1870–1914," *German History,* 18, no. 4 (2000): 413–38.

15. On the second part of this equation—the relation of ideology and sentiment to action—see van Rahden, "Ideas, Words, and Actions." See also van Rahden, "Ideologie und Gewalt," 11–29.

As I see it, the deadliest kind of antisemitism, the kind that results in massacre and attempted genocide, has little to do with real conflicts of interest between living people, or even with racial prejudice as such. At its heart lies the belief that Jews—all Jews everywhere—form a conspiratorial body set on running and then dominating the rest of mankind. And this belief is simply a modernized, secularized version of the popular medieval view.[16]

In this way of seeing the problem, an antisemitic belief rests deep in the unconscious of the Western mind. At certain points, the latent idea surfaces, sometimes manifesting itself in violence. It is perhaps interesting to understand when, and under what conditions, the idea manifests itself in violent ways, but this surely does not get to the heart of the real. The real is the structure of the belief. In *Hitler's Willing Executioners,* Daniel Goldhagen put forward a version of this argument, emphasizing the permanence and ubiquity of a certain "cognitive model." In the late nineteenth century, he averred, Germans developed a "virulent and violent 'eliminationist' variant of antisemitism, which called for the elimination of Jewish influence or of Jews themselves from German society." This "cognitive model," he further argued, "was also extremely widespread in all social classes and sectors of German society, for it was deeply embedded in German culture and political life and conversation, as well as integrated into the moral structure of society." Thus when Hitler seized power in 1933, many Germans already adhered to an ideology "pregnant with murder."[17] Consequently, when Hitler called upon his countrymen to murder Jews, they did so eagerly. Ordinary Germans were willing executioners, Goldhagen concluded.

Cohn and Goldhagen share a methodological assumption that posits incidents of antisemitic violence across time and space as the result of, in Goldhagen's words, "a generally constant antisemitism becoming more or less manifest."[18] This approach, however, does not allow us to take seriously the changing meanings of antisemitism, or to discern the shifting sociological contexts in which antisemitic violence is deployed. It assumes rather than demonstrates the motivations of antisemitic rioters. It discourages a close understanding of context, and it effaces differences across time and space, the stuff that historical insight is made of. Finally, it is sim-

---

16. Norman Cohn, *Warrant for Genocide: The Myth of the Jewish World-Conspiracy and the "Protocols of the Elders of Zion"* (New York, 1967), 16.

17. Daniel Jonah Goldhagen, *Hitler's Willing Executioners: Ordinary Germans and the Holocaust* (New York, 1996), 23, 77, 75.

18. Ibid., 39.

ply too simple. It adduces one cause, one motivation. The rest is merely accretion.[19]

The history of antisemitic violence is not so easily explained. What we need instead is an approach that takes the events of antisemitic violence seriously, that restores volition to those engaged in violent acts, that renders actors accountable, and not dominated by a transhistorical discourse.[20] Here one does not wish to deny continuities in the form of antisemitism. Many of the epithets directed against Jews, whether as "Christ killers" or as "usurers," have exhibited an unsettling degree of tenacity over time. Yet they have been deployed in different circumstances, by different kinds of people, to very different ends. These things, too, are important. For they reveal clues as to the meaning of antisemitic actions, and they suggest how people appropriate and reshape antisemitic discourses.[21]

The contexts that gave rise to exclusionary violence include grain shortages, social and political revolution, the sometimes deleterious effects of modern electioneering in an economically depressed area, an unsolved murder, runaway inflation, and the opportunistic policies of a racist state. These contexts may have something to do with relations between Christians and Jews. But, conversely, they may not. In most cases, the analytical problem is to explain why antisemitic violence, and not something else, constituted a popular response to problems extraneous to Christian-Jewish relations. The answer cannot be the preexistence of an antisemitic discourse. For a simple appeal to "the longest hatred" does not tell us why Christians, now in this context, now in another, appropriated a persecutory discourse directed against a minority rather than, say, a discourse about the abuses of rulers or about the inequalities of class.[22] Moreover, an explanation that focuses on the "structure of belief" or a "cognitive model" tells us little about the specific uses for which historical agents employed, and thus changed, vocabularies of hatred. As David Nirenberg

---

19. For a brilliant criticism of this approach generally, see David Nirenberg, *Communities of Violence: Persecution of Minorities in the Middle Ages* (Princeton, 1996), 1–7. Among the many essays critical of Goldhagen, see in particular Dieter Pohl, "Die Holocaust-Forschung und Goldhagens Thesen," *Vierteljahrshefte für Zeitgeschichte* 45, no. 1 (1997): 1–48; Norman G. Finkelstein and Ruth Bettina Birn, *A Nation on Trial: The Goldhagen Thesis and Historical Truth* (New York, 1998), esp. 101–48; and Istvan Deak, "Holocaust Views: The Goldhagen Controversy in Retrospect," *Central European History* 30, no. 2 (1997): 295–308. See also the essays collected in Julius H. Schoeps, ed., *Ein Volk von Mördern?* (Hamburg, 1996).

20. For this critique more generally, see Steven Feierman, *Peasant Intellectuals: Anthropology and History in Tanzania* (Madison, Wis.), 3–8.

21. Ibid., 3–17. See also Sherry B. Ortner, "Theory in Anthropology since the Sixties," in *Culture/Power/History: A Reader in Contemporary Social Theory,* edited by Nicholas B. Dirks, Geoff Eley, and Sherry B. Ortner (Princeton, 1994), 388–96.

22. See, for a different context, Feierman, *Peasant Intellectuals,* 8.

put it in *Communities of Violence:* "We need no longer insist on continuities of meaning in claims about minorities wherever we find continuities in form, since we can now see how the meanings of existing forms are altered by the work that they are asked to do, and by the uses to which they are put."[23]

Microhistories get us closer to seeing how people appropriate vocabularies of hatred in specific contexts. They thus offer a way out of two kinds of reductionism, the first that sees Christian antipathy toward Jews as a reflection of the social, the second that sees their enmity as existing independently of what happens in real life.[24] Sterile debates over what part drives the whole, whether base determines superstructure, the unconscious the life of the conscious, or structure event are thus rendered superfluous.[25] Moreover, by focusing on collective violence, we train our analysis on public acts and attempt to discern their meaning for those who carry them out as well as their significance in the larger context in which the violence occurs.[26] We can thus see the way in which society and discourse structure exclusionary violence without regarding either society or discourse as determinative. We can take ideology seriously and not see it as merely mask and shield for something else. This approach does not obviate a close understanding of the societal underpinnings (see section II) of collective violence. Nevertheless, it pays equal attention to agency and its meaning in specific contexts. And it admits that actions themselves can transform structures.[27] Not simply a window onto a culture steeped in antisemitic antipathy, exclusionary violence was also a transforming event and a constitutive process.[28]

The process was to a significant degree a ritual process. From the gathering in the streets, to the occupation of the marketplace, to the aspersions cast at Jews, to the rocks thrown, to the threats to beat the last Jew

---

23. Nirenberg, *Communities of Violence,* 6–7.

24. Jacques Revel, "Microanalysis and the Construction of the Social," in *Histories: French Constructions of the Past,* edited by Jacques Revel and Lynn Hunt (New York, 1995), 492–502.

25. See Ortner, "Theory in Anthropology since the Sixties," 392.

26. For a restatement of this approach, see Clifford Geertz, *After the Fact: Two Countries, Four Decades, One Anthropologist* (Cambridge, Mass., 1995), 126. Within the field of history, see Roger Chartier, *On the Edge of the Cliff: History, Language, and Practices* (Baltimore, 1997), 4–5.

27. See William H. Sewell Jr., "Three Temporalities: Toward an Eventful Sociology," in *The Historic Turn in the Human Sciences,* edited by Terrence J. McDonald (Ann Arbor, 1996), 263.

28. This distinction is an important one: violence is not merely a sign to be read, it also transforms culture. See, in particular, criticisms of Geertz on this point—for example, William H. Sewell Jr., "Geertz, Cultural Systems, and History: From Synchrony to Transformation," in *The Fate of "Culture,"* edited by Sherry B. Ortner (Berkeley, 1999), 46–51.

to death, to the smashing of windows and the beating of walls and doors of Jewish houses with sticks, the drama and serious play of antisemitic violence revealed a great many characteristics of ritual.[29] This did not make it any less terrifying for Jews. They could not know when a physical threat would be made good upon, or when a brick tossed through a window would strike a family member. There were, moreover, cases where the restraints inherent in ritualized violence were transgressed, where, to borrow from E. Valentine Daniel, the "taming capacities of culture" failed.[30] In Russia this happened in 1881, when at least fifty Jews were killed in the course of pogroms that raged throughout the spring and summer.[31] It also happened in Kishinev in April 1903, when "at the end of two days," according to one scholar, "47 Jews had been murdered, 424 wounded, 700 houses burned, 600 shops looted."[32] And it happened in a still more sustained and serious way in hundreds of pogroms throughout the Pale of Settlement in the three years following Kishinev, with a death toll of more than three thousand Jewish men, women, and children.[33] In Germany, "Kristallnacht," the state-supported pogrom of November 9–10, 1938, also entailed severe violence: the ruthless beatings and killings of an untold number of Jews.[34] But in nineteenth- and twentieth-century Germany previous to Kristallnacht, the incidents of exclusionary violence did not, as a rule, claim Jewish lives. To state this is not to belittle the violence perpetrated, but rather to focus attention on the way in which the riots followed rules, evinced patterns, were restrained from within (as well as by the authorities), and assumed the character of public theater.

"Rituals of degradation" constituted the principal acts marking out the progression of the public play—"theaters of conquest."[35] For violence forced Jews to cease to go out at night, to retreat to the corners of their private homes, to huddle for their own safety, and to supplicate the authorities for protection. It also put an abrupt, if sometimes temporary, end to

---

29. For a comparison with Holy Week riots, see Nirenberg, *Communities of Violence,* 200–230.

30. E. Valentine Daniel, "The Limits of Culture," in *In Near Ruins: Cultural Theory at the End of the Century* (Minneapolis, 1998), 69. Daniel's important larger argument, that violence (especially extreme violence) lies outside culture, is unconvincing, however. See Daniel, *Charred Lullabies: Chapters in an Anthropology of Violence* (Princeton, 1996), esp. 194–212. For a different approach, see Rolf Peter Sieferle and Helga Breuninger, eds., *Kulturen der Gewalt: Ritualisierung und Symbolisierung von Gewalt in der Geschichte* (Frankfurt, 1998).

31. Hans Rogger, "Conclusion and Overview," in Klier and Lambroza, *Pogroms,* 328.

32. Shlomo Lambroza, "The Pogroms of 1903–1906," ibid., 200.

33. Ibid., 228.

34. Marion A. Kaplan, *Between Dignity and Despair: Jewish Life in Nazi Germany* (New York, 1998), 123.

35. Peter Loewenberg, "The Kristallnacht as a Public Degradation Ritual," *Leo Baeck Institute Year Book* 33 (1987): 309–23.

social integration and, as an event transformative of structure, redrew local lines of segregation. Intended to reaffirm relations of power, outbreaks of exclusionary violence thus reminded Jews that theirs was a precarious position, and that they lived in a society defined by Gentile supremacy. In this respect, the history of exclusionary violence in Germany suggests parallels to white lynching of African Americans in the American South. Between the end of the Civil War and 1968, there were over five thousand lynchings of African American people in the United States. Concentrated in the period between 1880 and 1930, these lynchings dramatically demonstrated the violent face of white supremacy, imprinting, in one local context after the next, the rules of racial hierarchy and the prerogatives of white power in an increasingly segregated South.[36] They were also, as Orlando Patterson has brilliantly shown, highly ritualized events, involving drama, celebration, and play, culminating in the killing of the victim. The drama was, then, a sacrificial drama: it followed established patterns of human sacrifice and appropriated well-known symbols of Christianity, such as the burning cross. Moreover, lynchings were communal events: "ritualized killing," in Patterson's words, "in communal acts of human sacrifice."[37]

Exclusionary violence was also a communal act, a fact central to its meaning and significance.[38] In the antisemitic riots of nineteenth-century Germany, exceedingly large local crowds were involved, creating concentric circles of active participants, complicitous supporters, and curious onlookers: the actors, the chorus, and the audience. As the rituals of violence were not the stuff of the everyday, the events took place outside the weave of the quotidian—in the selvage that the ethnologist Victor Turner has identified as the "liminal." The liminal refers to the margins, to the threshold of a given structure, to the space betwixt and between. If everyday life is marked by structure and hierarchy, the liminal is the site of the world turned upside down, the reversal of assigned roles, the leavening of the social order, the loosening of controls.[39] Collective violence against Jews happened in this space, with participation in the ritual of violence

36. W. Fitzhugh Brundage, *Under Sentence of Death: Lynching in the South* (Chapel Hill, 1997), 11.

37. Orlando Patterson, *Rituals of Blood: Consequences of Slavery in Two American Centuries* (New York, 1998), 172.

38. See, for a slightly different context, Hillel J. Kieval, "The Importance of Place: Comparative Aspects of the Ritual Murder Trial in Modern Central Europe," in *Comparing Jewish Societies,* edited by Todd M. Endelman (Ann Arbor, 1997), 137.

39. Victor Turner, *Dramas, Fields, and Metaphors: Symbolic Action in Human Society* (Ithaca, 1974), 23–59; idem, *The Ritual Process: Structure and Anti-Structure* (Chicago, 1969); idem, *From Ritual to Theatre: The Human Seriousness of Play* (New York, 1982).

engendering what Turner considered the fundamental characteristic of the liminal stage in the ritual process: "communitas."[40] An including "we" thus became predicated on an excluding "they." By dint of antisemitic violence, non-Jews created community, reaffirming in their own mind the terms of their power to humiliate Jews and to show that, whatever the legal documents might affirm, Jews did not belong. In this sense, too, the violence perpetrated was exclusionary violence.

II

Since the 1980s, historical and sociological research on violence has intensified considerably, with scholarly interest focusing on ethnic conflict and ranging from forms of local collective violence, such as lynching, anti-immigrant riots, race riots, and pogroms, to organized forms of mass violence, such as massacres and genocide.[41] Because ethnic violence takes such different forms, it is important to distinguish between the forms of violence being discussed.[42] Collective violence can be aimed at an individual member of another group or at a group as a whole. It can be committed either by a majority against a minority or the reverse. It can also be directed against the state, and the state and its control agencies can respond in many ways.[43] Finally, collective violence can be either spontaneous or highly organized.

Building upon a typology proposed by Roberta Senechal de la Roche

---

40. Turner, *Dramas, Fields, and Metaphors,* 47.

41. See the overview of research in Dirk Schumann, "Gewalt als Grenzüberschreitung: Überlegungen zur Sozialgeschichte der Gewalt im 19. und 20. Jahrhundert," *Archiv für Sozialgeschichte* 37 (1997): 366–86. The causes of this communal violence continue to be interpreted in varying ways. See, for example, Walter Korpi, "Conflict, Power, and Relative Deprivation," *American Political Science Review* 38 (1974): 1569–78; John Bohstedt, "The Dynamics of Riots: Escalation and Diffusion/Contagion," in *The Dynamics of Aggression: Biological and Social Processes in Dyads and Groups,* edited by Michael Potegal and John F. Knutson (Hillsdale, N.J., 1994), 257–306; Clark McPhail, *The Myth of the Madding Crowd* (New York, 1991); and Clark McPhail and Ronald T. Wohlstein, "Individual and Collective Behaviors within Gatherings, Demonstrations, and Riots," *Annual Review of Sociology* 9 (1983): 579–600. On massacres, see most recently Mark Levene and Penny Roberts, eds., *The Massacre in History* (Oxford, 1999).

42. Rogers Brubaker and David D. Laitin, "Ethnic and Nationalist Violence," *Annual Review of Sociology* 24 (1998): 423–52, 446, and Robin W. Williams, "The Sociology of Ethnic Conflicts: Comparative International Perspectives," *Annual Review of Sociology* 20 (1994): 49–79, argue for a disaggregation of the forms of violence in discussion. In 1992 Craig C. Jenkins and Kurt Schock also found that a "huge empirical gap currently limits our understanding of ethnic antagonisms." "Global Structures and Political Processes in the Study of Domestic Political Conflict," *Annual Review of Sociology* 18 (1992): 161–85, 181.

43. For a definition of *pogrom,* see Robert Melson, *Revolution and Genocide: On the Origins of the Armenian Genocide and the Holocaust* (Chicago, 1992), 26.

for distinguishing between various types of collective violence, we would suggest that exclusionary ethnic riots (pogroms) be defined as a *one-sided, nongovernmental* form of collective violence against an ethnic group that occurs when one ethnic group (usually the majority) no longer expects to receive redress from the state for the (perceived) threat caused by another ethnic group (usually the minority).[44] Sometimes this violence can be a form of perceived "self-help" by a majority punishing a minority for an alleged violation of norms.[45] The perceived threat, which usually has a long history and has been entrenched in prejudices, is often openly discussed and dramatized over a period of time. But agitators, leaders, and organizations fulfill an important function in the mobilization of violence. In this model, the state plays an ambivalent role. As guarantor for peace and order, it must intervene against collective violence of any kind and can, as a result, become itself a target of the rioters. By its stance toward the group being discriminated against, the state can also indicate its tacit agreement with the goals of the ethnic majority. It may react haltingly, thereby encouraging rioters.[46]

The exclusionary riot may be distinguished from other forms of violence along a range of criteria.[47] The assumption that the minority group constitutes a *collective threat* makes the exclusionary riot different from a lynching, which, while operating from general prejudice, is directed at a single member of a minority.[48] The extreme *asymmetry of power* in favor of the rioters distinguishes exclusionary riots from other forms of rioting, such as food or race riots. The *low level of organization* makes them differ-

---

44. Roberta Senechal de la Roche, "Collective Violence as Social Control," *Sociological Forum* 11 (1996): 97–128.

45. How violent the punishment is can vary to a large degree: it can range from a ritualized, contained form of degradation to the destruction of subsistence means (causing damage to houses and shops, plundering) and go as far as the expulsion, injury, or murder of members of the group.

46. The organized anti-Jewish violence of the Nazi regime during the so-called June Action and Kristallnacht in 1938 is an exception: in these cases, the form of the pogrom was orchestrated by the regime, even though no one believed in the "wrath of the people" that it propagated. The decreed pogrom did, however, manage to develop on a local level into a real pogrom with the spontaneous participation of the population (see the article by Wolfgang Benz in this volume).

47. The term *pogrom* has come to stand for collective violence against a minority. See Rogger, "Conclusion and Overview," 314–72. General terms such as *demonstration, persecution,* or *fight* were initially used to designate anti-Jewish pogroms in Russia. The government used the word *besporiadok* (unrest, riot) to stress the disruption of public order. See John D. Klier, "The Pogrom Paradigm in Russian History," in Klier and Lambroza, *Pogroms,* 35.

48. During the upheavals of 1848, we also find these kinds of punishment acts against individual Jews (and non-Jews) who were accused of being "crop profiteers" (see the article by Manfred Gailus in this volume).

ent from vigilantism and terrorism, and the comparative absence of state participation sometimes, but not always, distinguishes exclusionary violence from large-scale massacres and genocide.[49] But because exclusionary ethnic riots often occur in the context of social unrest, revolution, war, civil war, and genocide, these distinctions cannot always be maintained empirically. The same caveat that applies to theoretical terms such as *revolution* and *totalitarianism* also applies to the typologies of riots: in most cases, there will be a discrepancy between the ideal type and the actual historical situations.

As no general theory of exclusionary riots (pogroms) exists, we present a series of open questions and outline alternative answers along with their (political) implications. When social scientists attempt to understand why an exclusionary riot breaks out at a certain time and place, they often seek causes in structural tensions and societal crises in which the attacks on the minority appear as a displacement of aggression or as part of a larger social movement. They also seek causes in competitive group relations that draw their élan from economic, political, and religious rivalry. In some cases, they consider ideological factors (racial hostilities and prejudice) as independent causes that cannot be reduced to objective, structural factors.

Taken together, our cases show that relationships between factors must be considered in each instance. In the riots of the 1840s and in 1923, a general social crisis centrally structured the anti-Jewish riots. In 1819, conflicts between groups played a more central role. And in Konitz in 1900, a murder and the subsequent accusation of the Jews seems to have been decisive. Not only must the factors be weighed differently, it is also necessary to differentiate between central and peripheral issues, as well as between specific, immediate causes and generally supportive factors. The case studies also

---

49. With these criteria, we are able to distinguish our approach from the "pogrom paradigm of Russian history," which viewed the state's direction and approval of violence as the central defining characteristic of a pogrom and which has meanwhile been superseded by historical research. In *Webster's Third New International Dictionary* (1964), a pogrom is defined as "an organized massacre and looting of helpless people, usually with the connivance of officials, specifically, such a massacre of Jews." A more recent publication by Paul R. Brass defines a pogrom as "attacks on person and property of a particular ethnic, racial, or communal group in which the state and/or its agents are implicated to a significant degree, but which are given the appearance, by design of the authorities or otherwise, of a riot." Paul R. Brass, "Introduction: Discourses of Ethnicity, Communalism, and Violence," in idem, ed., *Riots and Pogroms* (Hampshire, 1996), 1–55, 33. The more recent research has identified the common characteristics of the Russian wave of pogroms to be their spontaneous and confused character, the lack of a long-term political goal, their urban origins, and the lack of state direction. See Klier, "Pogrom Paradigm," 14. This description also applies to the anti-Jewish exclusionary riots of the nineteenth and twentieth century in Germany, with Kristallnacht remaining the exception (see n. 46).

make clear that structural tensions and objective crises have to take shape within the local situation—for example, through agitation or a specific triggering event—in order to actually lead to collective violence.

Depending on which explanation is adopted, the conclusions drawn regarding the role, motive, and responsibility of the actors can be very different—often, as Paul Brass has emphasized, with diverging political consequences. "But the interpretive process is not only political," Brass argues, "it also generates competing systems of knowledge concerning interethnic relations."[50] A theory on riots or pogroms is not neutral toward the interests of those who attempt to interpret the events, and it is not uninfluenced by the prominent ideological and scholarly paradigms.

Stressing economic competition and exploitation, for example, opens a space for the guilt to be localized onto the attacked group, thus blaming the victim. Similarly, a crisis theory based on the idea of the displacement of aggression may underestimate the importance of antisemitism in determining violent action. This is also true for the various answers provided to explain who the rioters are. The "pogrom paradigm in Russian history," which suggests that the riots were organized by the state, helped the Russian intellectuals to relieve the "Russian masses" of responsibility and to shift blame onto the reactionary state or the "exploitative" Jews.[51] Other theories, one of which might be called the "riffraff" theory, places the burden of responsibility onto social outsiders, thereby relieving the local community of guilt. The obverse hypothesis, that participants in a pogrom come from all strata of the population, emphasizes the responsibility of the local community as a whole.

Each of these theories can be supported by empirical evidence, since people with very different motives may participate in a violent action (defending against a threat, hate, enrichment through plundering, desire for violence, etc.). This means that in every single case, the social composition and the motives of rioters, as well as of peripheral participants, must be empirically determined.

As the cases in this volume illustrate, there are also very different answers regarding the questions of to what degree exclusionary riots or pogroms are spontaneous events, what role organized groups, agitators, and leaders play, and whether the authorities are involved. Because pogroms tend to come in waves, people have often suspected that the state alone is usually behind such actions. Our case studies show that this is true only for Kristallnacht, not for the Hep Hep riots, the antisemitic violence of 1848, the riots in Pomerania and West Prussia, or the riots in Berlin in

---

50. Brass, "Introduction," 1.
51. Klier, "Pogrom Paradigm."

1923. Rather, to explain how riots spread and how they break out on the local level, scholars must consider more strongly the role that communication (such as rumors and agitation) and intermediary specialists in what Brass has called "institutionalized riot systems" play in the dynamics of riots.[52] In addition to the analysis of events, the level of discourse that accompanies the participants and observers must also be taken into consideration, since that is what places the events into a specific context (e.g., the "Jewish question") and can serve to set off later riots.[53]

The beginning, course, and severity of exclusionary riots vary according to the *degree of organization.* A continuum can be drawn between two poles: a highly organized form typically involving a high level of violence, and a spontaneous disturbance usually involving a lower level of violence. The mechanisms of the pogrom might be imagined as follows.

Before an *outbreak* of pogrom violence, there is a significantly low measure of social relations between the parties in conflict. In contrast to the subsistence riots of the early nineteenth century, for example, where social networks existed and violence was limited by negotiations and customs, there exist fewer overlapping relationships between ethnic groups, and these continue to decrease during the escalating conflict. Broken communication with the outside is coupled with intensive local in-group communication (rumors, agitation, fliers, etc.), creating a "pogrom atmosphere." The lack of knowledge across ethnic groups results in a lack of information regarding the members and the behavior of the other group. This means that, for example, if a criminal incident occurs, the person who is actually guilty cannot be easily identified, and the out-group is punished collectively. Whether a pogrom breaks out depends on the occurrence of a *trigger event,* in which the group conflict manifests itself and collective action begins. For exclusionary riots, such events function as release mechanisms when they symbolize the threat to the majority. Everyday knowledge, often learned from childhood (for example, the ritual murder myth or the association of Jews with usury), is used to interpret these triggering events. The "infuriating occasion" releases feelings of rage and revenge, intensifying the in-group communication and leading to the assembly of a mass of people who are prepared to participate in a collective act. Leadership plays a role here, since it is usually the "ethnic ideologues" and "entrepreneurs" who direct the joint action and offer a model to follow and who can have an escalating or de-escalating effect on the crowd.

Unlike social movements, which mobilize their networks for a general

52. Brass, "Introduction," 12, passim.
53. Ibid., 2.

cause, riots require a mass of people who can be mobilized at a certain location. The sociologist Clark McPhail stressed the structural availability of rioters for the process of mobilization.[54] This dynamic of collective action has not yet been closely examined. Familiar research models of race riots apply to some aspects of this dynamic, for example, to the ecological preconditions of a riot: the triggering event, space, timing, weather. But there are important aspects of an exclusionary riot that make it a different kind of mobilization. This does not mean that a violent conflict must be planned from the very start. It can also be a result of the escalation of daily conflicts between members of ethnic groups or a displacement of other collective actions mobilizing a mass of people—for example, during a food riot, a strike, or a revolutionary movement.[55] At the local level, groups or organizations can be formed ad hoc into an effective mass that has the appearance of being organized and harboring the intention to use violence from the very start.[56] Often the rioters have an easily identifiable target area, especially if the minority is concentrated within an ethnic colony or in identifiable places of worship or business.

Exclusionary riots typically *spread in waves.* A riot at one site usually serves as the most important triggering event for subsequent actions, not only in the same local area, but in a larger geographical and temporal frame as well. *Diffusion* is significantly influenced both by social density— that is, the potential to recruit participants en bloc—and by the density and routes of communication.[57] When a pogrom is raging, it changes the cost/benefit relationship to the advantage of the participants. If the exclusionary riot is large and the state reacts sluggishly, this lessens the risk of sanctions and makes the diffuse willingness to use violence concrete. We still know very little about this dynamic of escalation, but imitative behavior, induced by communication, does seem to play a role here and has been observed in other public acts of violence, such as terrorist acts and suicides.

Exclusionary riots possess an *episodic character.* Typically, the crowd is not mobilized for a long time, and the mobilization is seldom based on permanent social networks. Moreover, the state cannot countenance a long-lasting disturbance. Scholars have tended to attribute to militant

---

54. Clark McPhail, "Presidential Address: The Dark Side of Purpose: Individual and Collective Violence in Riots," *Sociological Quarterly* 35 (1994): 1–32, 8, passim.

55. Charters Wynn, *Workers, Strikes, and Pogroms: The Donbass–Dnepr Bend in Late Imperial Russia, 1870–1905* (Princeton, 1992).

56. On the Kishinev pogrom of 1903, see Otto H. Dahlke, "Race and Minority Riots: A Study in the Typology of Violence," *Social Forces* 30 (1951/52): 419–25.

57. Aronson, *Troubled Waters.*

social movements, as well as to race riots, a high degree of rationality, thereby neglecting their emotional aspect. Under certain circumstances, violence appears as a merely rational means of achieving an aim. But there are violent acts that are not merely rational, such as lynching and pogroms. Indeed, for episodic violence in a local area, the pursuance of rational interests can be unimportant.[58] Exclusionary violence can have a ritualized character and thus be less violent, but we often find excessive violence, which cannot be easily categorized as purely rational or merely symbolic action. This kind of violence cannot be understood without the inclusion of moments of expressiveness, the release of emotional tension and hostile aggression, the demonstration of power and strength, and the desire for violence. This is especially true when the participants come from subcultural milieus or criminal gangs in which the exceptional character of violence is much less instrumental. The rate of criminality and phases of uncontained collective violence correlate with one another, as does rioting with the male gender and youth.[59]

The action of pogrom participants also has a utilitarian component (improving or securing the group's position), but its aim is to defend against a perceived threat. The actors want literally to remove the members of the attacked group, rob them of their material basis (through plundering and arson), degrade them, or even kill them. Through an exclusionary riot, the participants also indirectly demand, often successfully, that the state take measures against the minority that serve to benefit the majority. The aim is to instill insecurity and fear in the minority, to cause a deterioration of their social situation, and to destroy their economic livelihood.

III

Historians have been slow to address the legacy of anti-Jewish violence in modern German history. For a long time, studies of antisemitic violence focused on the Russian pogroms, and it was not until the late 1960s and early 1970s, when Jacob Toury and Jacob Katz published their work, that scholars began to study antisemitic violence in its early-nineteenth-century German context. Yet until the early 1980s, these investigations were available only in Hebrew. They then appeared in English, and later still in Ger-

---

58. James Rule, *Theories of Civil Violence* (Berkeley, 1988).
59. Bert Useem, "Breakdown Theories of Collective Action," *Annual Review of Sociology* 24 (1998): 215–38, 224.

man.[60] Toury and Katz located the source of anti-Jewish violence in the struggles for Jewish emancipation, thus interpreting the violence as a matter of ideology or as part of real conflict between Jews and non-Jews. The previously dominant interpretation viewed anti-Jewish riots in the first half of the nineteenth century as a displacement of social protest. Developed by Eleonore Sterling as early as 1950, this approach focused on anti-semitism as a product of general societal crisis, and thus as a secondary phenomenon.[61] According to this theory, the Jews became victims of a dissatisfaction that was "actually" directed against the ruling body or upper classes. In the 1970s, Sterling's thesis found fertile ground in social protest research, which, given sociology's predilection for modernization theory, gave primacy to class conflict over religious or ethnic conflict.[62] At least in Germany, it was not until the 1980s that scholars began to emphasize anti-semitism as an independent factor fueling anti-Jewish riots. These competing interpretations, one emphasizing social factors, the other mental dispositions, continue to divide historians.

Our book addresses recent scholarly discussions by placing case studies of pogrom-like riots in modern German history within a comparative theoretical framework. We limit our study to the nineteenth and early twentieth centuries, because pogrom-like anti-Jewish violence in the Middle Ages and the early modern period emerged within different structures of social conflict, and the role of authority differed from that which emerged in the developing modern nation-states after the late eighteenth century. Modern societies differ from the premodern in at least three respects that are central to pogrom actions: the existence of the constitutional nation-state, the state monopoly of power, and the inclusion of the entire population in functional subsystems on equal terms (such as equal rights, participation as formally equal consumers in a market economy, universal suffrage, and compulsory education). Only in this process of

---

60. Jacob Toury, "Turmoil and Confusion in the Revolution of 1848: The Anti-Jewish Riots in the 'Year of Freedom' and Their Influence on Modern Anti-semitism" (in Hebrew), *Merchavia,* 1968, 224, passim; idem, "Self-Defense in the Days of the 'Hep Hep' Riots" (in Hebrew), *Yalkut Moreshet* 14 (1972): 107–16; Jacob Katz, "The Hep Hep Riots in Germany of 1819: The Historical Background" (in Hebrew), *Zion* 38 (1973): 62–117. Katz's study was not published in German until 1994: Jacob Katz, *Die Hep-Hep-Verfolgungen des Jahres 1819* (Berlin, 1994). On the lack of critical attention received by Katz and Toury, see Stefan Rohrbacher, "Nachwort," ibid., 130, passim.

61. Eleonore O. Sterling, "Anti-Jewish Riots in Germany in 1819: A Displacement of Social Protest," *Historia Judaica* 12 (October 1950): 105–42.

62. See, for example, Rainer Wirtz, *"Widersetzlichkeiten, Excesse, Crawalle, Tumulte und Skandale": Soziale Bewegung und gewalthafter sozialer Protest in Baden, 1815–1848* (Frankfurt, 1981); Heinrich Volkmann and Jürgen Bergmann, eds., *Sozialer Protest: Studien zu traditioneller Resistenz und kollektiver Gewalt in Deutschland vom Vormärz bis zur Reichsgründung* (Opladen, 1984); and Arno Herzig, *Unterschichtenprotest in Deutschland, 1790–1870* (Göttingen, 1988).

nation-building has ethnicity become politicized, because the question arises as to who makes up the nation of the state. Ethnic conflicts occur primarily when states are being established or during crisis-ridden periods of reorganization when ethnic difference gains such importance that a struggle erupts over how state benefits will be parceled out.

This was the situation during the nineteenth century, when, through a process of emancipation and acculturation, the Jewish minority "entered" Christian societies all over Europe. It was a process supported by the state but opposed by parts of the population. In many cases, this opposition affiliated itself with social protest against the nobility and against state authorities, as well as with revolutionary movements. It could also take nonviolent forms, such as petitions and peaceful protests against the state, or dissemination of anti-Jewish publications attacking either individual Jews or all Jewish fellow citizens. Within the wide spectrum of anti-Jewish expression in Germany, collective violence remained the exception, especially within narrow local frameworks. Nevertheless, from the Hep Hep riots of 1819 to Kristallnacht in 1938, there were scores of violent riots in Germany. They occurred in cities as well as in the countryside. They happened in Protestant areas and in Catholic areas. And they happened in nearly every decade. In broad terms, there were at least three phases of violence.

Phase I: Jewish Emancipation

The emancipation of the Jews, the gradual process by which they became citizens with equal rights, was accompanied by public campaigns of pamphlets and petitions protesting the laws and by anti-Jewish harassment, rumors, and physical assaults. This phase incorporates two waves of pogrom-like riots: the Hep Hep riots of 1819, which constituted Germany's first large wave of anti-Jewish violence since the Middle Ages, and the anti-Jewish unrest that emerged with the revolutions of 1848. In the emancipation period, numerous other instances of anti-Jewish violence also occurred. They included the violence in Hamburg's coffeehouses in 1830 and 1835, in the Rhineland throughout the 1830s, and among university students in Breslau in 1844.[63] More generally, instances of anti-

---

63. See Moshe Zimmermann, "Antijüdischer Sozialprotest? Proteste von Unter- und Mittelschichten, 1819–1835," in *Arbeiter in Hamburg: Unterschichten, Arbeiter und Arbeiterbewegung seit dem ausgehenden 18. Jahrhundert,* edited by Arno Herzig, Dieter Langewiesche, and Arnold Sywottek (Hamburg, 1983), 89–94. See also Wirtz, *"Widersetzlichkeiten";* and Herbert A. Strauss, "Die preussische Bürokratie und die anti-jüdischen Unruhen im Jahre 1834," in *Gegenwart im Rückblick: Festgabe für die Jüdische Gemeinde zu Berlin 25 Jahre nach dem Neubeginn,* edited by Herbert A. Strauss and Kurt R. Grossmann (Heidelberg, 1970), 27–55.

Jewish violence happened in the context of revolutionary unrest in the years 1830, 1832, 1847, and 1850.[64]

Phase II: The Development of Modern Antisemitism

Modern antisemitism emerged in the late nineteenth century in Germany with the revocation of Jewish emancipation as its goal. Anti-Jewish violence became a means to protest "Jewish domination" and to stop the immigration of Polish and Russian Jews. The three case studies in this volume for the period between 1881 and 1923 illuminate three different aspects of this movement's development. The anti-Jewish riots in Pomerania and West Prussia in 1881 demonstrate how the antisemitic movement kindled agitation against Jews in positions of power within the German Empire. The accusation of blood libel in Konitz in 1900 shows that traditional religious prejudices could be mobilized into political action against the Jews. Ritual murder cases, too, reemerged during this period and frequently triggered local anti-Jewish violence, not only in the German Empire, but also in Hungary, Russia, and other European countries: the Buschhoff case in Xanten, 1891—92; the case in Tisza-Eslár in Hungary, 1882; and the prominent Beilis case in Russia, 1911.[65] Riots also broke out against Jews in many Bohemian villages and towns after the case in Polná in 1899. Indeed, not a single year during the 1890s had passed there without an accusation of ritual murder.[66] The third case study, of the 1923 *Scheunenviertelkrawalle* in Berlin, describes yet another facet of antisemitism, namely, resistance to east European Jewish immigration during the severe political and economic crisis following the First World War. This violence was linked to the Weimar government's efforts to expel Polish Jews.

The three case studies chosen to represent the emergence of modern antisemitism reflect the development of other incidents as well. There were

---

64. Michael Anthony Riff, "The Anti-Jewish Aspect of the Revolutionary Unrest of 1848 in Baden and Its Impact on Emancipation," *Leo Baeck Institute Year Book* 21 (1976): 21–41; Daniel Gerson, "Die Ausschreitungen gegen die Juden im Elsaß, 1848," *Bulletin des Leo Baeck Instituts* 87 (1990): 29–44.

65. On the riots in the Buschhoff case, cf. Barbara Suchy, "Antisemitismus in den Jahren vor dem Ersten Weltkrieg," in *Köln und das rheinische Judentum: Festschrift Germania Judaica, 1959–1984* (Cologne, 1984), 252–85; and Stefan Rohrbacher, *Juden in Neuss* (Neuss, 1986), 128–35. See also Andrew Handler, *Blood Libel at Tiszaezlar* (New York, 1980); and Hans Rogger, "The Beilis Case: Anti-semitism and Politics in the Reign of Nicolas II," *Slavic Review* 25, no. 4 (1966): 615–29.

66. Georg R. Schroubek, "Der 'Ritualmord' von Polná: Traditioneller und moderner Wahnglaube," in *Antisemitismus und jüdische Geschichte: Studien zu Ehren von Herbert A. Strauss,* edited by Rainer Erb and Michael Schmidt (Berlin, 1987), 149–71, 157.

anti-Jewish tumults in Berlin in 1880; riots against Viennese Jews and their property in 1885, 1925, and 1931; and in 1923, the year of the *Scheunenviertelkrawalle,* riots in Neidenburg (East Prussia) and in Beuthen (Silesia). Toward the end of the Weimar Republic, National Socialist units began to stage antisemitic violence. Riots accompanied the opening of the Reichstag in October 1930; Jews were beaten during the so-called *Kurfürstendammkrawall* in September 1931; and assassination attempts with bombs, as well as other violent acts against Jews, began under the direction of the regional SA leadership in August 1932.[67] The desire for the persistent, and physical, persecution of Jews in Germany was already apparent, and it would become state policy after 1933.

Phase III: State Antisemitism

The pogrom of November 1938, known as Kristallnacht, differed significantly from the incidents described above. For the first time since the Middle Ages, the state not only initiated a pogrom, but also largely organized and implemented it. Although the National Socialists insistently attributed the events of Kristallnacht to "the spontaneous wrath of the people" and thus to a tradition of collective anti-Jewish violence generated within the population, the pogrom signified the radicalization of the state-run process of persecution that led to the organized mass murders of the Holocaust. It also foreshadowed a series of extremely bloody pogroms initiated by the Einsatzgruppen among local populations (especially in Lithuania, Latvia, Galicia, and the Ukraine) following the German invasion in 1941.

The cases selected for this volume have been chosen both for their historical significance and for their ability to represent their particular historical epoch. Our time frame is not meant to suggest that pogroms were a daily, or even a common, occurrence in modern Germany. Rather, it permits an analytically precise examination of the causes, the motives, and the political, economic, and sociocultural contexts of pogroms. The detailed case studies enable the reader to evaluate the relative influence of different factors in the development of anti-Jewish violence: the underlying hostility toward Jews, exacerbated by contemporary social developments and transformed into violence by particular incidents within local contexts. Our goal is to achieve a clearer, more refined picture of the relationship between the ideology and the violent practice of antisemitism.

---

67. Walter, *Antisemitische Kriminalität,* 209–43.

The "Hep Hep" Riots of 1819: Anti-Jewish Ideology, Agitation, and Violence

Stefan Rohrbacher

On the evening of August 2, 1819, an anti-Jewish uproar erupted in the town of Würzburg, the capital of the Bavarian province of Lower Franconia (Unterfranken). A noisy crowd gathered in the streets, shouting "Hep hep!"—that ominous and enigmatic exclamation that was to become the battle cry of the Jew-baiters of the nineteenth century. Police were unable to handle the situation, and the military had to be called in to disperse the riotous mob. With some effort the disorders were quelled, and quiet was restored late at night. The authorities were alarmed at this sudden outbreak of disorder, but in spite of various measures taken to prevent a recurrence, the very next morning the uproar was repeated, developing into serious and prolonged riots. An even larger and more aggressive crowd gathered in the streets that day to shout "Hep hep!", "Schlagt die Juden tot!" (kill the Jews), and the like. Contrary to assertions by city officials, it is evident that among "the urchins and other rabble from the streets" who roamed the city there were some honorable citizens as well, and some soldiers of the Würzburg garrison had sided with these bands. This time, the rioters did not confine themselves to verbal aggression but systematically smashed the windows of Jewish-owned houses, tore off the signboards of Jewish-owned shops, and pillaged several shops and private homes. Jewish passersby were abused and chased through the streets; some were shot at, although they escaped unhurt.[1] The house of a wealthy

---

1. Cf. the report (in Yiddish) by an eyewitness in Moses Loeb Bamberger, *Beiträge zur Geschichte der Juden in Würzburg-Heidingsfeld* (Würzburg, 1905), 18–25.

Jewish banker, Jacob von Hirsch, was attacked by a gang of sixty to eighty individuals under the "military" command of a leader who later turned out to be a government employee. When the police, who had lowered their bayonets, tried to disperse the crowd, they met with violent resistance. Paving stones were thrown at them on command, auxiliary policemen trying to take rioters into custody were maltreated badly, and some of those arrested were freed by the mob. In the tumult, one of the rioters received lethal gunshot wounds. As the rioting continued, the Jewish inhabitants fled the town. It was not until August 5 that the military and police were able to finally crush the violent disorders, during which two people lost their lives.[2]

The Würzburg riots appeared to serve as a starting signal for a general persecution of the Jews in Germany. Out of the blue, anti-Jewish violence seemed to flare up everywhere in Germany, spreading within a few weeks as far as Denmark. Serious rioting erupted in a number of large towns, including Frankfurt and Hamburg, where it lasted for several days; and physical attacks against Jews were reported from numerous small towns and villages in Franconia, Baden, Hesse, the Rhineland, Westphalia, and elsewhere. In two Bavarian villages, the synagogues were demolished and Torah scrolls destroyed. Elsewhere, village Jews were terrorized by arson attacks. In Heidelberg the pillaging of the Jewish lane went on for hours, with the police standing by, before it was finally stopped by university students. In Danzig a large crowd attacked two synagogues and several Jewish-owned houses on the eve of the Day of Atonement, the highest Jewish holiday. "Hep hep" was heard far and near. Thus, for the first time since the Middle Ages, Jewish communities in all of Germany saw themselves exposed to the threat of large-scale violent persecution.[3]

Anti-Jewish Violence—A Displacement of Social Protest?

Few contemporaries seem to have shared the apprehensive presentiment claimed by the famous salonnière Rahel Varnhagen in August 1819: "I

---

2. For a detailed and reliable account of the riots in Würzburg, see Ursula Gehring-Münzel, *Vom Schutzjuden zum Staatsbürger: Die gesellschaftliche Integration der Würzburger Juden, 1803–1871* (Würzburg, 1992), 133–53. Many other accounts in the historiographic literature are seriously flawed by inaccuracies and exaggerations that seem to reflect the tendencies of contemporary newspaper reports. For example, contrary to oft-repeated assertions, there were no casualties among Würzburg's Jewish population.

3. For a general survey of the Hep Hep riots in Germany and Denmark, see Stefan Rohrbacher, *Gewalt im Biedermeier: Antijüdische Ausschreitungen in Vormärz und Revolution (1815–1848/49)* (Frankfurt/Main, 1993), 98–124.

know my country, alas! An unfortunate Cassandra. For three years I have kept saying: The Jews are going to be assaulted."[4] Rahel put the blame on the patriotic and religious zeal that had made itself felt among Christian intellectuals in recent years, which nurtured a continual agitation against the Jewish minority. To most observers, however, the anti-Jewish outbreaks came as a surprise, and because they occurred at a time of mounting political tension in Germany, they appeared in an altogether different light. Just a few months earlier, the diplomat and playwright August Friedrich von Kotzebue, an exponent of reactionary politics, had been killed by a member of the *Burschenschaften,* and only a couple of weeks had passed since the attempted assassination of a high-ranking government official in Hesse. In Prussia and other German states, police agents were hunting for suspected demagogues, as well as for inflammatory books and papers. In the early days of August 1819, on the eve of the Carlsbad Decrees, the awareness of revolutionary unrest and the fear of conspiracies were omnipresent in public life as well as in the politicians' minds. It was only natural, therefore, that the disorders in Würzburg and elsewhere should be interpreted in the light of these general circumstances: the anti-Jewish riots, it seemed to many contemporaries, had been instigated and concerted by some secret plotters who used the widespread anti-Jewish bias to arouse general political unrest. This notion was supported by the seemingly inexplicable suddenness of the first outbursts, by their rapid and wide diffusion, by the similarity of reports about incidents in places far apart, and last but not least by that mysterious battle cry that was heard wherever anti-Jewish sentiment made itself felt, and that many believed to contain a cryptic message.[5]

While historians have in general found little reason to share the belief of contemporaries in the existence of such conspiracies, they have, in a sense, followed the main logic of this notion: behind the attacks against the Jews there were other, deeper motives, and in order to adequately understand these eruptions of violence and to properly assess the motivations and the objectives of the rioters, one had to first and foremost learn about the *general* political, social, and economic situation in Germany during the years after the Congress of Vienna. In 1950 Eleonore Sterling published her influential article on the Hep Hep riots, which she termed a

---

4. Quotation from a letter to her brother, Robert Ludwig, published for the first time in Wilhelm Freund, *Zur Judenfrage in Deutschland vom Standpunkte des Rechts und der Gewissensfreiheit,* vol. 1 (Berlin, 1843), 182.

5. It is indicative of this situation that quite frequently more attention was given to the battle cry of the rioters than to the rioting itself: it was assumed that solving the riddle of the enigmatic "Hep hep!" might help to reveal the identity of the instigators as well as their ultimate aims. See Rohrbacher, *Gewalt im Biedermeier,* 94–98.

"displacement of social protest." She meant to show how at a time of political frustration, social tension, and even famine, social protest was redirected against a defenseless minority. To her, the Hep Hep riots of 1819 were just one example of the many incidents of anti-Jewish violence in German history:

> All these incidents have occurred at moments of grave crisis and at times when oppression and the thwarting of the people's aspirations have been most severe. Finding their human and social needs frustrated, the people turned their agony against the nearest, most vulnerable objects—the Jews.[6]

Sterling did acknowledge that there were acute conflicts in the relationship between the Jewish minority and the Christian majority at the time of the Hep Hep riots, but she regarded them as secondary. As the true reasons behind the disturbances she saw the outcome of the Congress of Vienna, the aftereffects of the great famine of 1816–17, and the pauperization of the artisans, which had resulted from the influx of English manufactured goods after the continental blockade was lifted. When the general malaise became unbearable, the populace found relief in lashing out against an easy target.

Many other historians have since applied this explanatory pattern to identify the causes that led to anti-Jewish violence, and a scenario of grave crisis has been suggested for virtually every instance of anti-Jewish rioting in nineteenth-century Germany.[7] Jacob Katz, on the other hand, has disputed that the general malaise was indeed a *prerequisite* and *necessarily* the prime mover for such occurrences.[8] I believe that there is ample reason for

---

6. Eleonore Sterling, "Anti-Jewish Riots in Germany in 1819: A Displacement of Social Protest," *Historia Judaica* 12 (October 1950): 106.

7. See Herbert A. Strauss, "Die preussische Bürokratie und die antijüdischen Unruhen im Jahre 1834," in *Gegenwart im Rückblick: Festgabe für die Jüdische Gemeinde zu Berlin 25 Jahre nach dem Neubeginn,* edited by Kurt R. Grossmann and Herbert A. Strauss (Heidelberg, 1970), 27–55; Rainer Wirtz, *"Widersetzlichkeiten, Excesse, Crawalle, Tumulte und Skandale": Soziale Bewegung und gewalthafter sozialer Protest in Baden, 1815–1848* (Frankfurt, 1981); Moshe Zimmermann, "Antijüdischer Sozialprotest? Proteste von Unter- und Mittelschichten, 1819–1835," in *Arbeiter in Hamburg: Unterschichten, Arbeiter und Arbeiterbewegung seit dem ausgehenden 18. Jahrhundert,* edited by Arno Herzig, Dieter Langewiesche, and Arnold Sywottek (Hamburg, 1983), 89–94; Hans-Gerhard Husung, *Protest und Repression: Norddeutschland zwischen Restauration und Revolution* (Göttingen, 1983); Helmut Berding, *Moderner Antisemitismus in Deutschland* (Frankfurt/Main, 1988), 69, 73–74; and Arno Herzig, *Unterschichtenprotest in Deutschland, 1790–1870* (Göttingen, 1988), 60–62.

8. Jacob Katz, "The Hep Hep Riots in Germany of 1819: The Historical Background" (in Hebrew), *Zion* 38 (1973): 62–117; idem, *From Prejudice to Destruction: Antisemitism,*

such doubts. To be sure, social and economic grievances often added to existing anti-Jewish tensions, and in some cases they were obviously a main factor in anti-Jewish disturbances.[9] However, while it is essential to understand the role that general socioeconomic and political problems play in the intensification of popular resentment toward minority groups, I would argue that there is no mechanism that would make all instances of general crisis invariably lead to the eruption of violent outbursts against the Jewish minority. Likewise, general socioeconomic and political problems are but one possible factor, and not a sine qua non, behind the upsurge of Jew-hatred. Thus, anti-Jewish rioting in itself should not be taken as sufficient evidence of the acuteness of general problems in society.[10] By far not "all these incidents" of anti-Jewish violence in German history are to be seen against a background of "grave crisis" and "oppression and the thwarting of the people's aspirations," as Eleonore Sterling would have it. The Hep Hep riots of 1819 may be a case in point.

Würzburg at the Time of the Rioting

There certainly was a grave crisis in the general political, social, and economic conditions in Germany in 1819, but the characteristics of this crisis do not fit with the specific patterns of the rioting. To illustrate this, let us focus our attention on Würzburg for a moment. It would be sound to assume that the main factors behind the riots were of particular significance in that town, as it was the scene of the initial outbursts. However, in spite of the convergence of adverse developments that so strongly dominated the

---

1700–1933 (Cambridge, Mass., 1980), 97–104. Katz carried his argument much further in his "Misreadings of Antisemitism," *Commentary* 76, no. 1 (1983): 39–44; I do not concern myself here with this more generalizing denial of causal interrelations between general conditions in society and the rise of antisemitism.

9. This seems to be true for the anti-Jewish disturbances in Hesse and Bavaria during the revolution of 1830, for example; see Rohrbacher, *Gewalt im Biedermeier,* 176–77. The most obvious examples of anti-Jewish violence in the context of general social and economic suffering may be the disturbances in a few places in the eastern provinces of Prussia in 1847 and 1849; see Manfred Gailus, *Straße und Brot: Sozialer Protest in den deutschen Staaten unter besonderer Berücksichtigung Preußens, 1847–1849* (Göttingen, 1990), 282–301. However, the anti-Jewish aspect was secondary in these incidents. Overall, anti-Jewish tendencies did not play a dominant role in disturbances caused by the subsistence crisis of 1846–47. See Rohrbacher, *Gewalt im Biedermeier,* 230–32. For an altogether different view, see the contribution by Manfred Gailus to this volume.

10. See Strauss, "Die preussische Bürokratie," for a vivid description of misery and want that assumed crisis proportions in the Rhineland in 1834, when anti-Jewish rioting broke out. However, there was in fact no such crisis, and some of the main elements in the scenario described by Strauss (e.g., mass emigration of pauperized farmers and artisans to America) were entirely unknown to the Rhineland at that time.

Fig. 1.   Johann Michael Voltz, "Hepp! Hepp!" Copper engraving, 1819, 16.0 × 21.3 cm. (Courtesy Nürnberg, Germanisches Nationalmuseum, Graphische Sammlung. © Germanisches Nationalmuseum.)

overall picture, conditions varied considerably in different localities and regions in Germany. As it turns out, the various elements of the general malaise were conspicuously absent in the town of Würzburg.

1. Würzburg was no hotbed of political unrest, and there are hardly any signs that its citizens were very sensitive to political oppression in general. Even Würzburg's university was exceptionally calm during this uneasy period, and reports on the political activities of its students are rare and insignificant.[11] If the general frustration over the political situation had indeed been a major factor behind the outbreak of violence, one would assume that those who took a particular interest in politics—and revolutionary, nationalist members of the *Burschenschaften* in particular—would have taken a noticeable part in the disturbances. However, contrary to assertions by various historians, the rioting did not start at the university, nor were university students involved in any other way.[12] There were antigovernment overtones during the riots, but they were clearly secondary and reflected the grievances of Franconian particularism rather than any of the acutely pressing political questions of the years after the Congress of Vienna.[13] Thus it is unlikely that the general political situation should have generated the anti-Jewish riots in Würzburg.

2. It is highly improbable that the riots of 1819 were a belated reaction to the famine of 1816–17: *during* the famine, there had been violent outbursts that had aimed at a number of individuals—mostly Christian, sometimes Jewish—who were held directly responsible for the situation,

---

11. A delegation of students from Würzburg had participated in the famous convention at the Wartburg in 1817, but revolutionary and nationalist ideas do not seem to have had many ardent followers at the university in Würzburg. It ought to be mentioned that one year after the rioting, a Jewish graduate gave a public speech at the university. In spite of his passionate advocacy of Jewish emancipation and his outright denunciation of the ultranationalist attitude of the Burschenschaften as "un-German Germanness," he did not meet with any hostile reactions from his large audience.

12. See Sterling, "Anti-Jewish Riots," 121; Monika Richarz, *Der Eintritt der Juden in die akademischen Berufe: Jüdische Studenten und Akademiker in Deutschland, 1678–1848* (Tübingen, 1974), 119–20; Berding, *Moderner Antisemitismus,* 67. Sterling even asserts that the students had formed secret tribunals to "either expel the Jews or to extirpate them by means of sword and dagger." Eleonore Sterling, *Judenhaß: Die Anfänge des politischen Antisemitismus in Deutschland (1815–1850)* (Frankfurt, 1969), 149–50. Sterling took this quotation, however, from a threatening letter that was written only after the rioting had been quelled and that is unrelated to any student activities. Gehring-Münzel, *Vom Schutzjuden zum Staatsbürger,* 134–35. Later, the rector and the senate of Würzburg's university would explicitly compliment the students on their impeccable conduct during the anti-Jewish disturbances of 1819.

13. Gehring-Münzel, *Vom Schutzjuden zum Staatsbürger,* 153–64; Rohrbacher, *Gewalt im Biedermeier,* 138–41.

without ever threatening the Jews as such.[14] If such a displacement of aggression did not occur at the time of deepest misery, it is hard to explain why it should have happened so much later. Moreover, in 1819 there were no aftereffects of the famine in Würzburg that we can identify with any certainty. Wages being comparatively high and prices rather low, ordinary people hardly suffered from unusual want.[15]

3. ·The economic calamities and social tensions that accompanied the transformation from a largely agricultural to a predominantly commercial-industrial society were unlikely to be felt very strongly in an area where this transformation progressed at a moderate pace and on a limited scale. In the town of Würzburg, a gradual decline of traditional crafts was obvious, but it was far from assuming dramatic proportions. To be sure, the incorporation of the Grand Duchy of Würzburg into Bavaria and the loss of the town's status as a capital city in 1814 had dealt the local economy a blow. However, most complaints concerning economic conditions focused on irksome and costly tariff barriers and other obstacles to commerce, which residents had bemoaned in much the same manner before. The lifting of the continental blockade does not seem to have had the devastating effects on local trade that Sterling and others claim it did. There are no indications that artisans or tradespeople in Würzburg felt they were going through an acute crisis, and indeed there is no evidence that artisans or tradespeople played a significant part in the rioting.[16] Local conditions contrasted sharply with the crisis that plagued Nuremberg, for instance. There, local industry was hit hard when the market was flooded with English manufactured goods. In Nuremberg, however, there were no anti-Jewish riots in 1819.[17]

---

14. Wilhelm Abel, *Massenarmut und Hungerkrisen im vorindustriellen Europa: Versuch einer Synopse* (Hamburg, 1974), 323, 416; John Dexter Post, *The Last Great Subsistence Crisis in the Western World* (Baltimore, 1977), 75. In Franconia, Jews seem not to have been implicated in the dearth of 1816–17, and no incidents of violence against Jews were reported in the area at that time.

15. Rohrbacher, *Gewalt im Biedermeier,* 132–33. City authorities even intimated that the disturbances were furthered by high wages and low prices, which let the riffraff indulge in heavier drinking than usual. Prices had dropped well below the pre-1816 level as early as summer 1818 and had remained more or less stable since then. See Moritz J. Elsas, *Umriß einer Geschichte der Preise und Löhne in Deutschland,* vols. 1, 2 (Leiden, 1936–40).

16. Gehring-Münzel, *Vom Schutzjuden zum Staatsbürger,* 156–57. It should be stressed that contrary to oft-repeated assertions, there is no evidence that merchants and artisans instigated the rioting. Several threatening letters reflecting the interests of tradespeople were circulated in Würzburg only *after* the riots had been quelled, and while they testify to an attempt to exploit the situation created by the riots, they should not be mistaken for documents exposing the motivations of the rioters.

17. Rohrbacher, *Gewalt im Biedermeier,* 134–35. There was also no evidence of anti-Jewish disturbances in nearby Fürth and Zirndorf. See Jacob Toury, "Self-Defense in the Days of the 'Hep Hep' Riots" (in Hebrew), *Yalkut Moreshet* 14 (1972): 114.

Different Patterns of Action Testifying to a Common Cause

It is evident that in the summer of 1819 Würzburg was not a scene of general, unspeakable misery and despair, and there was no gloomy awareness of the imminent end of the world that would have made people turn against the Jews, as has been suggested.[18] The repercussions of the general crisis appear to have had only very limited effects on local conditions of life. Thus, while this crisis may in some ways have facilitated the eruption and diffusion of violent disorder, it hardly engendered it, and an outright *displacement* of social protest is a most unlikely assumption. Instead, I agree with Jacob Katz that the riots were a genuine expression of Christian-Jewish conflict proper. Moreover, I would argue that the specific local peculiarities of the rioting are indicative of its immediate causes and objectives: in each of the main locations—Würzburg, Frankfurt, and Hamburg—the riots adopted a peculiar pattern, and it is the *differences* in these patterns that may help us to identify the *common* cause of the rioters.

In Würzburg there were two targets that stand out: first, the residence of the wealthiest Jewish family, which was attacked with particular fervor; and second, the signboards that were torn off from literally all Jewish-owned shops. In Frankfurt the attacks began with Jewish pedestrians' being chased away from the public promenade and Jewish customers being ejected from the post office. In Hamburg the riots centered upon the fashionable cafés, where Jewish customers were thrown out. In a second phase, three Jewish-owned houses were singled out to be attacked, and only at a later stage did these attacks against selected targets turn into an indiscriminate persecution of Hamburg's Jews.[19]

Heterogeneous as they may seem, the main targets in Würzburg, Frankfurt, and Hamburg have one quality in common: they were the most conspicuous local symbols of Jewish aspirations for emancipation and of Christian unwillingness to accept profound changes in the status of the Jews.

1. By acquiring their palatial residence at an auction in 1803, the von Hirsch family had forced the Bavarian government to grant them a residence permit, making them the first Jews to be readmitted to Würzburg since the expulsion of 1642. To make matters worse, their new home had previously belonged to a monastery, and its acquisition by a Jewish family was a direct result of the secularization of church property

---

18. See Rainer Erb and Werner Bergmann, *Die Nachtseite der Judenemanzipation: Der Widerstand gegen die Integration der Juden in Deutschland, 1780–1860* (Berlin, 1989), 237–38. The apocalyptic circle that Erb and Bergmann refer to was in fact entirely marginal—comprising probably no more than one household in 1819—and completely isolated, and it did not concern itself with the Jews at all. See Rohrbacher, *Gewalt im Biedermeier,* 133–34.

19. Rohrbacher, *Gewalt im Biedermeier,* 105–6, 120–22.

by the Bavarian government.[20] The secularization, in which Jewish traders played a major role, must have seemed an abominable sacrilege to Würzburg's Catholic citizens and a symbol of political humiliation as well, as it signified that the sovereignty of the episcopal principality had come to an end.[21] Thus the splendid home of the von Hirsch family was highly symbolic of the change of times and of the transgression of traditional limits by the Jews in more than one respect. The same goes for the other main target of the attacks. While Jews had been banned from living in Würzburg since 1642, they had been allowed storage rooms for their merchandise in the city. However, they had not been permitted to openly sell their goods nor to advertise their business. After the gradual readmission of Jews beginning in 1803, these regulations remained in force until 1816. The signboards of Jewish-owned shops were therefore a conspicuous novelty that also "advertised" that the times of traditional restrictions on Jewish life were coming to an end.

2.   Frankfurt had been the only German city with a walled-in Jewish ghetto. The city's Jews were cooped up in an overpopulated, dark, unhealthy lane, which they were not allowed to leave at night nor on Sundays and Christian holidays. With the bombardment of the city by the French in 1796, the ghetto walls came down, and most restrictions on Jews' freedom of movement were abolished shortly thereafter. However, entry to the public promenade remained forbidden to Jews until it was granted by the government in 1806—and it is significant of the symbolic character of this highly controversial issue that this was the very first official act of Dalberg's "Napoleonic" rule over the city.[22] One other conspicuous restriction remained even longer: Jews were not allowed to enter the post office. Like the admission of Jews to the city's promenade, this had been the subject of passionate debates for a long time, and it was not until 1817 that this peculiarity was finally done away with.[23] By their very presence on the promenade and in the post office, Frankfurt's Jews confronted Christians with the evident changes in their status, signifying at the

---

20. Gehring-Münzel, *Vom Schutzjuden zum Staatsbürger,* 77–79.

21. See the auction lists in Leo Günther, *Würzburger Chronik,* vol. 3 (Würzburg, 1925), 14–18, where Jews are identified as the sole buyers of jewels and other precious objects formerly in the possession of the church. On the vicious exploitation of this issue in later anti-Jewish polemics, see Erb and Bergmann, *Die Nachtseite der Judenemanzipation,* 221. The episcopal principality of Würzburg had ceased to exist in 1802, when its territory came under Bavarian rule for the first time. After the interlude of the independent Grand Duchy, established in 1806, the principality of Würzburg was incorporated into Bavaria in 1814.

22. Isidor Kracauer, *Geschichte der Juden in Frankfurt am Main,* vol. 2 (Frankfurt, 1927), 360.

23. Ibid., 291–92.

same time that the traditional, exclusive prerogatives of Frankfurt's Christian citizens could be validated no longer.

3. In Hamburg there was no ghetto, but Jewish residence had been restricted to two areas. While the precise designation of the boundaries of these areas was hotly debated in the late eighteenth century, the abolition of these restrictions remained unthinkable even much later.[24] During French rule, however, a few wealthy families had moved to streets that were, by tradition, forbidden to Jews, and in 1819 the rioters literally went out of their way to attack these houses while taking no notice of many others that would have been much easier to reach.[25] The presence of Jewish customers in the fashionable cafés had been a subject of heated public argument in Hamburg before—and here we enter the sphere of agitation at last. Traditionally, Jews were not allowed entry to sites of public amusement in Hamburg. In 1798 and again in 1810, a literary debate had flared up over this issue, and it is evident from the articles and pamphlets that debating the presence of Jews in the cafés was equivalent to debating their right to a place in civic society.[26] One pamphleteer held that the differentiation between various social classes was an inherent quality of cultured states, and therefore the places where they enjoyed the pleasures of social life had to be kept apart as well. Tellingly, his coffeehouse argument culminated in the general statement that as long as the Jews separated themselves from the rest of mankind by adhering to their specific laws and customs, they could not gain full citizenship and therefore could not participate in the privileges of civic society.[27]

Anti-Jewish Literary Agitation on the Eve of the Rioting

Hamburg is also exemplary of the local repercussions of the general anti-Jewish literary agitation of that time. A plethora of tracts and pamphlets

---

24. Jürgen Ellermeyer, "Schranken der Freien Reichsstadt: Gegen Grundeigentum und Wohnungswahl der Hamburger Juden bis ins Zeitalter der Aufklärung," in *Die Hamburger Juden in der Emanzipationsphase (1780–1870)*, edited by Peter Freimark and Arno Herzig (Hamburg, 1989), 194–202. As a matter of fact, it took the disastrous Great Fire of 1842, which left the city largely in ruins, to bring freedom of settlement to Hamburg's Jews. See Helga Krohn, *Die Juden in Hamburg, 1800–1850* (Frankfurt: a.M., 1967), 64, 100.

25. Rohrbacher, *Gewalt im Biedermeier*, 146–47.

26. Franklin Kopitzsch, *Grundzüge einer Sozialgeschichte der Aufklärung in Hamburg und Altona*, vol. 2 (Hamburg, 1982), 510–11.

27. *Critische Beleuchtung und Rüge der in den Hamburgischen gemeinnützigen Nachrichten erschienenen Abhandlung: Über das gesellschaftliche Verhältniß der Juden zu den Christen in Hamburg, in besonderer Rücksicht auf öffentliche Gast-, Caffee-, Restaurations- und Speise-Häuser* (Hamburg, 1810), 8–9, 11.

were written against the Jews during those years in Germany, many in the spirit of German nationalism and Christian romanticism.[28] After the Congress of Vienna, which had frustrated all aspirations for national strength and unity, the quest for German national identity made it all the more important to expose the characteristics of the outside enemies—the French—and of the outsiders within, namely, the Jews. In fact, the French and the Jews were described in much the same way, and their alleged marks of character served to illustrate the opposing characteristics that supposedly forged the corporate identity of the Germans.[29] Friedrich Ludwig Jahn, the influential *Turnvater,* had coined the motto that "hatred of everything foreign was the German's duty"; but with the French living mostly in France, the Jewish minority in Germany was the more immediate target of such hatred. To many pamphleteers who rallied to the defense of German Christians against the unjustified pretensions of the Jews, this was first and foremost a question of religion. Achim von Arnim's Christlich-deutsche Tischgesellschaft, however, refused to accept even baptized Jews, and protoracist overtones are noticeable in many anti-Jewish writings of this time.[30]

Indeed, the voices that were raised against the Jews were far from sounding in unison, but they formed a vociferous chorus. For all their ideological differences, rationalistic liberals adhering to the concept of enlightenment seemed to join forces with romanticists idealizing the political, social, and religious homogeneity of the Middle Ages. Respectable intellectuals appeared to side with journalists who specialized in scandal-mongering and with playwrights of limited literary merits. The contents of anti-Jewish tracts written by university professors such as the historian Friedrich Rühs and the philosopher Jakob Friedrich Fries were propagated well beyond a learned readership, being broadly echoed by newspa-

---

28. For a general survey, see Selma Stern-Täubler, "Der literarische Kampf um die Emanzipation in den Jahren 1816–1820 und seine ideologischen und soziologischen Voraussetzungen," *Hebrew Union College Annual* 23, pt. 2 (1950/51): 171–96. A broader historical perspective is provided by Katz, *From Prejudice to Destruction,* 51–91.

29. See Michael Jeismann, *Das Vaterland der Feinde: Studien zum nationalen Feindbegriff und Selbstverständnis in Deutschland und Frankreich, 1792–1918* (Stuttgart, 1992).

30. See Heinz Härtl, "Romantischer Antisemitismus: Arnim und die Tischgesellschaft," *Weimarer Beiträge* 33 (1987): 1159–73; Wolfgang Frühwald, "Antijudaismus in der Zeit der Romantik," in *Conditio Judaica: Judentum, Antisemitismus und deutschsprachige Literatur vom 18. Jahrhundert bis zum Ersten Weltkrieg,* edited by Hans Otto Horch and Horst Denkler, vol. 2 (Tübingen, 1989), 72–91. See also Uriel Tal, "Young German Intellectuals on Romanticism and Judaism: Spiritual Turbulence in the Early Nineteenth Century," in *Salo W. Baron Jubilee Volume,* vol. 2 (New York, 1974–75), 919–38. Naturally, this is especially true for the more rationalistic and secularist strands in anti-Jewish ideology. For a revealing analysis of the vocabulary of early-nineteenth-century anti-Jewish polemicists, see Nicoline Hortzitz, *"Früh-Antisemitismus" in Deutschland (1789–1871/2)* (Tübingen, 1988).

per writers and even read out to people in taverns.[31] In the spring and summer of 1819, the popular weekly *Dorfzeitung* devoted no fewer than six lead articles to a markedly aggressive campaign against Jewish economic activities and emancipation.[32] Anti-Jewish plays, full of venom, were staged; some of them were extremely successful, drawing large audiences for weeks on end.[33] In addition, several newspapers took to printing such plays in full. Reviews of anti-Jewish pamphlets offered the opportunity for newspapers to quote them at length or even reprint them, and anti-Jewish poems and inflammatory articles contributed to a continual undertone of Jew-hatred in the press. Thus the waves of agitation against the Jews had been running high in Germany in the years before the Hep Hep riots.

Like officials elsewhere, local authorities in Hamburg sought to curb these tendencies, which they feared might lead to political unrest. However, in spite of their efforts, anti-Jewish plays appear to have been staged in the city, and their spiteful message was disseminated by other means as well.[34] Beginning in August 1815, a local journal, the *Niederdeutsche Blätter*, printed several such plays in full, including the extremely popular *Unser Verkehr* (Our crowd) by Karl Borromäus Alexander Sessa; and before long another paper, the *Norddeutsche Blätter*, followed suit. Although many of the more notorious plays and pamphlets were banned by the authorities, that could not prevent ordinary newspaper readers from devouring such antisemitic outpouring—and they did not have to

---

31. Friedrich Rühs, *Über die Ansprüche der Juden an das deutsche Bürgerrecht* (Berlin, 1816); idem, *Die Rechte des Christenthums und des deutschen Volks, vertheidigt gegen die Ansprüche der Juden und ihrer Verfechter* (Berlin, 1816); Jakob Friedrich Fries, *Über die Gefährdung des Wohlstandes und Charakters der Deutschen durch die Juden* (Heidelberg, 1816). Both tracts by Rühs had been published for the first time in *Zeitschrift für die neueste Geschichte, die Staaten- und Völkerkunde* in 1815–16. While Rühs did not gain much renown as a historian, Fries was among the most influential philosophers of his time, and his adaptions of Kantian teachings had a lasting impact on German philosophical thought. A liberal thinker and an ardent nationalist, Fries had participated in the convention at the Wartburg in 1817 and was suspended from lecturing at the University of Heidelberg on charges of demagogy in 1819. See Hans Kraft, "Jakob Friedrich Fries (1773–1843) im Urteil der Philosophiegeschichtsschreibung" (Düsseldorf: Univ. Diss., 1980), where Fries's anti-Jewish tendencies are minimized. His brochure *Über die Gefährdung des Wohlstandes und Charakters,* originally a review of the tract *Über die Ansprüche der Juden* by Rühs, is reprinted in the recent multivolume edition of his complete works: Jakob Friedrich Fries, *Sämtliche Schriften,* vol. 25 (Aalen, 1996), 150–73. See Erb and Bergmann, *Die Nachtseite der Judenemanzipation,* 262–63.

32. Erb and Bergmann, *Die Nachtseite der Judenemanzipation,* 267.

33. See Hans-Joachim Neubauer, *Judenfiguren: Drama und Theater im frühen 19. Jahrhundert* (Frankfurt/Main, 1994).

34. Hans-Joachim Neubauer, "Auf Begehr—Unser Verkehr: Über eine judenfeindliche Theaterposse im Jahre 1815," in *Antisemitismus und jüdische Geschichte: Studien zu Ehren von Herbert A. Strauss,* edited by Rainer Erb and Michael Schmidt (Berlin, 1987), 318.

look very hard to find more of it: in 1816 the *Orient oder das Hamburger Morgenblatt* carried a near-complete reprint of the pamphlet *Über die Gefährdung des Wohlstandes und Charakters der Deutschen durch die Juden* by Fries, supplemented by a euphorically approving commentary, while *Hamburgs Wächter* quoted extensively from the anti-Jewish tracts by Rühs. In 1817 the same journal featured a series of articles on Albert Wurm, an actor whose appearances in plays such as *Unser Verkehr* had gained him much popularity and whose supposedly Jewish way of declamation was greatly admired by those who took delight in mocking the Jews.[35] Some weeks later, *Hamburgs Wächter* treated its Protestant readership to Martin Luther's most vicious anti-Jewish rhetoric and went on to comment on the deliberations of the national assembly:

> Germany's expectancy of the verdict of the illustrious assembly in Frankfurt is getting more and more tense and anxious. May the genius of Christianity light it on its way. . . . May a Christian Cato rise among the assembled nobles, and, like the old Roman exclaiming "Down with Carthago" at every vote taken in the Senate, may he let the general motto of the German people be heard every day: "Out with the Jews!"—His name will mark a page in history, and it will live on in honor and fame among future generations.[36]

In the meantime, the Lutheran *Lesefrüchte vom Felde der neueren Literatur* had taken to systematically preaching Jew-hatred as well. Other local papers would print an occasional poem mocking Jewish soldiers and invariably proving they were unfit for military service; or they would complain about the allegedly provocative behavior of Jewish youths, demanding vigorous reaction from Hamburg's hearty Christians. Allusions to violence as an appropriate means of putting the Jews in their place were no rare occurrence. When in 1818 the Hamburg lawyer and theologian Johann Ludolf Holst published his influential anti-Jewish tract *Über das Verhältniß der Juden zu den Christen in den deutschen Handelsstädten,* the display of Jew-hatred had already been on a firm footing in local public life for quite some time.

Anti-Jewish Agitation and Action in Würzburg

There was more than just a continual undertone of anti-Jewish agitation in the years before the Hep Hep riots. Like Hamburg, Würzburg had its own

---

35. See Julius von Voß, "Ueber des Schauspielers Herrn Wurm jüdische Deklamation," in *Jüdische Romantik und Wahrheit* (Berlin, 1817), 291–300.

36. *Hamburgs Wächter* 29 (1817): 229.

anti-Jewish pamphleteer. In May 1819 Thomas August Scheuring had published the memorandum *Das Staatsbürgerrecht der Juden,* a rejoinder to a pro-emancipation petition to the Bavarian Diet that had been filed by a member of the von Hirsch family.[37] Scheuring reflects the spirit of Christian-Germanic romanticism but at the same time betrays a rationalistic attitude; he is remarkable for his nationalistic approach and for his implicit equating of civic society and national entity. The Jews, it was obvious, could partake in neither. They were Orientals who had merely infiltrated European societies without ever being able to be anything but foreigners to European nations. Emancipation and integration of the Jews were unthinkable, since civic rights were the exclusive property of the "indigenous" nation in which no foreign "tribe" could have a share.[38]

While few may have read Scheuring's pamphlet, its publication certainly caused a stir in Würzburg. The excitement culminated two months later when a scathing review appeared in the local *Intelligenzblatt,* on July 20. The author, Sebald Brendel, a law professor at the University of Würzburg, was widely believed to have written the petition for emancipation that had been published in the name of Salomon Hirsch.[39] Scheuring's coarse and provocative response to Brendel's review article was published in the *Intelligenzblatt* on July 29.[40] Just a few days before the outbreak of the anti-Jewish violence in Würzburg, then, a passionate exchange between two well-known citizens over the emancipation of the Jews had reached its climax. Again, few may have actually read the *Intelligenzblatt,* and many may have known little of the arguments employed by the adversaries, but it was public knowledge that Scheuring had written "against the Jews" while Brendel was "in favor of the Jews." There can be little doubt that in early August 1819, Scheuring's scandalous conflict with Brendel was a popular topic of discussion among ordinary people in the streets of Würzburg.[41]

---

37. Thomas A. Scheuring, *Das Staatsbürgerrecht der Juden: Eine unpartheiische Würdigung in Beziehung auf die von Salomon Hirsch in Würzburg an die Ständeversammlung in Baiern eingereichte Vorstellung* (Würzburg, 1819); Salomon Hirsch, *Unterthänigste Bitte um Revision derjenigen Edikte und Anordnungen, welche die Rechte der Bekenner der mosaischen Religion betreffen* (Würzburg, 1819).

38. Scheuring, *Das Staatsbürgerrecht der Juden,* 36, 41.

39. Gehring-Münzel, *Vom Schutzjuden zum Staatsbürger,* 128.

40. Both Brendel's review and Scheuring's rejoinder are reprinted in the appendix to Katz, "The Hep Hep Riots," 109–12.

41. Even a poorly educated Jewish eyewitness to the rioting was able to provide many details about Scheuring, his pamphlet, and the controversy it caused. This witness, who was barely capable of writing decent Yiddish, would have made a most unlikely reader of the *Intelligenzblatt* or of any German-language pamphlets. The errors and unfounded assumptions contained in his account may be all the more indicative of the general hearsay that permeated the city in those days. See Bamberger, *Beiträge zur Geschichte der Juden,* 18.

However, it took a peculiar coincidence to finally trigger the rioting. Scheuring's tract and his heated argument with Brendel had focused the attention of the local public on a question that was at the top of the political agenda in Bavaria at exactly that time. In February 1819 the Bavarian Diet had convened in Munich, and it seemed likely from the outset of its deliberations that wide-ranging reforms would be initiated. One of the topics of parliamentary debate was a clause in the federal act of 1815 that ruled that religious freedom must be granted by the member states. On July 22, the king declared that a revision of the laws concerning the Jews was imminent.[42] Speculations about the eventual results of the drawn-out consultations of the Diet were mounting—and tension in the streets of Würzburg was running high. For some days, occasional shouts of "Hep hep!" had been heard in the city, and on the evening of August 2 more severe disorders occurred for the first time. The next day Wilhelm Josef Behr, the University of Würzburg delegate to the Diet, was to return from Munich. He was a liberal and had spoken in support of Jewish emancipation, albeit with some caution.[43] However, there are no indications that his support of Jews was known to the citizens of his hometown, where he enjoyed considerable popularity. On August 3 a large crowd gathered in the streets of Würzburg to greet Behr upon his arrival and to learn about the outcome of the deliberations of the Diet. University professors and students had set out to meet him and lead him into town in a procession. In this excited atmosphere, the rioting flared up.[44]

The Hep Hep riots, it seems to me, are first and foremost an example of "violent politics." In the main locations where they occurred, they display a remarkable degree of logic and accuracy in striking at specific targets that were symbolic of their primary cause. Local conflicts over the rights of the Jewish minority made it easy for local citizens to identify the points at issue in the wider debate over Jewish emancipation, as the general ideological argument seemed closely connected to local civic affairs. It is certainly sound to assume that the subtleties of the reasoning evolved by the various anti-Jewish agitators were lost upon the public at large. Yet the continual flow of anti-Jewish agitation, which was disseminated in many different ways, added considerably to the sense of acuteness of the problem, and some of its more vicious varieties supported the notion that violence was an adequate and legitimate means of dealing with the Jews. In Würzburg the local debate over Jewish emancipation, fueled by literary

---

42. See Adolf Eckstein, *Der Kampf der Juden um ihre Emanzipation in Bayern* (Fürth, 1905), 34–36.

43. See Katz, *From Prejudice to Destruction,* 98, where Behr is identified as "the foremost spokesman" defending the Jews. For an overall appraisal, see Max Domarus, *Bürgermeister Behr: Ein Kämpfer für den Rechtsstaat,* 3d ed. (Würzburg, 1985).

44. Günther, *Würzburger Chronik,* 381–82, 388, 394–97.

agitation, had just reached its climax when the delegate to the Diet was to return from the parliamentary debate, and it was at this very moment that the riots started. There is indeed a connection between ideology, agitation, and action that proved crucial in the events of 1819.

The Multiple Causes of the Rioting

This attempt at identifying the main factors that led to the eruption of anti-Jewish violence in 1819 does not maintain that resistance to Jewish emancipation was the one and only motivation for the rioting; indeed, the riots of 1819 were heterogeneous in many ways. But that does not invalidate the identification of their main causes and their primary goals.

1. While it appears justified to state that the rioters acted with obvious determination in places such as Würzburg, Frankfurt, and Hamburg, purposefully striking at specific targets that symbolized the questions at issue, such a statement is not necessarily valid for every individual involved in the rioting in these places. From official reports and other testimony, it is evident that those who joined in the rioting against the Jews in Würzburg may indeed have done so for the most varied reasons—and sometimes perhaps for no specific reason at all. Some of them were drunk; others just ran after the riotous mob to take part in the excitement. And it certainly took much less Jew-hatred than greed to participate in the pillaging, or to take advantage of the situation and add to the damage done to a competitor.[45] Yet it is apparent that for all their heterogeneity, and for all the different elements involved, the riots in Würzburg, Frankfurt, and Hamburg had a highly specific profile that distinguished them from mere acts of violence serving no particular purpose beyond looting and just dealing the Jews a powerful blow.

2. What holds true for Würzburg, Frankfurt, and Hamburg may not be true for other places in the chain of events. In some instances—especially in rural areas—there are no indications of specific reasons for the rioting, unless we are willing to give credence to the stereotyped accusation of usurious practices brought against the Jewish population in the countryside.[46] The systematic pillage of the Jewish lane in Heidelberg

---

45. A report by state authorities on their investigation of the rioting in Würzburg contains data on twelve defendants, information that is quite telling in this respect. See Jacob Katz, *Die Hep-Hep-Verfolgungen des Jahres 1819* (Berlin, 1994), 97–106.

46. For a discussion of this stereotype as an explanatory pattern in the context of the anti-Jewish rioting during the Revolution of 1848, see Rohrbacher, *Gewalt im Biedermeier,* 234–40. There are no indications that numerous non-Jewish debtors in rural areas went bankrupt around 1819 because of contracts made with Jewish creditors during the famine of 1816, as has been suggested by Post, *The Last Great Subsistence Crisis,* 172–73, and Berding, *Moderner Antisemitismus,* 70.

betrays little similarity to the attacks in Würzburg, Frankfurt, and Hamburg, where looting was an exception in the rioting.[47] In the Rhineland, the Hep Hep riots were echoed in October 1819, when a ritual murder accusation made Catholic villagers turn against their Jewish neighbors.[48] It is uncertain whether the issue of Jewish emancipation played a decisive role in any of these incidents, and it is most likely that in some of them it did not play a role at all. Yet despite these important qualifications, and despite the other factors that can be identified in the rioting, the conflict over Jewish emancipation was the decisive element that triggered it; and after the initial outbreak of violence in Würzburg, it was the recurrent, central issue at other main locations of the rioting.

In view of the heterogeneity of the riots, and considering the multitude of motivations that may have nurtured them, it appears essential to differentiate between central and peripheral issues—between specific, immediate causes and generally supportive factors. In this latter category, the explanatory pattern provided by Eleonore Sterling does make an important contribution to our insight into the historical background of the riots: somehow or other, the Jews were implicated in more or less all ills that befell the Christian population and the German nation—not necessarily in reality, to be sure, but certainly in the imagination of Christians. In this way, the general crisis—or, rather, the perception of a general crisis—may indeed have constituted an important factor in the outbreak and spread of the Hep Hep riots.[49] However, it is not the general crisis but the

---

47. A detailed and reliable account of events in Heidelberg is provided by Martin Krauss, "Zwischen Emanzipation und Antisemitismus (1802–1862)," in *Geschichte der Juden in Heidelberg* (Heidelberg, 1996), 181–89.

48. See Stefan Rohrbacher, "Die 'Hep-Hep-Krawalle' und der 'Ritualmord' des Jahres 1819 zu Dormagen," in Erb and Schmidt, *Antisemitismus und jüdische Geschichte,* 135–47.

49. Just a few days before the riots flared up in Würzburg, a letter was published in the local *Intelligenzblatt* of faraway Ravensburg, in the Kingdom of Württemberg, unmasking the Jews in Germany as secret agents for a London trade firm: the English firm thanked the Jews in Germany for their tireless activities on the firm's behalf. The Jews had succeeded in flooding the market in Germany with cheap English manufactured goods, thereby ruining German factories and German artisans and tradespeople. Thanks to this ideal partnership, the Jews would soon be able to gain supremacy over the impoverished non-Jews in Germany; and once they had made them totally dependent on imported English goods, the English would be quite willing to be circumcised and to receive some shiploads of rabbis. *Intelligenzblatt* (Donau-Kreis), Ravensburg, July 26, 1819, 129–30. The publication of this fake letter in the newspaper of a remote provincial town shortly before the riots started is a mere coincidence as far as potential effects on events in Würzburg are concerned, but it is indicative of the range of allegations that were circulated against the Jews in Germany at that specific time.

resistance to the process of Jewish emancipation and its local repercussions that can be identified as the immediate cause and the primary reason for the eruption of anti-Jewish violence in 1819, and that ultimately accounts for the specific élan, the emotional force, and the destructive energy of the rioting.

The Hep Hep riots of 1819 were not to be the last wave of anti-Jewish violence in Germany during the first half of the nineteenth century. During the revolutionary unrest of 1830, violent acts against the Jewish minority occurred in numerous towns and villages, mostly in Hesse, Bavaria, and Baden, but also in Hamburg, where violent anti-Jewish rioting eventually turned into a general revolt against municipal authorities and the military.[50] While the political aspects of the riots in Hamburg are fairly obvious, the incidents of anti-Jewish rioting in 1830 in general appear to be closely linked with the subsistence crisis that plagued many areas at that time and in which the Jews were widely believed to be implicated.[51] Thus the explanatory pattern applied by Eleonore Sterling and others to the Hep Hep riots of 1819 might make a more convincing case with regard to the incidents of 1830.

A much more serious wave of anti-Jewish violence, however, occurred during the revolution of 1848, particularly in its initial phase. Incidents of violence were reported from most parts of Germany, but they were especially harsh and widespread in some rural areas of Baden, where hardly a Jewish community seems to have been spared.[52] While it is certainly safe to assume that the most varied motives were involved in these acts, and that more often than not general grievances about social and economic conditions and the alleged implication of the Jews in these conditions may have been a decisive factor, there can be little doubt that the question of Jewish emancipation stands out as the most important single factor in the anti-Jewish rioting of 1848.[53] Thus it is important to note that in several places, complaints about the alleged implication of the Jews in social and economic misery led to attacks on individual Jewish "profiteers," and anti-Jewish bias certainly added to the aggressive zeal of their attackers. However, these incidents were not typical of the widespread and violent anti-Jewish rioting that occurred during the revolution of 1848; it was conflicts over the emancipation of the Jews, par-

---

50. See Rohrbacher, *Gewalt im Biedermeier,* 161–64.

51. Ibid., 165–80.

52. Ibid., 181–220.

53. For an altogether different view, see the contribution by Manfred Gailus to this volume.

ticularly over their status in local society, that resulted in indiscriminate persecutions of the Jewish minority.[54] In this perspective, the Hep Hep riots of 1819 could be seen as the first significant manifestation of the exclusionary anti-Jewish violence that accompanied the process of emancipation in Germany and that reached its peak, ironically, during the "Year of Freedom."

---

54. The importance of conflicts over Jewish emancipation and its local repercussions is highlighted by the fact that these conflicts account for numerous cases of very serious anti-Jewish rioting. Of the incidents of anti-Jewish violence reported in March 1848 in Baden, at least 25 percent can be ascribed with certainty to conflicts over Jewish emancipation, with no specific causes being recognizable in 60 percent of all cases. Of the worst cases of rioting, however, over 62 percent were evidently caused by conflicts over emancipation. See Stefan Rohrbacher, "Deutsche Revolution und antijüdische Gewalt (1815–1848/49)," in *Die Konstruktion der Nation gegen die Juden,* edited by Peter Alter, Claus-Ekkehard Bärsch, and Peter Berghoff (Munich, 1999), 45.

Anti-Jewish Emotion and Violence in the 1848 Crisis of German Society

Manfred Gailus
Translated by Miriamne Fields

At no other time in nineteenth-century German history were outburts of collective violence so widespread as during the severe crisis of the late 1840s.[1] This was true not only in 1848, the year of the revolution—the so-called mad year of violent conflicts between diverse groups—but also, at the very least, in 1846, 1847, and 1849. Over a long transitional period, a corporative-feudal society developed into a bourgeois-capitalistic society. This was a full-blown and far-reaching societal crisis of modernization. A survey of all the actions, rebellions, and excesses of these crisis years initially reveals a chaotic and tangled web of confrontations, conflicts, group solidarity, and collective phobias. Many contemporaries, witnessing their society caught in a period of extreme tumult, saw everything familiar coming apart. Traditional group identities, in danger of partially disintegrat-

Translated from the German. I would like to thank Ulrich Wyrwa (Berlin) for his suggestions and criticism.

　　1. For general information, see Richard Tilly, "Unruhen und Proteste in Deutschland im 19. Jahrhundert: Ein erster Überblick," in idem, *Kapital, Staat und sozialer Protest in der deutschen Industrialisierung* (Göttingen, 1980), 143–74; and Manfred Gailus, *Straße und Brot: Sozialer Protest in den deutschen Staaten unter besonderer Berücksichtigung Preußens, 1847–1849* (Göttingen, 1990). For the most recent review of research on the revolution, see Dieter Dowe, Heinz-Gerhard Haupt, and Dieter Langewiesche, eds., *Europa 1848: Revolution und Reform* (Bonn, 1998).

ing, reasserted and consolidated themselves while other identities were just beginning to take shape.

In part, the crisis involved contradictory processes that were occurring simultaneously: on the one hand, new feelings of community and brotherhood were unfolding; on the other, a newly intensified polarization and espousal of hostile images developed. Everywhere, stricter demarcations of the "other," of groups with competing interests or opposing aims, were drawn. The disintegration of group relations as well as abrupt about-faces were the order of the day. The exceptional revolutionary situation demanded that "one's own" be secured against every "other" or "outsider." In the few weeks of March and April 1848, during which the revolutionary mood grew ever stronger, collective self-perceptions and views of the "other," "outsiders," "friends," and "enemies" intensified much more than in previous years or decades.

The temporary rediscovery of "the Jew," both as friend and foe, was also part of this broad reorganization of identities. Anti-Jewish actions, embedded in a widely expanding range of anti-Jewish resentment, rumors, and emotions, constituted one component of the conflict in this highly mobilized society, although, when viewed in a larger context, they were not central to the violent conflict.[2] Violent group behavior in its many different forms, ranging from the invention of hostile rumors to malicious anonymous threats and threatening public gestures, to symbolic acts of punishment and even excessive physical violence, was part of the shared repertoire of behavior. Antifeudal peasant riots and social rebellions of the rural lower classes dominated the countryside; subsistence riots (price increase unrest), politicized charivari (collective acts of censure), communal political unrest and uprisings, worker protests (strikes and violent acts such as Luddism), and crowd actions over major issues of national policy characterized the events in the cities.

I

Anti-Jewish riots occupied a special place among the violent social disturbances of this epoch. The number of anti-Jewish acts was smaller than the number of previously mentioned types of conflict, but in some regions,

---

2. Cf. Jacob Toury, *Soziale und politische Geschichte der Juden in Deutschland, 1847–1871: Zwischen Revolution, Reaktion und Emanzipation* (Düsseldorf, 1977); Reinhard Rürup, "The European Revolutions of 1848 and Jewish Emancipation," in *Revolution and Evolution: 1848 in German-Jewish History,* edited by Werner E. Mosse, Arnold Paucker, and Reinhard Rürup (Tübingen, 1981), 1–53; and Stefan Rohrbacher, *Gewalt im Biedermeier: Antijüdische Ausschreitungen in Vormärz und Revolution (1815–1848/49)* (Frankfurt/Main, 1993), 181–244.

such as northern Baden, they appeared for a short time as the dominant form of violence.[3] The Jewish experience during the revolutionary period was shaped primarily by a paradox of simultaneous hope and fear: hope for progress in emancipation legislation, national policy, and complete equal rights; and fear of the revival of aggressive anti-Jewish myths and rumors, emotional outbursts, and collective outbreaks of violence, particularly in the countryside and in small towns.[4] A closer examination finds an increase in anti-Jewish emotion and actions, primarily in connection with widespread food riots, already in the prerevolutionary crisis period of 1846 and 1847.

For the prerevolutionary year of 1847, in non-Habsburg Germany alone, there is evidence of more than 210 food revolts related to the wave of price increases throughout the country.[5] These revolts demonstrate the almost ubiquitous presence of severe social dissent over the market and the way in which the basic food supply was managed in times of shortage. Should it continue to be controlled by the authoritarian state as a public matter of welfare policy, or should it be seen as each individual's private problem, determined by the market? Collective actions were aimed not only at authorities, who were appealed to for protection, but, more importantly, at all groups involved in the production, marketing, and processing of basic foods: landowners, prosperous farmers, grain and other crop merchants, millers, bakers, and others.

In a considerable number of these food riots, participants adopted traditional and clearly popular hostile rhetorical expressions to stigmatize those who were profit-hungry. Epithets such as "forestaller," "corn Jew," and "usurer" suggest an explicit anti-Jewish component. Take, for instance, the example of Landsberg an der Warthe (Neumark, in the Prussian province of Brandenburg) in the spring of 1847.[6] For weeks, the Jewish landowner Louis Boas had been buying up the potato stock in Landsberg and the surrounding area for use in his distillery. This caused great bitterness among the "poorer inhabitants." On April 19, a few days after several truckloads had been plundered, the mayor received a pamphlet "threatening the Jews with death and ruin" and saying that "the food

---

3. On the entire spectrum of collective actions in the 1848 era, see Gailus, *Straße und Brot,* 107–200.

4. On paradoxical Jewish perceptions and experiences of the whole revolutionary period, see Rürup, "European Revolutions of 1848"; and Reinhard Rürup, "Der Fortschritt und seine Grenzen: Die Revolution von 1848 und die europäischen Juden," in Dowe, Haupt, Langewiesche, *Europa 1848,* 985–1005.

5. Manfred Gailus, "Food Riots in Germany in the late 1840s," *Past and Present* 145 (November 1994): 157–93; idem, "Nahrungsmangel, Versorgungspolitik und Protest in Deutschland (ca. 1770–1873)" (manuscript, Berlin, 1996), 99–159.

6. Cited in Gailus, *Straße und Brot,* 282–301.

price increase was just used as a pretext . . . to provoke the people to revolt."[7] Disregarding the increased security measures, a large crowd gathered on the same day at the road leading to the feudal estate, ready to plunder other wagons. During questioning, the people explained to the mayor that they had gathered "to take from the Jew the potatoes that he had bought only in order to make them more expensive through his distillery. All queries and admonitions, all warnings, were unsuccessful. The people asserted that they and their families were forced to live destitute and to starve, that only 'the Jews' were to blame, and that it served them right when they received a heavy thrashing for it."[8] In the end, the crowd stormed a number of crop warehouses, including the cellar storeroom of the Jewish landowner. During these actions, bitter complaints were expressed repeatedly about "the Jews." Franz Kaufmann, a twenty-eight-year-old married worker, addressed the mayor: "Look here, it is not correct that the Jews have such freedom, that they can buy up everything without bringing a single potato to the market. I now have rent debts for three-quarters of a year and school debts for four months."[9]

Although non-Jewish merchants and owners were also attacked during these riots, Boas was without doubt at the center of the unrest. Widespread anti-Jewish antipathy toward him was apparently reinforced by an anonymous pamphlet against the "Jews and crop profiteers." Many participants in the violent action viewed their attack on the property of the landowner, and what was regarded as his "immoral" and self-interested agrarian capitalistic conduct, as slightly more legitimate because they were dealing with someone from outside the community. Documentation exists of a number of anti-Jewish statements expressed by the rioters. Moreover, the distribution of the aforementioned pamphlet, as well as other evidence that surfaced during the legal investigation, indicates that the actions were planned in advance.

A year later, at the start of the March Revolution, anonymous notices on buildings were discovered, signed by an obscure "association for the promotion of the community spirit and for the repression of spreading injustices." A year had passed, said the notice, since the repression of the "Jews and crop profiteers" had been called for. Now it was time for the liberation of the entire fatherland from arbitrary power and despotism: "Just take a look at our city, my friends, look around you, is it not as the saying goes: 'the petty thieves are caught, the big ones go free'? Why is it, then, noble friends, that this cheating Jewish people always gets off good, be it by milling or by cheating, if not because the authorities accept their bribes?

---

7. Ibid., 284.
8. Ibid., 284–85.
9. Ibid., 286.

Take the example of the 'hungry dog' police inspector. That is why you have to speak up, dear friends, and show what you are capable of when you are unified."[10] This was a renewed appeal to violent action against an assumed cartel of local notables and Jews—an attempt that apparently could be suppressed only temporarily by the formation of a large militia. On May 29, 1848, the windows of the home of a Jewish salesman and city councilor were smashed "as a consequence of unpopular comments" he had made.[11]

Another example comes from Koblenz, in the Prussian province of the Rhineland. On May 9, 1847, according to a report from the authorities, a notice was found in the city calling for the people to gather in order "to give the profiteering grain merchants and bakers a thrashing."[12] A large number of people did assemble in the evening at a central square, and they conducted themselves peacefully at first.

> Suddenly, however, at around half past nine, a commotion formed in the mass, and a number of people, unrecognizable in the dark, ran across the small parade square into the Rheinstraße to the very narrow entranceway to the Kastorpfaffengasse, where Reinhold, a Jewish grain merchant who a few years earlier had immigrated from the Nassau region, lived in a house he had recently purchased. . . . Before the police officers and constables, who were hurrying after them, could make their way through the throng of people and reach the narrow street, the mob, amongst wild screams and shrill whistling, had thrown stones through most of the windows of Reinhold's house.[13]

An added explanation states that the merchant, according to hearsay, had drawn attention to himself by doing a significant grain trade with high profits during the recent crisis period. He was a wealthy stranger who had moved to the town, a Jew, unscrupulous in making a profit, and, moreover, apparently leading an immoral life—that is what an agitated public charged him with, according to a report from the authorities. Following this event, a crowd of people gathered in front of the house of another grain merchant (this time not Jewish) but did not erupt in violence.[14]

---

10. Ibid., 300.

11. *National-Zeitung* (Berlin), no. 60, June 1, 1848.

12. Geheimes Staatsarchiv Preußischer Kulturbesitz (GStAPK), Rep. 77, Tit. 505, No. 4, Bd. 3, Bl. 11, 93–95: Govt. of Koblenz to the Berlin Ministry of Internal Affairs, May 11, 1847; cited in Hans-Heinrich Bass, *Hungerkrisen in Preussen während der ersten Hälfte des 19. Jahrhunderts* (St. Katharinen, 1991), 259–61.

13. Ibid., 260.

14. Ibid. One of the many public reproaches against the merchant was "malicious desertion of his previous bride, who suffered in shame and desperation."

It is not difficult to compile a sizable number of other relevant cases. As early as fall 1846, a series of food protests broke out in the North Hessian district of Hünfeld, focusing on the business transactions of the Jewish grain merchant Somborn from Gelnhausen. He has been described as the indisputable "key figure" in a large-scale interregional grain trade. Somborn, whose business practices were the focal point of diverse rumors, did not have a good reputation.[15] From the small mountain town of Glatz in Silesia, on May 5, 1847, came a report of a Jewish corn merchant who sold grain at excessive prices, was caught "profiteering," and was brought to the police station among "loud shouts of approval." Another merchant, however, received life-threatening injuries.[16]

The Prussian province of Posen (Posnan), where the population consisted primarily of three groups—an agrarian-rural Polish majority, a large German minority, and a smaller but still strong Jewish minority[17]—was the scene of an unusually rapid succession of food revolts in April and May 1847. For at least six of some thirty cases, there is evidence of an anti-Jewish component, and it is likely that the rate was even higher. Notable incidents include Gnesen (the plundering of Jewish grain merchants and stores on May 2); Trzemeszno (the plundering of stores, storerooms, and apartments of twelve Jewish merchants on May 2); and Rogasen (an attack on the homes of Jewish and Prussian inhabitants on May 3).[18] From the small town of Rogowo, north of Gnesen, came the following report:

> In the town of Rogowo with its population of ca. 2,500, three-fourths are Jews, many of whom have acquired considerable wealth from grain trading and profiteering. In response to the turmoil that broke out on the 2nd in Gnesen and Trzemeszno, the Jews in Rogowo were warned in time by fellow Jews, and on the 4th they turned to the district chief administrative officer for help; he called for the District Commissar, who didn't arrive in Rogowo until 8 o'clock in the morn-

---

15. See Hermann-Josef Hohmann, "Die lokale Bedingtheit von sozialem Protest: Proteste gegen den Lebensmittelhandel im Kreis Hünfeld 1846 und ihr Umfeld," *Hessische Blätter für Volks- und Kulturforschung* 26 (1990): 47–61, esp. 51–52.

16. *Augsburger Allgemeine Zeitung,* no. 136, May 16, 1847.

17. At 5.7 percent, the Jewish proportion of the entire population in the Posen province (1848) was much larger than in other Prussian provinces. West Prussia had the next largest Jewish population, with 2.2 percent, and Silesia and the Rhineland followed with 1.1 percent each. See Michael Brenner, Stefi Jersch-Wenzel, and Michael A. Meyer, *Deutsch-Jüdische Geschichte in der Neuzeit,* vol. 2, *Emanzipation und Akkulturation, 1780–1871* (Munich, 1996), 59.

18. Bass, *Hungerkrisen,* 245–58.

ing on the fifth. He found around 300 people there with clubs and empty sacks. When asked what it was they wanted, the answer came, "We're hungry." Admonishments and warnings were to no avail; the crowd of people, which had grown to 1,200 men by evening, plundered the homes of the Jewish bakers and grain merchants and carried on until 11 o'clock at night. Word spread throughout the area; on the 6th, another crowd, estimated at 3–5,000 people, had collected to begin plundering anew at 8 o'clock, and this time it was not just limited to grain.[19]

Numerous factors played a role in the province of Posen to make the anti-Jewish focus of the protests emerge so starkly: a strained Prussian Protestant administration that evidently implemented only lax security and precautionary measures; a large and for the most part poor agrarian Polish Catholic rural population; and finally, in some areas, a strong Jewish presence in trading, particularly grain and crop trading. The "Jewish profiteers" continued to be held responsible for the rising prices, food shortages, and hunger, which led to a militant invasion by a large rural population, with traditionally strong anti-Jewish attitudes, into the small towns, where, without exception, an insufficient detachment of police officers operated.[20]

"Corn profiteers," "forestallers," "money and corn speculators," "grain profiteers," "corn Jews," "Jewish profiteers," and "grain speculators"—this is a sample of the general terminology used by the rioters but also found in newspaper articles and, in a somewhat more subdued form, in official reports. These terms have their roots in the early modern period, when Jews dominated the money and trading business and when profit-oriented market behavior, at least in periods of crisis and high prices, was stigmatized as immoral, self-interested, and ultimately unchristian. Those who engaged in unauthorized collective actions in response to these kinds of practices believed they were more or less meting out a legitimate punishment, which they were permitted to administer in the name of, or in place of, an authority that inadequately cared for and protected its citizens.

This concerns not only the question "as to what were legitimate and what were illegitimate practices in marketing, milling, baking, etc.," as

---

19. Quoted in Bass, *Hungerkrisen,* 252.

20. Ibid., 257–58, 262–64. On the situation for Jews in Posen province, see Sophia Kemlein, *Die Posener Juden, 1815–1848: Entwicklungsprozesse einer polnischen Judenheit unter preußischer Herrschaft* (Hamburg, 1997).

Edward P. Thompson writes in his classic formulation of the "moral economy." Equally important is the question of which individuals in each business and commercial sphere worked on the supplier side of the market.[21] When only non-Jewish producers and merchants controlled the market, they could also become the target of such attacks. When both Christian and Jewish merchants were present, they were equally affected, regardless of their religion. It became clear during the period of inflation, however, that two people with the same or similar business practices could be judged differently according to their position in the community. Whereas certain business transactions by local Christian grain producers, merchants, and shopkeepers were still tolerated, a comparable market behavior could be sufficient cause for violence if the merchant was a so-called outsider, particularly if he was Jewish.[22]

II

A component of the March Revolution in March and April of 1848 was a broad wave of anti-Jewish violence in central and east European regions, including attacks on Jews in at least 180 localities affected by the revolution. In the regions of non-Habsburg Germany, close to one hundred incidents have to date been identified with certainty. Helmut Berding called it "the worst persecution of Jews in the entire epoch of emancipation."[23] (French) Alsace, with approximately sixty cases, counted the highest number of incidents, as did the south and southwest German regions, in particular the Grand Duchy of Baden. In Baden, thirty-four incidents that broke out into anti-Jewish riots have been documented.[24] In these cases, anti-Jewish protest was intertwined with antifeudal actions against manor lords and persons of rank (nobility). In some cases, roaming peasants would simultaneously assault feudal lords and Jews: the feudal lords for

---

21. Edward P. Thompson, "The Moral Economy of the English Crowd in the Eighteenth Century," *Past and Present* 50 (1971): 76–136, 79.

22. Other examples are given in Gailus, *Straße und Brot,* 135, 299.

23. Rürup, "Der Fortschritt," 987–88; Rohrbacher, *Gewalt im Biedermeier,* 220–21; Helmut Berding, *Moderner Antisemitismus in Deutschland* (Frankfurt/Main, 1988), 74.

24. For Alsace, see Daniel Gerson, "Die Ausschreitungen gegen die Juden im Elsaß, 1848," *Bulletin des Leo-Baeck-Instituts* 87 (1990): 29–44; for Baden, see Michael Anthony Riff, "The Anti-Jewish Aspect of the Revolutionary Unrest of 1848 in Baden and Its Impact on Emancipation," *Leo Baeck Institute Year Book* 21 (1976): 21–41; Rohrbacher, *Gewalt im Biedermeier,* 186–201, 221–22 (33 locations). See also Stefan J. Dietrich, "Gegen eine Minderheit: 'Freiheit, Gleichheit soll leben; die Juden müssen sterben,'" in *"Heute ist Freiheit!":* *Bauernkrieg im Odenwald, 1848,* edited by Haus der Geschichte Baden-Württemberg (Stuttgart, 1998), 74–81.

repression of their subjects, and Jewish "money lords" for moneylending practices in the countryside.[25]

A new, careful examination of sources, however, has ascertained that, for all the incidents in northern Baden, a number of overlapping motives must be considered: socioeconomic aspects were intertwined with political and general cultural aspects, including religious mentalities. Particularly revealing are anonymous threatening letters, sometimes written prior to the event and sometimes accompanying or following an action. Consider, for example, the following letter to the Jews of Krautheim in April 1848:

> To the Jews in Krautheim: For what reason should we tolerate the Jews any longer, why should we consider it, nothing more than the swindling of us Christians, that is your main cause. No matter what it is, you always want the best. Why should we Christians of both confessions, Catholic and Protestant, allow ourselves to be cheated by Jews when our Savior himself says: You are cast out and should be dispersed like lost sheep. Our confessions Cath. and Prot. are the main religions and they take revenge on the blood of our Savior, which remained unavenged for 1815 years. But this moment brings us the best opportunity to avenge the blood of our Lord and Savior Jesus Christ.[26]

Shortly before this, an anonymous threatening letter to Joel Hersch Rotschild, the synagogue official in Krautheim, contained the following:

> Jul Hersch Rothschilt. After work, gather together the Jews and tell them if they do not leave Krautheim in 3 days, then on the fourth day all those who are still here will be hung and Krautheim will be burned to the ground. I have spoken, and mark my words.[27]

It is not a coincidence that such letters became more frequent around Easter, a traditionally dangerous period for a Jewish minority living in a Christian environment, during which religious references to the crucifixion of Jesus Christ, with its clear anti-Jewish elements, experience a revival.[28]

---

25. Riff, "Anti-Jewish Aspects"; Rainer Wirtz, "*Widersetzlichkeiten, Excesse, Crawalle, Tumulte und Skandale": Soziale Bewegung und gewalthafter sozialer Protest in Baden, 1815–1848* (Frankfurt/Main, 1981), 169–246, esp. 233–38.

26. Dietrich, "Gegen eine Minderheit," 78.

27. Ibid., 80.

28. Cf. Stefan Rohrbacher and Michael Schmidt, *Judenbilder: Kulturgeschichte antijüdischer Mythen und antisemitischer Vorurteile* (Hamburg, 1991), 256–63.

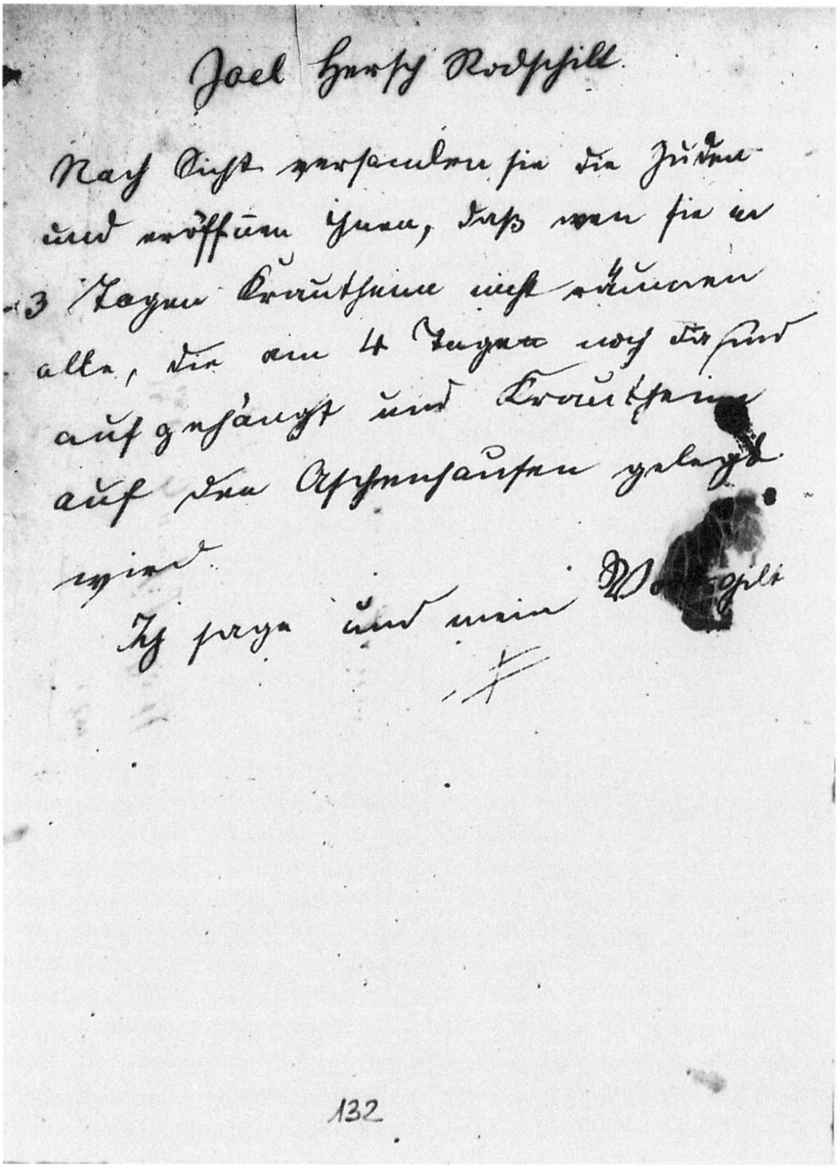

Fig. 1. Anonymous threatening letter to Joel Hersch Rothschild, member of the synagogue council in Krautheim, dated April 7, 1848. "Jul Hersch Rothschilt. After work, gather together the Jews and tell them if they do not leave Krautheim in 3 days, then on the fourth all those who are still here will be hung and Krautheim burned to the ground. I have spoken, and mark my words." (Vorlage und Aufnahme: Generallandesarchiv Karlsruhe GLA 313/4329, © Generallandesarchiv Karlsruhe.)

A similar threatening letter was found around the same time in the nearby district of Boxberg:

> On the holy Good Friday it will be 1,815 years since the Jews crucified our divine Savior, and on Good Friday, on this day of his death, we also want to hold a day of death, not that kind, but rather a much more dreadful day of death for the Jews . . . , although we won't rob, we want solely to avenge the blood of our Lord Jesus Christ gallantly, spiritually, and steadfastly in accordance with our duty, and there are no earthly powers that can stop us, we are a sworn alliance and therefore not one single Jew-child clinging to his mother will be spared, each one will be cut to pieces. Then we Christian brothers will have served our purpose, we don't want anything else from anyone here. Written on holy Palm Sunday—the leaders.[29]

One can only speculate as to who the writers of such letters were. All three were written *after* the wave of anti-Jewish violence in Baden. As was the case in Landsberg/Warthe, they probably did not originate from the circle of people who directly participated in the violent attacks. For reasons of respectability, the letter writers kept a distance from the riots, but they were eager for them to occur. The representation of the Jews as enemies of the Christians, and the appeal to retaliate against the so-called Christ or God killers, signified a deeply rooted religious mentality, which, one can certainly assume, was widespread among the rural population during this period.

The events in the northern Baden community of Unterschüpf, where, on the evening of March 8, a severe assault on Jewish homes occurred, are relatively well documented.[30] Many days before the attack, rumors had spread throughout the area that violence against "the Jews" was imminent. On the day before the attack (March 7), a group of people from outside the village had arrived, running through the streets wearing masks. One of the masked men, a Jewish witness reported afterward, carried a whetstone in one hand and a knife in the other. Standing in front of Jewish houses, he demonstratively sharpened his knife and made the gesture of slitting someone's throat.[31] Two soldiers had already extorted money from Jews on that day. During the course of the riot, seven Jewish homes were demolished and plundered (mostly of porcelain and kitchenware), and numerous promissory notes were stolen. The local militia did not interfere, and individual members even helped the rioters where they

---

29. Dietrich, "Gegen eine Minderheit," 78–79.
30. Ibid., 79–80.
31. Statement from Moses Höchheimer, March 16, 1848, ibid., 80.

could. One of the participants from the next village explained afterward to an inquiry judge that one of the main perpetrators, the son of a butcher from Unterschüpf, had angrily complained to him on the day of the riot that he had found it extremely inappropriate that certain individuals had attacked on March 7 already. This, he said, had given the Jews a warning and time to hide money and valuable papers: "I could have killed the fellows for being so stupid: just show the Schüpfer Christians that we are coming but not to touch anything, that was the signal, and then to retreat and the Jews feel secure and afterward to attack, that was the plan."[32] According to the statement of a local official, before the agitators stormed the Jewish homes, they hollered, "Freedom lives, one religion, one God, and one ruler."[33] Contrary to the self-protecting claims of the Christian majorities in the villages involved that "outsiders" were responsible for the excesses, locals of Unterschüpf (and other areas) were indeed involved: six of the ten defendants in the Unterschüpf case were members of the local community.[34]

If one observes the unrest in Baden as a whole, one finds a combination of three major motives for the anti-Jewish assaults. There was, for one thing, the old tradition of Christian anti-Judaism—a more or less ubiquitous religious mentality, more dominant among peasants than in the cities, kept alive and reinforced through rumors, anonymous threatening letters and fliers, pamphlets, and other forms of communication. It was the oldest and most widespread form of anti-Jewish attitudes, which each year in the period leading up to Easter could be virulently recharged, as the threatening letters of April 1848 quoted above clearly illustrate.

In addition, there was the equally popular tradition of denouncing Jews as usurers and hagglers. "As a result of the dissolution of certain feudal rights, a need for money developed in areas inhabited by nobility and manor lords, which, with public credit agencies lacking, was often met by Jewish businessmen. When heavy debts led to bankruptcy proceedings and auctioning, the creditor was usually blamed. He was immediately accused of being a 'profiteering Jew' who used unscrupulous methods to bleed the unsuspecting countryman, reducing him to penury while the Jew got richer and richer. This explains why the movement against the nobility and manor lords and the attack on the Jewish population were regarded as closely connected: both events were directed at people by whom the peasants felt mistreated and oppressed."[35] It is correct to stress that only a small minority of rural Jews were in a position to actually engage in major credit operations. Moreover, a number of wealthy Christians (business-

---

32. Ibid.
33. Ibid., 78.
34. Ibid., 80.
35. Ibid., 76.

men, lodging proprietors, lawyers, priests, officials, and other well-off people) emerged as creditors in the country. Although they, too, were accused of charging exorbitant interest, they were for the most part spared from similar attacks of violence in the Baden region. As was the case during the wave of price increases in 1846–47, people were less hesitant to use violence against Jews—the domestic "other," the cultural and religious "foreigner"—than against Christian creditors or businessmen, who in the very same way used the country people's money shortage and hard times to make profits.[36]

Finally, another factor in the anti-Jewish assaults was an immediate and direct consequence of the revolution: a resistance to what appeared to be the approach of ultimate political standing for the Jews as equal citizens in the community. Such strongly status-oriented protests played a primary role in the unrest in some communities in the Kraichgau region. In some places, Jews were forced to sign a document renouncing their share of equal rights in the community, thereby relinquishing their claim to local benefits (poverty aid, for example). As a result of massive pressure from below, the Second Chamber, the traditionally liberal state parliament of Baden, left the question of Jewish emancipation unresolved for a long time during the revolutionary period. In the Emancipation Law, which was not passed until February 1849, the explosive issue of regulating the communal rights of Jews was postponed to a later date.[37]

III

The violent attacks on Jews evidently did not differ much from other conflicts during the revolutionary period. In general, from the point of view of the perpetrators, just as in other kinds of confrontations, the attacks involved a collective punishment or act of revenge, a symbolic destruction of property, and the demolishing of houses and apartment furnishings. Beyond that, the relatively base act of plundering food, equipment, and valuables, or the extortion of money, also played a considerable role. Collective theft occurred against Jews more often than in other conflicts. The assumption made by the actors was that they were engaging in the more or less justified reappropriation of valuables and objects that had been illegitimately taken away from them or their countrymen—conceived of as the "community" or the "people."[38] Attacks on synagogues

---

36. Rohrbacher, *Gewalt im Biedermeier,* 35–61; Dietrich, "Gegen eine Minderheit," 78.

37. Rohrbacher, *Gewalt im Biedermeier,* esp. 193–95; Reinhard Rürup, "Das Doppelgesicht der Revolution: Zur Geschichte der Juden in der badischen Revolution, 1848/49," in Haus der Geschichte Baden-Württemberg, *"Heute ist Freiheit!"* 82–86.

38. On the problem of plundering in social unrest, see Gailus, *Straße und Brot,* 121–25, 218, 240–51, 282–89, 296, 303–4.

and the vandalism or destruction of sacred objects could be a part of the unrest, but generally such behavior was merely incidental to actions that were motivated by other interests.[39] To the extent that generalizations can be drawn from the few detailed case studies that are available, it appears that severe physical violence against Jews occurred only in a few cases.[40] This seems on par with the (rather limited) presence of excessive physical violence in other actions, such as peasant riots, attacks by the agrarian lower classes, hunger unrest, charivaris, and worker protests.[41]

What stands out in anti-Jewish unrest is the perpetrators' distinctive fantasies of collective violence and their extremely aggressive threats within the context of the conflict. The rhetoric of anti-Jewish letters and fliers, rumors, and public speeches incorporated a graphic, symbolic language of gestures and often expressed the use of direct violence to the point of physical annihilation: bloody revenge for crucifying the Savior, death and misfortune, physical punishment, dismembering of adults and children, pillaging, arson, hanging, slitting of throats. Such was the dreadful language of late medieval or early modern pogroms. The perpetrators, more or less consciously, used references to established custom in order to conjure up the atavistic mood of a bygone time.[42] Examples exist even from Berlin, the revolutionized Prussian capital. In July 1848, a Jewish sales clerk found himself accused on the street of having torn down a politically conservative poster. In spite of his denials, he was immediately surrounded by a crowd and suffered injuries. A minor flour merchant and two carriage coachmen stood out for their violent behavior. The flour merchant supposedly screamed, "That is a Jew, he must be beaten to death."[43]

The emphasis on fundamental difference, the rejection of equal standing, the sharpening of the contours of an insurmountable division, and the instillment of fear through fomenting a mood ripe for a pogrom—all this

---

39. Examples are in Dietrich, "Gegen eine Minderheit," 78 (for Merchingen, Baden); and Rainer Erb and Werner Bergmann, *Die Nachtseite der Judenemanzipation: Der Widerstand gegen die Integration der Juden in Deutschland, 1780–1860* (Berlin, 1989), 254–56 (for Baisingen, Württemberg).

40. Strikingly violent and dreadful excesses are mentioned in Rohrbacher, *Gewalt im Biedermeier,* for the province of Posen in connection with the Polish uprising against Prussian rule in spring 1848 (219–20).

41. For an overview, see Gailus, *Straße und Brot.*

42. In addition to the examples cited, see Gerson, "Ausschreitungen gegen die Juden," 37. On early modern anti-Jewish violence, see Rohrbacher, *Gewalt im Biedermeier,* 37–61; for a typical example of a violent early modern anti-Jewish rebellion, see Rudolf Endres, "Ein antijüdischer Bauernaufstand im Hochstift Bamberg im Jahre 1699," *Historischer Verein für die Pflege der Geschichte des ehemaligen Fürstbistums Bamberg* 117 (1981): 67–81.

43. *"Der Publicist"* (Berlin), no. 71, August 19, 1848.

occurred amid the violence and represented another, subtle form of anti-Jewish aggression. More often than in other confrontations, "shady characters," acting undetected, played a distinct role by writing anonymous letters. Another singular factor was that core groups often met prior to an attack to coordinate the action. That the fear and terror experienced by Jews had a major impact is demonstrated by an example from the Baden region: in Krautheim, where there was not even an open attack on the Jewish community, a Jewish woman reportedly gave birth to a stillborn as a result of the terror and died herself shortly thereafter.[44]

IV

Other areas of prevalent anti-Jewish violence included the Grand Duchy of Hesse, a region to the north of Baden that had the highest proportion of Jews in the entire territory of Germany (up to 3.45%, in comparison to Baden with 1.78% and Prussia with 1.38%); and some parts of Franconia.[45] In Prussia around 1848, anti-Jewish violence was underrepresented, although there was a regional concentration of incidents in the provinces of Silesia, Posen (subsistence riots in 1847 and riots in connection with the Polish protest movement in 1848), and Westphalia.[46] In comparison to the Hep Hep unrest of 1819 and other violent protests of the revolutionary period, anti-Jewish violence around 1848 was strikingly a phenomenon of the countryside and small towns: in Baden, Württemberg, Hesse, and Bavaria, it was the small Jewish communities in villages and small country towns that were primarily afflicted.[47] In the southwest and south, it was not uncommon for threatened Jewish families to flee to nearby larger cities, seeking the protection offered by the urban area's more pronounced civil culture with its public authorities and security forces. From Alsace, Jews fled to Basel or to Baden on the other side of the Rhine. In Baden, for example, Heidelsheimer Jews found safety in Bruchsal after outbursts of violence on March 6, and Jewish families from the Franconia localities of

44. See Dietrich, "Gegen eine Minderheit," 79.

45. On anti-Jewish unrest in Hesse, in addition to Rohrbacher, *Gewalt im Biedermeier,* see also Michael Wettengel, *Die Revolution von 1848/49 im Rhein-Main-Raum: Politische Vereine und Revolutionsalltag im Großherzogtum Hessen, Herzogtum Nassau und in der Freien Stadt Frankfurt* (Wiesbaden, 1989), 76–80; and Robert von Friedeburg, "Kommunaler Antisemitismus: Christliche Landgemeinden und Juden zwischen Eder und Werra vom späten 18. bis zur Mitte des 19. Jahrhunderts," in *Jüdisches Leben auf dem Lande: Studien zur deutsch-jüdischen Geschichte,* edited by Monika Richarz and Reinhard Rürup (Tübingen, 1997), 139–71, 165–66.

46. Gailus, *Straße und Brot,* 132–35; Rohrbacher, *Gewalt im Biedermeier,* 215–20.

47. Gailus, *Straße und Brot,* 89–93; Rohrbacher, *Gewalt im Biedermeier,* 94–156.

Burgkunstadt, Lichtenfels, Unterlangenfeld, and others sought refuge around March 13 in Bamberg.[48]

When anti-Jewish acts occurred in large cities, they usually originated in the artisan milieu and were directed against the supposed or actual Jewish competition posed by larger shops that did not belong to the guild. This was the case in Heidelberg (where there was an attack by tailors on a Jewish-run clothes shop on February 29); Hirschberg, Silesia (an attack on two fancy-goods shops on March 20); Karlsruhe (an assault on Jewish homes on March 21); Breslau (an attack on shops, including Jewish-owned shops, on April 18); Fulda (charivari and pillaging in the Jewish passage on April 22–21); Gleiwitz and Ratibor, Silesia (an assault on Jewish homes and stores on May 1–2), Löbau, West Prussia (a particularly destructive attack on Jewish market stalls and shops on June 28–29); and Lüben, Silesia (the demolition of a Jewish cloth merchant's house and the plundering and destruction of the bookkeeping accounts on October 16).[49]

In general, anti-Jewish acts in the larger cities, under the liberal, democratic revolutionary conditions of 1848, hardly gained support and were stifled before they could get started. Berlin, which along with Vienna was the most turbulent city in the revolutionary period, experienced a single incident, in which a group of journeyman tailors were about to attack a Jewish clothes shop. On the street such cries could be heard as, "The Jews must close their shops immediately or else they will be plundered." The action never got beyond its initial phase and was soon followed by a legal investigation.[50] Only in a few large eastern cities of the Habsburg monarchy, including Prague, Pressburg (Bratislava), and Budapest, did anti-Jewish riots take on a larger role within the metropolitan revolutionary events.[51]

---

48. On Alsace, see Gerson, "Ausschreitungen gegen die Juden," esp. 37. On Heidelsheim, see *Vossische Zeitung* (Berlin), no. 61, March 13, 1848; and *Trier'sche Zeitung*, no. 73, March 13, 1848. On Franconia, see *Augsburger Allgemeine Zeitung*, no. 77, March 17, 1848; no. 78, March 18, 1848.

49. Heidelberg: *Frankfurter Journal*, no. 63, March 3, 1848; *Trier'sche Zeitung*, no. 65, March 5, 1848; Hirschberg: *Breslauer Zeitung*, no. 70, March 23, 1848; *Vossische Zeitung*, no. 122, May 27, 1848; Karlsruhe: *Karlsruher Zeitung*, no. 82, March 23, 1848; *Kölnische Zeitung*, no. 85, March 25, 1848; Breslau: *Breslauer Zeitung*, no. 93, April 19, 1848; *Kölnische Zeitung*, no. 133, April 22, 1848; no. 134, April 23, 1848; Fulda: *Westfälischer Merkur* (Münster), no. 104, April 30, 1848; Gleiwitz and Ratibor: *Schlesische Zeitung*, no. 103, May 4, 1848; no. 104, May 5, 1848; *Frankfurter Journal*, no. 130, May 10, 1848; Löbau: *Vossische Zeitung*, no. 154, July 6, 1848; no. 155, July 7, 1848; Lüben: *Vossische Zeitung*, no. 247, October 22, 1848.

50. *Der Publicist*, no. 30, April 19, 1848 (documentary report on the court proceedings against the major defendants, three journeyman tailors).

51. Rürup, "Der Fortschritt," 991.

Fig. 2. Bachmann-Hohmann, "Persecution of the Jews in Pressburg," April 24, 1848. (Courtesy Historisches Museum, Vienna.)

Like other riots, the anti-Jewish actions were predominantly limited to the months of March and April 1848; they were thus a component of the general March movements at the onset of the revolution. Of the forty-five relevant cases making up a systematic sample of protests for the period between 1847 and July 1849, a good 55 percent transpired in the month of March 1848.[52] As the revolution continued to unfold and the first stages of a modern German party system were established, a process began that could be described as a transformation of long-standing anti-Jewish attitudes and sentiments.

---

52. Gailus, *Straße und Brot,* 135.

Fig. 3. "Uprising against the Jews in Wreschen," colored lithograph, 1848. (Courtesy Bayerisches Nationalmuseum, inventory no. 47/21.677.)

V

Anti-Jewish attitudes began to appear less often in the context of direct and spontaneous acts of violence and instead occurred with increasing frequency as a political instrument within the formation of a Christian conservative party milieu, which embraced all social strata. Thus in Bavaria, for example, following the decision by the Second Chamber of the Parliament in December 1849 to grant the general emancipation of the Jews, a comprehensive antisemitic petition movement began.[53] The first signs of a new kind of ideological antisemitism in a conservative party milieu began to emerge, as Michael Wettengel's study also shows to be true for the Rhine-Main region.[54]

In Prussia, in the intellectual world of the influential *Evangelische Kirchenzeitung* of the Berlin theology professor Ernst Wilhelm Hengstenberg, in the *Kreuzzeitung,* in the social milieu of the conservative associations movement, in the numerous military, peasant, and fatherland associations that were forming, and among the "throne and altar" revolts that occurred more frequently beginning in late summer 1848 against all of the so-called friends of the revolution, a hostile stance developed toward the presumed instigators of the revolution. Targets included propagandists of a God-denying supremacy of rationalism and intellectualism—as it was called in the terminology of the time—as well as supporters of Western-democratic thinking and political culture; enemies of the semiofficial beliefs of the church; enemies of the king and his divine right; and enemies of "the real Prussia." In the eyes of these conservatives, "the Jews," especially, embodied all of these identities.[55] An aggressive nationalistic cult of the "real Prussia," which contained the beginnings of a strong and exclusive ethnic (*völkisch*) collective thinking, evolved in response to the conservative Christians' nightmare of a (more feared than actually achieved) "upheaval."

A pogromlike attack on August 20, 1848, on the small Charlottenburg democratic association, which stood isolated in the practically closed monarchic-conservative milieu of this small royal residency outside the gates of Berlin, testifies to the altered intellectual climate during this period

---

53. James F. Harris, *The People Speak! Anti-Semitism and Emancipation in Nineteenth-Century Bavaria* (Ann Arbor, 1994), esp. 123–87.

54. Wettengel, *Revolution von 1848/49,* 452.

55. For fundamental background on the conservative Prussian Associations movement of the counterrevolution, see Wolfgang Schwentker, *Konservative Vereine und Revolution in Preußen, 1848/49: Die Konstituierung des Konservativismus als Partei* (Düsseldorf, 1988); and Eckhard Trox, *Militärischer Konservatismus: Kriegervereine und "Militärpartei" in Preußen zwischen 1815 und 1848/49* (Stuttgart, 1990). On "throne and altar" unrest in East Prussia, see Gailus, *Straße und Brot,* 431–94.

of transformation. On that Sunday morning, a group of many hundred robust men and local Royalists assaulted and brutally mistreated the few members of the recently founded association in their homes, including the prominent literary figures Bruno and Edgar Bauer.[56] The aim of the atavistic hunting scene in Charlottenburg, which came close to achieving the hate-filled and excessively violent atmosphere of traditional Jewish pogroms, was the expulsion, or even the physical extermination, of the "anti-Christians" and "major traitors." An eyewitness reported that a young man was mistreated and forced under the threat of violence to declare "whether or not he believed in God and wanted to be faithful to the king. The young man replied that he had never denied that, upon which he received a terrible beating and was then thrown out onto the street. Another member of the association was able to save himself only after he gave in to the attackers' demand that he place his left hand on his heart, raise three fingers of his right hand, and swear to believe in God, to be faithful to the king, and to never again join the Republicans."[57]

A similar pogrom mood broke out on October 22, 1848, targeting the Jewish doctor and prominent Berlin Democrat Moritz Lövinson as he reported to roll call in his (middle- and lower-middle-class) reserve army unit in nearby Wilmersdorf. Shouts of "the Jew must leave; beat the Jew to death" could be heard. After he had registered according to regulations and was about to leave the room, "a general pulling, charging, and pushing transpired around me with the words 'beat the Jews to death!' They blocked my way, fists pounded on my hat and back, I was pushed out the door, and in the corridor I received such a blow to the back of my head from some kind of instrument that blood started streaming down."[58]

In the conservative countermilieu, the revolution was depicted more and more as a heinous conspiracy of "outsiders," "foreigners," and "the godless." And who could represent this antitype better than the classic native "outsider," the Jew? Democrats and Republicans, therefore, were soon regarded as potential "Jews," and "Jews" were in turn seen as the true plotters and actual propagandists of the revolution: one saw in them disrespectful enemies of the king, anti-Christians who had strayed from God, unpatriotic outsiders.[59] Such circular argumentation functioned in

---

56. Gailus, *Straße und Brot,* 447–48; Rüdiger Hachtmann, *Berlin 1848: Eine Politik-und Gesellschaftsgeschichte der Revolution* (Bonn, 1997), 693–94; idem, "'Rote Hauptstadt' und 'schwarze Provinz': Zum spannungsgeladenen Verhältnis zwischen dem demokratischen Berlin und seinen 'Vororten' Charlottenburg, Spandau und Potsdam im Revolutionsjahr," in *Demokratie, Liberalismus und Konterrevolution: Studien zur deutschen Revolution von 1848/49,* edited by Walter Schmidt (Berlin, 1998), 159–95.

57. Eyewitness report cited in Hachtmann, "Rote Hauptstadt," 169.

58. Report of the victim, in Hachtmann, *Berlin 1848,* 532–33.

59. Ibid., 530–36, 541–42.

the advancing counterrevolution in a successful interplay between a developing conservative party and its ideological ideas on the one hand and Prussian nationalist thinking on the other, particularly in the smaller cities and in the countryside east of the Elbe. It palpably narrowed the room in which all Jews could freely move about. A conflict in Bütow (Pomerania) toward the end of the revolutionary period is a symptomatic example. On July 8, 1849, after a crowd of people had stormed the home of Naumann, a Jewish grain merchant, and forced him to sell his grain at the very lowest price, an official report expressing threefold approval legitimized the violation of otherwise inviolable property rights: The militia and police guard need not have acted against the attackers, "since even the citizens say it was a Jew, a Democrat, and therefore a 'nice' friend of the people, who raises the price of rye. And he should warrant our protection? Previous comments and subversive activities also seem to be involved. He got what he deserves."[60]

VI

If one considers the entire long-term history of Jewish-Christian relations in Germany, then the crisis years around 1848 represent an intensified and severely contradictory experience for Jews. There was hope and fear: prospects for complete emancipation and for political and social equality, but at the same time a newly intensified discrimination, a new form of exclusion that went so far as to threaten the Jews with expulsion from villages and small country towns, as well as with direct violence against property and person. The enduring, profound social crisis of the late 1840s, during which resources were extremely limited and traditional claims to entitlements were endangered, sharpened the collective understanding that "one's own" competed with perceived illegitimate rivals, and "outsiders" in particular. The crisis created or reinforced an inclusionary and exclusionary sense of identity of very different forms. "True" Germans joined together against non-Germans and against foreigners, and "real" Prussians separated themselves more strictly than ever from non-Prussians and anti-Prussians. Even dedicated Christians assembled themselves anew against supposed or actual non-Christians. Churchgoers drew a line separating themselves from anti-clerics, dangerous rationalists, enlightened thinkers, followers of different faiths, and "the godless"; monarchists distanced themselves from democrats, republicans, and Westerners; individualistic liberals divided themselves more sharply from communalists, who were committed to the common good; free-market economists opposed supporters of a protected market

---

60. GStAPK, Rep. 77, Tit. 502, No. 3, Bd. 2, Bl. 10–11.

and guaranteed welfare; the poor and impoverished formed a threatening union against the prosperous and the social climbers; the bourgeoisie distanced themselves from the workers and vice versa.

In this rapidly changing society, in which few found anything still stable and secure, the rediscovery of "the Jew" also took place. This was another factor in the people's reassertion of what was "one's own," a notion that had become blurry in its differentiation of the supposed or actual "outsiders." Among all those declared as "other," the Jews were placed in a singular role. Whereas common "outsiders" were confronted with a revived and vehement xenophobia, the Jews were seen as natives and therefore special "strangers." Traditionally, the Jews, as special "outsiders," were perceived as negatively connecting their central (religious) identity to one of the most essential identity traits of the German majority culture, namely, a basic Christian mentality, defined in the broadest sense. The Christian perceived himself not only as a non-Jew, but also as an anti-Jew, and saw the Jew not only as non-Christian, but also as the unredeemable, impenitent anti-Christ.

This construed or supposed relationship of a specific mutual negation of basic religious tenets linked the two groups in an almost fateful way. It was compounded by the long-standing tradition of labeling Jews as profiteers and hagglers—to the point where such traits were regarded as Jewish "national characteristics"—and by the strong bias against granting Jews political and social equality. The crisis era of 1848, in light of the newly revived anti-Jewish emotions and violent actions, was therefore not only an important landmark on the long and thorny road to Jewish emancipation, but also a decisive event in the development of a modern antisemitic counterposition, a cultural and increasingly national and ethnic exclusion of Jews as the "incorrigible" and totally distinct "outsiders."[61]

Conclusion

Anti-Jewish emotions and actions around 1848 were anything but a uniform, one-issue movement. It is instead their multidimensionality that should be emphasized. They were based on a variety of overlapping causes and motives, fears, rumors, suspicions, and, not least of all, discourses. They were determined sometimes more by economic, sometimes more by social, and sometimes more by political factors. Equally important were the cultural, intellectual, and religious aspects. Depending on the specific context, one component or another played a more dominant role. The fact that they found more clear expression in the rural and provincial areas has

---

61. See also Erb and Bergmann, *Die Nachtseite der Judenemanzipation,* 251–68; and Harris, *The People Speak!* 209–37.

to do with a number of factors, including, for example, that in the countryside there was a more sharply contoured cultural clash in the understanding of what was "one's own" versus the "other"; there was a widespread absence of intermediary forces (such as a bourgeoisie and civil
servants or the new liberal-democratic revolutionary public); a relative
closeness of traditional religious Christian thinking (represented by the
overly dominant personal presence of authority—the priest and the
church); but also by the relatively distant state security forces. It is exactly
under these kinds of conditions that the generally more symbolic social
protest aimed at banishing and punishing individual lawbreakers could
escalate into a more generalized, religious and ethnic violence aimed at the
expulsion of an entire group. For the Jews affected, flight to the nearest
urban administrative center as an "island of civilization" was often their
last chance to escape.

There is almost a consensus in historical protest research that around
1850, after the final crisis of the *type ancien* was surmounted, the early
modern European period of limited resources came to an end. Until then
it was true (for central Europe) that periodically recurring existential fears
caused by scarce resources (or in extreme cases by outbreaks of hunger
panic) went hand in hand with aggressive forms of xenophobia toward
Jews, other minorities, and generally "foreign" groups. In short, the struggle for resources intensified. And with a certain inevitability, the official
and popular definition of what was "one's own" versus what was perceived as the "other" radicalized: if food entitlements and other claims to
benefits were disputed, new checks and evaluations occurred; if an acute
selection process to determine who had a right to entitlements transpired,
those who believed they legitimately qualified for the benefits (of subsistence, existence, status, security) more acutely distanced themselves from
those who were identified as less legitimate or even illegitimate demanders,
competitors, rivals, and so on. These kinds of sharp distinctions are evident throughout the entire spectrum of anti-Jewish emotions and actions
around 1848. In particular, the simultaneous occurrence of food riots and
anti-Jewish excesses in the various regions of Germany in the early modern period up to the middle of the nineteenth century suggests a marked
coincidence. One could even speak of a certain intersection of the two
conflicts, which in times of crisis are likely to surface together—or at least
in temporal proximity—and which, as symptoms of the epoch, reflect
shared or similar mentalities. After these final massive social eruptions
around 1848, both the traditional form of protest and the era of scarce
resources came to an end, to be followed after 1850 by fundamental crises
of modernization in Germany.

Political Culture and Violence against Minorities: The Antisemitic Riots in Pomerania and West Prussia

Christhard Hoffmann
Translated by A. D. Moses

I. Introduction

In the summer of 1881, violent riots broke out in many towns and villages of Pomerania and West Prussia. Starting in the district town of Neustettin, ill-famed for the burning of its synagogue five months earlier, the pogroms spread throughout the region like wildfire, encompassing all of eastern Pomerania and parts of West Prussia and reaching even to the province of Posen. They followed the same pattern almost everywhere: hundreds of shouting demonstrators marched through the streets, chanting the traditional antisemitic catchword "Hep hep!" and "Jews to Palestine!" In the safety of numbers, they smashed the windows of stores, houses, and synagogues, destroying shop displays and casting them into the street. In the Pomeranian town of Schivelbein, the excesses were particularly severe. Here the rioters, using axes and jimmies, inflicted bodily harm, destroyed

Translated from the German. I am most grateful to Richard S. Levy for his helpful comments regarding style and content. This essay is a slightly revised and updated version of my German article "Politische Kultur und Gewalt gegen Minderheiten: Die antisemitischen Ausschreitungen in Pommern und Westpreußen, 1881," *Jahrbuch für Antisemitismusforschung* 3 (1994): 93–120.

shops and private residences of Jews, committed arson, and engaged in looting. For a while it seemed that the situation in the eastern Prussian provinces had gotten totally out of control. In many towns, the state authorities had to bring in the military, which took action against the tumultuous crowds, sometimes with fixed bayonets. Still, it took the authorities six weeks to end the attacks and restore order in the region.

The "Pomeranian Civil War," as the pogroms were called by contemporaries, shocked both Jews and non-Jews. The time of "medieval-style" persecution of German Jews was thought to have disappeared forever with Jewish emancipation (1869) and to have been impossible under the strict "law and order" standards of the *Kaiserreich*. Indeed, German towns and cities had witnessed almost no significant anti-Jewish riots since the 1840s.[1] The Jews of the Pomeranian and West Prussian towns were longtime, relatively well integrated residents, certainly not newcomers.[2] Some of them had been elected to town councils as early as the 1840s, and many others had been playing an active role in the social life of the towns for more than forty years as members of veterans' organizations, shooting clubs, and choirs.[3]

Contemporaries accounted for the sudden deterioration of these relations, culminating as it did in the violent excesses, with two diametrically opposed explanations and then proposed political solutions in keeping with each view. The conservative camp, which hoped to attract the support of the new antisemitic movement, blamed the Jews themselves: profiteers of the liberal economic order, Jews had provoked the ire of the people through their "usury," "arrogant behavior," and "interference in the relations of Christians." The situation could only be calmed, the conservatives said, by measures to rescue the economically troubled *Mittelstand* (middle classes) from "usurious exploitation." Radicals in the conservative camp went so far as to call for the partial or full abolition of the emancipation laws.[4] Liberals, by contrast, viewed the riots in the "most backward Prussian provinces" as the logical consequence of a two-year-long antisemitic propaganda campaign, which, they claimed, was toler-

---

1. Stefan Rohrbacher, *Gewalt im Biedermeier: Antijüdische Ausschreitungen in Vormärz und Revolution, 1815–1848/49* (Frankfurt/Main, 1993), 295–96.

2. For a brief historical overview, see Hans-Werner Rautenberg, "Zur Geschichte des Judentums in Pommern und Westpreußen zwischen Emanzipation und Erstem Weltkrieg," in *Juden in Ostmitteleuropa von der Emanzipation bis zum Ersten Weltkrieg* (Marburg, 1989), 49–72.

3. Jacob Toury, "Der Anteil der Juden an der städtischen Selbstverwaltung im vormärzlichen Deutschland," *Bulletin des Leo Baeck Instituts* 6 (1963): 279.

4. See, for example, "Wo liegt die Schuld," *Der Reichsbote,* August 20, 1881; "Aus Pommern," *Neue Preußische (Kreuz) Zeitung,* September 6, 1881; and "Über die Judenkrawalle," *Deutsche Tageblatt,* August 21, 1881.

ated or directly supported by the government. The violence showed in what direction the agitation against Jews led. The government could end the conflict, using its moral authority to condemn antisemitism and its police powers to punish perpetrators. For good measure, liberals also called for a ban on agitation that endangered public security.[5]

The opposing assessments of the anti-Jewish riots in the contemporary press have made their way into the historiography on the subject: the Jewish provocation thesis or the lax government thesis remain the favored interpretations of those who pay any attention at all to these events. But both are seriously reductionist, blacking out the general political context and the complex interplay of local sources.[6] Despite the importance of the Pomeranian riots of 1881 for the history of antisemitism in Germany, scholars have yet to subject these events to thorough historical analysis.[7] The following reconstruction of their causes, context, and development attempts to fill this gap on the basis of available source material and in light of the theoretical reflections of pogrom research.[8] It offers a multi-

---

5. See, for example, *Vossische Zeitung,* August 9, 1881; "Eine melancholische Betrachtung," *Vossische Zeitung,* August 20, 1881; "Politische Übersicht," *Frankfurter Zeitung,* July 20, 1881; the lead article in *Frankfurter Zeitung,* August 21, 1881; and *Allgemeine Zeitung des Judenthums* 45 (1881): 553–55.

6. Walter Frank, *Hofprediger Stoecker und die christlichsoziale Bewegung* (Berlin, 1928), 96. See also Martin Philippson, *Neueste Geschichte des jüdischen Volkes,* vol. 2 (Leipzig, 1910), 25–27; and Simon Dubnow, *Weltgeschichte des jüdischen Volkes,* vol. 10 (Berlin, 1929), 38–39.

7. For brief references, see Julia Männchen, "Der Antisemitismus seit der zweiten Hälfte des 19. Jahrhunderts in Deutschland," in *Der faschistische Pogrom vom 9,/10 November 1938—Zur Geschichte der Juden in Pommern,* edited by Wolfgang Wilhemus and Julia Männchen, Kolloquium der Sektionen Geschichtswissenschaft und Theologie der Ernst-Moritz-Arndt Universität, Greifswald (Greifswald, 1988), 18–31; and Marek Fijalkowski, "Z historii gminy zydowskiej w Szczecinku," *Szczecineckie Zapiski Historyczne* 2 (1987): 22–26. After the publication of my article in German ("Politische Kultur und Gewalt gegen Minderheiten," 1994), the following contributions on the topic have been published: Bernhard Vogt, "Antisemitismus und Justiz im Kaiserreich: Der Synagogenbrand in Neustettin," in *"Halte fern dem ganzen Lande jedes Verderben . . .": Geschichte und Kultur der Juden in Pommern,* edited by Margret Heitmann and Julius H. Schoeps (Hildesheim, 1995), 379–99; Gerd Hoffmann, *Der Prozeß um den Brand der Synagoge in Neustettin: Antisemitismus in Deutschland ausgangs des 19. Jahrhunderts* (Schifferstadt, 1998); and Stephen C. J. Nicholls, *The Burning of the Synagogue in Neustettin: Ideological Arson in the 1880s,* Centre for German-Jewish Studies, University of Sussex, Research Paper No. 2, spring 1999.

8. In addition to the contemporary press, the most important sources used are the reports of the local government offices and the state authorities of the Prussian Ministry of the Interior (Geheimes Staatsarchiv Preußischer Kulturbesitz Berlin [GStAPK], Rep. 76 III, Sekt. 1, Abt. XIIIa, Nr. 56, vols. 1–3 [Agitation gegen die Juden]); government statements and plans about the "Jewish Question" (Bundesarchiv [BA], Abtl. Potsdam, Reichskanzlei Nr. 679 ["Angelegenheiten der Juden"]); the documents of the Jewish community from the region in the former Gesamtarchiv der deutschen Juden (Stiftung "Neue Synagoge Berlin,"

layered explanation that attempts to do justice to the economic background, the catalyzing force of ideology, and, not least, the role of modern
politics. This approach is based on the insight that no one factor alone can
explain the riots.

II.   General Causes of the Riots

Socioeconomic Factors

The provincial governor (*Oberpräsident*) of Pomerania, Freiherr von
Münchhausen, wrote in his concluding report to the Prussian minister of
the interior that the riots were occasioned by social dissatisfaction, for
which the Jews were responsible:

> The cause of violence, which is by no means justifiable, lies . . . in the
> profound bitterness that the Jews have provoked in all sections of the
> population, from the small man to the educated and well-off, by their
> usury, their dividing land into lots [*Parcellierungen*], and the conse-
> quent ruin of many small and medium property owners in the
> province. . . . These relationships and conditions are especially preva-
> lent in the town of Stettin since Jewish businessmen have increasingly
> entered into competition with small merchants and tradesmen and
> have begun to reduce the food source of the aforementioned classes,
> especially the smaller craftsmen, by forcing down prices through fac-
> tory-style production and the use of greater capital. . . . Because of the
> substantial ruin that the Jews have caused in social life in Pomerania,
> the contrasts between them and the other parts of the population are
> sharper than in the other parts of Prussia.[9]

Münchhausen's explanation, which is representative of many other
reports from local government offices, clearly sought to blame the Jews
themselves for the riots so as to play down the possible negligence of the
authorities. His sweeping reproach against the exploitative business prac-

---

75a Ne 6 [Neustettin], 75a Sto 1 [Stolp]); letters from Jewish representatives in the region to
the "Comité vom 1. Dezember 1880" (ibid., 75c Ko 1); and letters of individual Pomeranian
antisemites to Adolf Stoecker (GStAPK, Rep. 92, Nachlaß Adolf Stoecker, I 7a–b [Briefe
1881–1882]). See Werner Bergmann, "Soziale und kulturelle Bedingungen kollektiver Gewalt
in Pogromen," in *Lerntag über Gewalt gegen Juden: Die Novemberpogrome von 1938 in historischer Perspektive,* edited by Herbert A. Strauss et al. (Berlin, 1989), 7–22. See also
Bergmann's contribution to this volume.
    9. Oberpräsident Pomerania, September 9, 1881, GStAPK, Rep. 76 III, Sekt. 1, Abt.
XIIIa, Nr. 56, Bd. 2, Bl. 17.

tices of the Jews is a product of the traditional cliché of the "Jewish usurer," and it evinces a stereotypical rejection of modern liberal economic development.[10] Because of its undifferentiated and value-laden portrayal, and its mixture of local politics and prejudice, Münchhausen's report says less about the actual social relationships than about the contemporary interpretation of the central points of social conflict. If one places these references in the context of the general economic and social development at the beginning of the 1880s, a differentiated picture emerges of the possible social causes of the riots.[11]

As elsewhere in Germany, Jews in the small towns of Pomerania and West Prussia formed a social group whose employment structure differed markedly from that of the majority population. In these largely unindustrialized areas, the townspeople had lived since time immemorial from agriculture and handcrafts, and often from both: small farmers also worked as craftsmen, and craftsmen had agricultural plots. The Jewish population, by contrast, which represented on the average about 5 percent of the town population, was overwhelmingly concentrated in commerce. In Neustettin, for example, 500 of the 8,500 inhabitants were Jews, of whom only seven worked as artisans; most of the others earned a living as salesmen or in retail trade. Only four families could be considered relatively well-off, most belonging "to that middle class [*Mittelstand*] that, without owning much capital, nevertheless ran a good business and [could] properly feed itself." The general social advancement of the town's Jewish families became evident in the fact that more and more Jewish students enrolled in the local *Gymnasium*.[12]

In the sparsely settled rural areas of East Elbia, Jewish merchants fulfilled the important roles of creditor, deliverer of raw materials (for example, wool and leather for craftsmen), agricultural middleman, and distributor of everyday consumer items. These traditional and mostly uneventful commercial relations were adversely affected by a long-term, structural economic and social transformation, which culminated in the cyclical downturn of the last quarter of the nineteenth century. The mod-

---

10. On this point, cf. Jacob Toury, *Soziale und politische Geschichte der Juden in Deutschland, 1847–1871: Zwischen Revolution, Reaktion und Emanzipation* (Düsseldorf, 1977), 371–81; and Stefan Rohrbacher and Michael Schmidt, *Judenbilder: Kulturgeschichte antijüdischer Mythen und antisemitischer Vorurteile* (Reinbek, 1991), 43–147.

11. Hans Rosenberg, *Grosse Depression und Bismarckzeit: Wirtschaftsablauf, Gesellschaft und Politik in Mitteleuropa* (Berlin, 1967); Reinhard Rürup, *Emanzipation und Antisemitismus: Studien zur 'Judenfrage' der bürgerlichen Gesellschaft* (Göttingen, 1975), 74–94.

12. Letter from the rabbi of Neustettin, Nathan Hoffmann, to the "Comité vom 1. Dezember 1880," February 2, 1881, Stiftung "Neue Synagogue Berlin—Centrum Judaicum," 75c Ko 1.

ernization of agriculture, for example, demanded greater investment by individual farmers, which was often possible only by taking out loans. Because banks and credit unions were very rare in country areas, the only source of credit was via private arrangement. That individual Christian and Jewish lenders used their monopoly position to their own advantage, especially before the "Usury Law" of May 24, 1880, can hardly be doubted, according to the available reports.[13]

The larger structural crisis was rooted in the growing competition from industrial products and modern marketing methods, which rendered small-scale production unprofitable.[14] This development was readily apparent in, for example, shoemaking, which dominated in the towns in which rioting took place. Jewish merchants often opened a shop (depot) that sold cheap (finished) shoes, and occasionally Jewish entrepreneurs employed workers who had hitherto been independent master shoemakers in their own small workshops.[15] In this regard, too, Jews, because of their specific employment profile, possessed "considerable advantages" in the transition to a capitalist economy, which contemporaries interpreted as unfair competition and a "permanent threat" rather than as a transition to modern marketing practices.[16] For the many small shoemakers, including those who made shoes on the side, who produced in advance for the autumn market, and who purchased leather mostly from local Jewish merchants, the Great Depression of the mid-1870s, with its extreme deflation, must have had a devastating effect; lower prices for their shoes made it difficult or impossible to meet payment deadlines for the raw materials. To the shoemakers, the business cycle was a mystery. They blamed "the Jews."[17]

Economics—even misperceived economic processes—cannot wholly explain the large-scale outbreak of violence in 1881. In other towns, such as Jastrow, shoemakers were largely independent of Jewish leather merchants, and in economic terms there was certainly no "special reason for

---

13. Ibid. On the general situation, see the partially antisemitic, tainted reports from the two investigations organized by the "Verein für Sozialpolitik": "Bäuerliche Zustände in Deutschland" and "Der Wucher auf dem Lande," in *Schriften des Vereins für Sozialpolitik*, vols. 22–24 (Leipzig, 1883) and 35–38 (1887–89).

14. See, in general, Shulamit Volkov, *The Rise of Popular Antimodernism in Germany: The Urban Master Artisans, 1873–1896* (Princeton, 1978).

15. Albert Heintze to Stoecker, January 1, 1882, GStAPK, Rep. 92, Nachlaß Stoecker, I 7a–b (Briefe 1881–1882); Regierungspräsident Marienwerder, January 1, 1882, ibid., Rep. 76 III, Sekt. 1, Abt. XIIIa, Nr. 56, Bd. 3, Bl. 112; ibid., Bl. 119.

16. Rürup, *Emanzipation und Antisemitismus*, 83.

17. Regierungspräsident Marienwerder, January 1, 1882, GStAPK, Rep. 76 III, Sekt. 1, Abt. XIIIa, Nr. 56, Bd. 3, Bl. 111–12.

mistrust of the Jews."[18] Yet here, too, anti-Jewish riots took place. This example shows that real social conflicts were not a sufficient condition for the emergence of anti-Jewish prejudices and violence. The general economic dissatisfaction, when tainted by traditional value preferences and the clichés of modern antisemitic propaganda, was enough to identify the "Jewish usurer" as a threat to one's own economic existence, the principal cause of the deplorable state of affairs, and a suitable target for violence.

Real economic and social tensions, sharpened by the structural and cyclical crisis, did indeed exist between Jews and non-Jews in the towns of Pomerania and West Prussia, a situation that was often understood—and presented in propaganda—as a gain in status for Jews ("Jewish domination") at the expense of Christians. But the outbreak of the riots cannot be satisfactorily understood in terms of the justifiable "wrath of the people," cited by self-serving conservative bureaucrats, because social relations and economic conditions in the two Prussian provinces did not differ substantially from those in other rural regions of the *Kaiserreich,* areas that experienced no similar outbreaks. Further factors must have been present in Neustettin before widespread social dissatisfaction could manifest itself in violence.

Antisemitic Agitation

Collective violence against a minority does not fall from the sky. It requires intellectual and propagandistic preparation. Liberal and Jewish opinion harbored no doubt about this, blaming the "mob unrest" on the long-term influence of the local antisemitic press and the direct effect of several public events involving the radical Berlin antisemitic leader Ernst Henrici.[19]

Indeed, the Neustettin-based newspaper *Norddeutsche Presse* had, since 1875, become a radical voice of the antisemitic movement and had loudly trumpeted the slogan of Otto Glagau: "The social question is the Jewish question."[20] Long before the outbreak of the riots, in April 1880, the executive board of Neustettin's Jewish community had tried to defend itself against the paper's blanket defamation through a libel suit. The court

---

18. Ibid., Bl. 119.

19. See, among other sources, *Allgemeine Zeitung des Judenthums* 45 (1881): 509–10, 558–59; and *Frankfurter Zeitung,* July 20, August 21, 1881.

20. See, for example, *Norddeutsche Presse,* January 20, 1880: "The Jewish question is in fact nothing other than the economic question, which has been raised by the freedom of usury, trade, and stocks, and it only becomes the Jewish question because the Jews have used these freedoms the most to exploit our people to their detriment."

in Köslin decided against the plaintiff on the basis of several technicalities: the newspaper's criticism was not directed against individual Jews, but against general social conditions; the executive board of the Jewish community was unable to speak for all Jews and therefore could not take legal action on their behalf.[21]

The *Norddeutsche Presse* was not the only antisemitic newspaper preparing the ground for violence. The *Deutsche Patriot,* the Berlin *Ostendzeitung,* and *Die Wahrheit* were disseminated in many towns— often in local pubs.[22] Antisemitic committees and associations had also sprung up in these places. Vehicles of the independent middle class and often masquerading behind harmless names such as "German Citizens Association," "Patriotic Club," or "Reform Association," these antisemitic organizations intensified their agitation at the beginning of the election campaign in the summer of 1881. Individual officials and a few clergymen joined the chorus of anti-Jewish voices.[23]

The antisemitic movement was gaining ground in several locales, as was evident from the massive crowds at appearances by Henrici in February 1881 and again in June of the same year.[24] Henrici, then a twenty-seven-year-old secondary-school teacher who had been forced out of his profession after several turbulent political meetings, was the most fanatical and unscrupulous agitator of the radically anti-Jewish and demagogic "Berlin Movement."[25] In contrast to the Christian conservative Adolf Stoecker, his antisemitism was based on a secular, anticlerical orientation and uncompromising racism. He called himself a "firebrand" and demanded the deportation of all Jews from Germany.[26] As one of the ini-

---

21. Köslin court to the congregation of the Neustettin synagogue, August 31, 1880, Stiftung "Neue Synagoge Berlin—Centrum Judaicum," 75a, Ne 6 (Neustettin), Bd. 5.

22. Regierungspräsident Marienwerder, January 19, 1882, GStAPK, Rep. 76 III, Sekt. 1, Abt. XIIIa, Nr. 56, Bd. 3, Bl. 107; *Frankfurter Zeitung,* August 20, 1881, evening edition; *Allgemeine Zeitung des Judenthums* 45 (1881): 558–59.

23. See the letters of the Neustettin congregational rabbi, Hoffmann, January 25, February 3, and February 9, 1881; of Josef Bauer (Köslin), January 26, 1881; and of Philipp Michaelis (Cammin), February 10, 1881, to the "Comité vom 1. Dezember 1880," Stiftung "Neue Synagoge Berlin—Centrum Judaicum," 75c Ko 1.

24. Besides Neustettin, Henrici had spoken at least in Bärwalde, Ratzebuhr, and Jastrow. He had been scheduled to speak in Hammerstein as well, but he did not appear after the outbreak of the unrest.

25. On Henrici's life and career, see Hoffmann, *Prozeß,* 247–81.

26. Werner Jochmann, *Gesellschaftskrise und Judenfeindschaft in Deutschland, 1870–1945* (Hamburg, 1988), 49–50; Peter G. J. Pulzer, *Die Entstehung des politischen Antisemitismus in Deutschland und Österreich, 1867–1914* (Gütersloh, 1966), 84–85; Hans-Gert Oomen and Hans-Dieter Schmid, eds., *Vorurteile gegen Minderheiten: Die Anfänge des modernen Antisemitismus am Beispiel Deutschlands* (Stuttgart, 1978), 32; Kurt Wawrzinek, *Die Entstehung der deutschen Antisemitenparteien (1873–1890)* (Berlin, 1927), 35–42.

tiators of the antisemitic petitions intended for Bismarck, which called for a ban on Jewish immigration, the exclusion of Jews from public office, and the reintroduction of a Jewish census, he traveled through the provinces to collect signatures, and in this way he arrived in Neustettin on February 13, 1881. His inflammatory rhetoric ("Protective measures are taken against epidemics in animals . . . why should there not be protective measures against the overgrowth of Jewry?") and malicious ridicule of the supposed special features of the "Jewish race" were enthusiastically greeted by the several hundred who had gathered to hear him, among them the *Landrat* (county official) of Neustettin district and other local notables and civil servants.[27] Henrici painted an utterly pessimistic picture of the future—all real estate would soon be in Jewish hands, while the German would be the "pigherdsmen of the Jews." He appealed to his audience to take "self-help" measures, by which he meant the boycott of Jewish shops and "Jewish newspapers," the signing of the antisemitic petition, and the readiness for unconditional struggle. He hoped to make it so difficult for the Jews in Germany that they would, in fact, emigrate: "Banish false fear and know that we 42 million Germans will bring the 700,000 Jews to heel. . . . If the Jews feel so oppressed that they want to leave us, after they have sucked us dry, we don't have to worry where they end up. We are not obliged to be concerned for them."

Five days after Henrici's appearance, the Neustettin synagogue went up in flames. When the inflammatory speech of the Berlin agitator was linked with the fire, Henrici and the local and national antisemitic press immediately accused the Jews of setting the fire themselves, first of all to cash in on a generous insurance policy, and second, to damage the reputation of the antisemitic movement, which threatened to expose their evildoing.[28] Henrici undertook a second trip through Pomerania and West Prussia only a few weeks before the outbreak of unrest, in June 1881, and this accusation stood at the center of his speeches, no doubt further stirring up emotions.

The continuous antisemitic agitation in Neustettin and adjacent areas, especially when radicalized by Henrici's appearances, fundamentally worsened the standing of the Jews in the eyes of the Christian population. Through the propaganda, the Jews were socially marginalized, denounced as "spoilers," and feared as overpowering enemies, against whom it was necessary to assume a defensive posture. This campaign was

---

27. Cf. Hoffmann, *Prozeß,* 26–27. My summary of Henrici's speech is based on the extensive report in *Norddeutsche Presse,* February 16, 1881.

28. Ernst Henrici, "Der Synagogenbrand in Neustettin," speech of March 11, 1881, Berlin, in *Norddeutsche Presse,* March 13, March 15, 1881. Henrici's blaming the Jews for insurance fraud was unfounded. Vogt, "Antisemitismus und Justiz," 382–83.

an essential prelude to the collective violence of July and August, providing the necessary "process of delegitimation and dehumanization of a group."[29]

But once again, it is unwarranted to assume an automatic causal connection between agitation and pogroms. Henrici and other antisemitic demagogues made appearances all over Germany, yet anti-Jewish riots occurred only in Pomerania and West Prussia at this time. One more ingredient was crucial to this outcome.

The Behavior of the Government

In modern societies in which the state has appropriated a monopoly of violence in the course of its formation, special conditions must obtain for violent unrest to occur against specific groups in the population. Of decisive importance is the attitude and willingness to act on the part of the state authorities, especially the government, the police, and the justice administration.

When the authorities are weak and there is a power vacuum at the heart of the state, as in revolutionary times, anti-Jewish activity is often associated with general protest movements or anarchic conditions. A historical example is the 1848 revolution, when anti-Jewish riots took place in many parts of Germany. But when the government is secure in the exercise of its power, anti-Jewish violence on a larger scale can basically occur only when the rioters think—with or without good reason—that the state authorities stand behind them and that their deeds will go unpunished. They understand themselves as agents of a "real" government policy that cannot be publicly articulated or officially sanctioned. The Russian pogromists of 1881–82, for example, believed that the czar had secretly authorized violence against the Jewish population in revenge for the murder of his predecessor. In such cases, anti-Jewish violence expresses subjects' loyalty to vested authority, rather than protest. The actual behavior of the state is completely irrelevant; the mere appearance of state legitimation is sufficient for violence to commence.[30] Finally, there is the special case of the state's purposefully inciting the "people's wrath" and organizing and staging violent riots, as in the Russian pogroms of 1905 and the "Reichskristallnacht" of November 1938. The all-important relations between rioters and the state authorities are the basis of a distinction that can be made between protest pogroms, loyalist pogroms, and state-led pogroms.

---

29. Bergmann, "Soziale und kulturelle Bedingungen," 8.

30. *Pace* the widespread legend, the Russian pogroms of 1881—82 were not planned or initiated by the government or other organizations. See I. Michael Aronson, *Troubled Waters: The Origins of the Anti-Jewish Pogroms in Russia* (Pittsburgh, 1991).

In this typology, the Pomeranian riots were loyalist pogroms. Count-less contemporary observers attested that "in regions in which the author-ity of the state is recognized and in which the loyalty of the population is almost proverbial," such riots could hardly have taken place without the "terrible delusion that the state promoted this movement or at least did not view it unfavorably," and without the "false belief of impunity."[31] In the West Prussian town of Jastrow, one inhabitant who had participated in the riots answered the subsequent interrogation by a civil servant with the statement that "this action was of course wished 'from above'—Bis-marck is Henrici's friend—so no one can and will punish us if we drive off the Jews."[32] Another witness informed a court that the rioters of Schivel-bein were motivated by the "belief that in the end they were doing the state a favor."[33]

On the basis of this widespread public opinion and because of Bis-marck's acceptance of the antisemitic petition and his exchange of formal greetings with several antisemitic organizations, the liberal press accused the chancellor of supporting antisemitism and therefore promoting the eruption of the tumults.[34] Bismarck took legal action against such accusa-tions, not always successfully.[35] His behavior toward the antisemitic movement was contradictory and essentially motivated by tactical rather than ideological considerations.[36] He was unsympathetic toward Stoecker's agitation, for example, because of its "socialist" populism, and he considered prohibiting the court preacher's appearances before mass audiences under the antisocialist laws.[37] But as opponents of the progres-sive party and the socialists, Stoecker and other antisemites were welcome allies, and Bismarck knew how to instrumentalize them for his political goals. It was no coincidence that in the run-up to the Reichstag elections of 1881—in which Bismarck hoped to bring about the decisive defeat of the left wing of the National Liberals, led by the Jewish politicians Ludwig

---

31. *Frankfurter Zeitung,* August 21, 1881.

32. *Allgemeine Zeitung des Judenthums* 45 (1881): 559.

33. Ibid., 828.

34. See, for example, *Nationalzeitung* 378 (1881); and *Vossische Zeitung,* August 9, 1881.

35. For example, a former editor of the *Berliner Nachrichten* who had asserted that Bis-marck was co-responsible for the antisemitic actions was pronounced not guilty of defama-tion after his lawyer detailed Bismarck's connections to antisemitic organizations. *Allgemeine Zeitung des Judenthums* 45 (1881): 570–72 (reprint of an article from the *Vossische Zeitung*).

36. Josef Popper-Lynkeus, *Fürst Bismarck und der Antisemitismus* (Vienna, 1925); Otto Jöhlinger, *Bismarck und die Juden* (Berlin, 1921); Paul W. Massing, *Rehearsal for Destruc-tion: A Study of Political Anti-Semitism in Imperial Germany* (New York, 1967), 37–50; Fritz Stern, *Gold und Eisen: Bismarck und sein Bankier Bleichröder* (Frankfurt/Main, 1978); Otto Pflanze, *Bismarck and the Development of Germany: The Period of Fortification, 1880–1889,* vol. 3 (Princeton, 1990), 49–51.

37. Massing, *Rehearsal for Destruction,* 38; Stern, *Gold und Eisen,* 625–26.

Bamberger and Eduard Lasker—he strongly played the antisemitic card and, in generous doses of public support, signaled his agreement with the antisemitic "reform policies." When after the election it became apparent that the Berlin Movement could not have prevented the victory of the progressives and secessionists, Bismarck began to distance himself from Stoecker and the antisemites.[38]

With his instrumentalization of the antisemitic movement as a weapon in domestic politics, Bismarck revealed himself as the "first great manipulator of anti-Semitism in modern Germany because of the very fact that he harbored neither racial nor religious prejudices against the Jewish group and that he did not aim at Jews *qua* Jews when he gave comfort to anti-Semitic agitation."[39] The craftsmen and rural workers of Pomerania and West Prussia, however, were naturally unable to see through such tactical finesse, taking his signs of public support for the antisemites at face value. For the antisemites in Neustettin, there was special reason to believe that Bismarck would support them. After the first mass meeting with Henrici on February 13, 1881, a telegram was sent to Bismarck expressing support for the economic and tariff policy of the chancellor. In return, Bismarck sent a letter of thanks to the leader of Neustettin's antisemites, which he signed personally.[40] As they fell violently upon their Jewish fellow citizens, the antisemites of Neustettin could easily convince themselves that they were acting on the authority of the chancellor—whose country estate of Varzin lay close by and who was held in particularly high esteem in the area. That Bismarck did not clear up this misunderstanding and permitted his enormous prestige to be misused by the agitators was without doubt an important factor in the outbreak and duration of the violence.[41]

The government's temporary backing of the antisemitic campaign created two important conditions for the outbreak of collective violence: it formed an impression of changed power balances and signaled a relaxation of social control.[42] For radical antisemites, domestic political struggles and social conflicts were always a fight "for or against the Jews." In this Manichean view, Bismarck's antiliberal turn in 1878–79 and his electoral maneuvering in 1881 had to appear as a loss of power for Jews and

---

38. Massing, *Rehearsal for Destruction,* 41–43; Stern, *Gold und Eisen,* 638–40.

39. Massing, *Rehearsal for Destruction,* 43.

40. Hoffmann, *Prozeß,* 25. The same exchange of telegrams between local antisemites and Bismarck took place a day later in Ratzebuhr.

41. Jöhlinger, in *Bismarck und die Juden,* 47–49, suggests that Bismarck did articulate his criticisms of the "vulgarity and meanness" of the antisemitic smear campaign in an article supposedly planted in the *Kölnische Zeitung* on July 24, 1881. Even if this is the case, for which Jöhlinger provides no evidence, such a measure—an anonymous article in a distant newspaper—was hardly likely to influence public opinion.

42. Bergmann, "Soziale und kulturelle Bedingungen," 11–12.

a commensurate gain for the antisemites. Inhibitions about committing illegal acts against the Jews were consequently reduced, because it was believed—falsely, as it later turned out—that state sanctions would not be applied.

Social tensions and frustrations, antisemitic propaganda, and the misunderstood signals of a cynically manipulative government were the general causes of the Pomeranian riots. Their specific origins must be sought in the immediate locality.

III. The Origins and Course of the Anti-Jewish Excesses

The Culmination of the Conflicts in Neustettin

The social movement of antisemitism, especially in the time of "awakening" after 1879, brought high hopes for a decisive breakthrough to "improvement" and the beginning of the end of the "deplorable state of affairs" caused by "Jewish domination." Every apparent setback, every new change in the power balance in favor of "the Jews," therefore demanded stronger countermeasures by, and mobilization of, antisemites, in order to compensate for the "loss of power."[43] This was the situation in Neustettin after the burning of the synagogue on February 18, 1881.

The cause of the fire was never firmly established, so that negligence or arson cannot be ruled out. The absurd accusation that the Jews had set their own synagogue ablaze was considered in two costly and lengthy court actions and can be dismissed.[44] It is also improbable that negligence was the cause, because the synagogue had not been used for some time before the fire. The probable, though in retrospect unprovable, cause is thus arson from anti-Jewish motives.[45]

That the cause of the fire was never cleared up was not just the result of tardy inquiries by the authorities—a criminal detective from Berlin was not sent until the time of the appeal case, which was held in the West

---

43. On a similar constellation in antiquity, see Werner Bergmann and Christhard Hoffmann, "'Kalkül oder Massenwahn'? Eine soziologische Interpretation der antijüdischen Unruhen in Alexandria, 38 n. Chr.," in *Antisemitismus und jüdische Geschichte: Studien zu Ehren von Herbert A. Strauss,* edited by Rainer Erb and Michael Schmidt (Berlin, 1987), 15–46, esp. 31–35.

44. Hugo Friedländer, "Der Brand der Neustettiner Synagoge vor den Schwurgerichten zu Köslin und Konitz," in idem, *Interessante Kriminalprozesse von kulturhistorischer Bedeutung,* vol. 9 (Berlin, 1913), 9–144.

45. Dubnow, *Weltgeschichte,* 10:38, asserts, "The perpetrator was a local blacksmith, an alcoholic and an inveterate antisemite." According to the court records, much speaks for the fact that the blacksmith Buchholz was the perpetrator, as he was the main witness against the Jewish defendants. Friedländer, "Brand der Neustettiner Synagoge," 118–20, 141.

Prussian town of Konitz in 1884[46]—but issued more from the political meaning of the case and the extreme political polarization of public opinion. The antisemites were faced with an immediate danger when the public reacted with general dismay to the fire. For should it have been confirmed, as most Jews and liberal newspapers asserted, that the blaze was a direct consequence of Henrici's agitation, then official measures would almost certainly be taken against the antisemites, and this would of course represent a blow to the "movement."[47] The antisemitic press accordingly spared no effort to avoid this scenario, countering with the accusation that the Jews had set the synagogue ablaze themselves in order to put the blame on the Christians and thereby damage the reputation of antisemitism. At the same time, they tried to exploit the town's damaged reputation, caused by the fire, in order to mobilize all local "patriots" against the Jewish "traitors who fouled their own nest." Independently of one another, the local *Landrat,* Bogislav von Bonin, and the editor of the *Norddeutsche Presse* conducted quite dubious inquiries and concocted a story to "prove" Jewish culpability in the arson.[48] It casts a telling light on the attitude of local bureaucrats and other interested parties that the antisemitic interpretation, based on transparent lies, rumors, and manipulated witness reports, was held credible enough for the public prosecutor to commence proceedings against five Jews for the crime.

In the highly charged atmosphere of early 1881, relations between Christians and Jews in Neustettin rapidly deteriorated. As is often the case in such situations, children and youths were the first to practice what the adults were thinking. Christian schoolchildren humiliated their Jewish classmates to the extent that they did not attend school for some time.[49] Business and social

---

46. The detective was sent only at the express wish of the defense. See Counsellor of Justice Makower to the Prussian Ministry of the Interior, February 8, 1884, GStAPK, Rep. 76 III, Sekt. 1, Abtl. XIIIa, Nr. 56, Bd. 3, Bl. 7–8. In early 1881, the Berlin police headquarters had rejected the request of the Jewish community in Neustettin to send a criminal detective. Royal Police Headquarters to the executive of the synagogue congregation of Neustettin, March 7, 1881, Stiftung "Neue Synagoge Berlin—Centrum Judaicum," 75a Ne 6, Bd. 5.

47. See, for example, *Neue Stettiner Zeitung* (cited from *Der Reichsbote,* February 22, 1881): "The flames of this burning synagogue throw a glaring light on the bottomless abyss of brutality and madness to which the leaders of the antisemitic movement and the whole rabble dizzily following them are rushing; these flames cast a glaring light on the urgent danger that a further tolerance of this odious swindle, which in Berlin and elsewhere celebrates its orgies, must bring with it. [. . .] [W]e hope that finally those in responsible positions will open their eyes to the fact that the distance from word to deed is not so far, and we energetically demand in sight of the smoking fire of this synagogue that the arsonistic demagogues will be laid by the heels."

48. Friedländer, "Brand der Neustettiner Synagoge," 142–43; *Der Israelit* 25 (1884): 378, 384.

49. Lawyer Stern to the "Comité vom 1. Dezember 1880," August 17, 1881, Stiftung "Neue Synagoge Berlin—Centrum Judaicum," 75c Ko 1.

contacts between Christians and Jews declined, Jewish shops were boycotted, and Jews were refused membership in clubs and associations.[50]

The Jews of Neustettin did not remain passive during the tense atmosphere in the spring of 1881. Through the distribution of publications of the Berlin-based Jewish self-defense association, "Comité of December 1," they attempted to enlighten at least those with an education and those with an open mind about the true nature of antisemitism.[51] Furthermore, the executive of the Jewish community sued Henrici for "defamation of religion" (section 166 of the German Penal Code) and individual antisemitic newspapers in Germany for slander. They also complained to the local consistory about a Lutheran pastor who had uttered anti-Jewish invective at one of Henrici's meetings.[52] However, the Jewish community of Neustettin placed their greatest hopes of countering the antisemitic climate of opinion in the town on the newly founded *Neustettiner Zeitung.* It was an adoption of the liberal *Cösliner Zeitung* with a special section for Neustettin.[53] In order to compete with the *Norddeutsche Presse,* the Neustettin rabbi attempted to organize subsidies from Jewish organizations elsewhere in Germany.[54] A free copy of the Berlin humor magazine *Ulk* was added after July 1, 1881, in hopes of substantially increasing the number of subscribers to the *Neustettiner Zeitung.*

The appearance of a local paper in which the anti-Jewish efforts were sharply criticized and ridiculed represented a great "Jewish" provocation for the antisemites, and with threats and abuse they attempted to intimidate its Jewish editors, the Cohn brothers.[55] This constellation ultimately led to the outbreak of the riots on July 17, 1881.[56] The president of the

50. Congregational rabbi of Neustettin, February 22, 1881, ibid.; *Norddeutsche Presse,* March 13, 1881.

51. Congregational rabbi of Neustettin, June 23, 1881, Stiftung "Neue Synagoge Berlin—Centrum Judaicum," 75c Ko 1.

52. Executive of the synagogue congregation of Neustettin to the state attorneys at Köslin, March 2, 1881; and to the provincial consistory of Pomerania, March 14, 1881. Both representations proved fruitless; see the answers of the state attorneys and the consistory, both of March 23, 1881, Stiftung "Neue Synagoge Berlin—Centrum Judaicum," 75a Ne 6, Bd. 5; and congregational rabbi of Neustettin, March 2, 16, 1881, ibid., 75c Ko 1.

53. Congregational rabbi of Neustettin, March 28, 1881, ibid. The newspaper had approximately two to three hundred subscribers at that time.

54. Congregational rabbi of Neustettin, April 24, June 8, 1881, ibid.

55. After the riots, the editor of the *Neustettiner Zeitung* received the following threatening letter: "A warning to the Jew Adolf Cohn of Neustettin. Because of vile offenses against Christians and rabble-rousing, noted for punishment. Association for the Extermination of the Jews [Verein zur Ausrottung der Juden]." *Der Israelit* 22 (1881): 804.

56. Regierungspräsident Köslin (represented by Count d'Haussonville), July 21, August 20, 1881, GStAPK, Rep. 76 III, Sekt. 1, Abtl. XIIIa, Nr. 56, Bd. 2, Bl. 230, 314, passim; Police administration, Neustettin, July 18, 1881, ibid., Bl. 237, passim; Oberpräsident Pomerania, September 20, 1881, ibid., Bd. 3, Bl. 19–20; *Allgemeine Zeitung des Judenthums* 45 (1881): 509–10; *Der Reichsbote,* July 20, 21, 22, 1881.

Neustettin "League of Antisemites," the building contractor Luttosch, felt insulted by an article in the *Neustettiner Zeitung* and attacked Cohn in the street. But Cohn's brother was close at hand, and together they repelled the furious antisemite. Bleeding from the head, Luttosch rushed around various taverns in the town and called upon the craftsmen and workers, who drank there on Sundays, to drive off the Jews and "beat them to death." In the course of the afternoon, some eight hundred to one thousand people gathered and marched through the streets chanting "Hep hep!" and smashing the windows of some Jewish shops with stones. The situation escalated that evening when the police arrested Luttosch. The mob demanded his release and became increasingly violent. Laying siege to the building of the *Neustettiner Zeitung,* they wrecked its editorial offices and damaged the printing machinery. Another twenty-one Jewish shops had their windows smashed, and two were totally destroyed. Despite police reinforcements and several warnings, events escalated the next evening. Nearly all Jewish houses now had their windows smashed, and out of fear their inhabitants slept in the open. On the third evening, after the arrival of the government representative from Köslin and further police reinforcements, another large gathering took place, but this time no further violence ensued.

The Spread of the Riots: Patterns of Dissemination and Development

What began in Neustettin could not be contained there. In the following weeks, riots spread in concentric circles around the Pomeranian provincial town: substantial rioting occurred in Hammerstein (July 20–24), Bärwalde (July 25 and 27), Baldenburg (August 2), Jastrow (August 3, 4, and 7), Schivelbein (August 6 and 7), Konitz (August 5 and 7), Pollnow (August 8), Falkenburg (August 11), Stettin (August 15–17), and Stolp (September 2–4). In other towns, for example Bublitz (July 31), Rummelsburg (August 4), Lauenburg (August 7), Zippnow (August 14), Tempelburg (August 14 and 15), and the Posen town of Rogasen (August 21), the outbreaks remained minor or were nipped in the bud.

   That the Neustettin incidents occasioned a whole series of anti-Jewish excesses has been explained as the doing of either "outside agitators" or "spontaneous copycats." In view of the sustained rioting, many government authorities replaced their "wrath of the people" thesis with an "agitation" thesis, and they suspected that the cause of the disturbances was a long-planned conspiracy from outside the area. Thus, for example, the Köslin-based *Oberregierungsrat* Count d'Haussonville wrote, "These occurrences, which began in Neustettin and were gradually repeated in all

Fig. 1.   Places of antisemitic rioting in summer 1881. (Layout and cartography by Karsten Bremer.)

towns, bear the stamp of an illegal agitation, which is directed by a certain party [. . .] Dr. Henrici is, in the first instance, the responsible person."[57] The Prussian minister of the interior, in his report to the kaiser, also adopted this interpretation, placing all blame on Henrici and ignoring the general connection between political culture and the pogrom atmosphere.[58] But in the subsequent police and judicial investigation, no direct connection could be proven between the tumults and antisemitic agents from outside the region, nor, tellingly, between one local organization and

57. Regierungspräsident Köslin (represented by Count d'Haussonville), August 10, 1881, GStAPK, Rep. 76 III, Sekt. 1, Abtl. XIIIa, Nr. 56, Bd. 2, Bl. 271.

58. Prussian minister of the interior, August 21, 1881, BA, Abtl. Potsdam, Reichskanzlei Nr. 679, Bl. 202–3.

that of another town.[59] Neither did the investigation of the individual disturbances indicate that they were planned in advance or centrally organized. Even if one cannot overestimate the significance of antisemitic propaganda for the preparation of a pogrom atmosphere, the riots themselves, with perhaps one exception, were not the work of individual agitators or less visible "string pullers." A less self-interested reading of the evidence strongly suggests spontaneous cases of imitation with low levels of organization and a diffuse circle of perpetrators. In some cases groups with former ties formed on an ad hoc basis; in other instances interested persons who, for example, wanted to neutralize a local Jewish competitor attempted to influence the tumults and steer them in a certain direction.[60]

The Neustettin conflict spread immediately to Hammerstein, because many Jews had fled there from Neustettin to avoid the violence and because Christian students who attended the Neustettin *Gymnasium* had returned to Hammerstein for the school vacation. The meeting of the two parties, with their divergent reports and interpretations of the happenings in Neustettin, led to an escalation of animosity and finally to the disturbances.[61]

In the other towns of the area, the anti-Jewish riots obviously did not occur so spontaneously. Here it is possible to distinguish between phases of preparation, escalation, and actual rioting. In the first phase, reports of witnesses or newspapers from Neustettin led to a general and uncertain atmosphere of disquiet: the streets were livelier than usual in the evenings, occasional cries of "Hep hep!" or "Out with Jews!" were heard, and the rumor circulated that action against the Jews would soon (in many cases, on a specific day) be "unleashed." In this way, a general mobilization of the population occurred over several days, and the expectation rose that something would happen. In some cases, it is possible to identify an even higher level of preparation and organization: in Lauenburg, Falkenburg, Stettin, and Rogasen, threatening letters were sent to Jewish citizens, and posters were hung up that called for agitation against Jews. One read, "Notice! Jew-baiting [*Judenhetze*]. Sunday, August 21, and Friday, September 2, 1881. Evening 9 P.M. Signal: fire in the Jewish street. Shout: Hep, Hep."[62] The authorities saw in these posters evidence of a planned organi-

---

59. Regierungspräsident Marienwerder, January 19, 1882, GStAPK, Rep. 76 III, Sekt. 1, Abt. XIIIa, Nr. 56, Bd. 3, Bl. 107.

60. Thus in Konitz, for example, a Christian butcher who was in dispute with a Jewish merchant paid youths for "Hep hep!" chants. Cf. *Vossische Zeitung,* August 10, 1881.

61. Regierungspräsident Marienwerder, July 19, 1881, GStAPK, Rep. 76 III, Sekt. 1, Abt. IIIa, Nr. 56, Bd. 1, Bl. 250; January 1, 1882, ibid., Bd. 3, Bl. 108–13; Oberpräsident West Prussia, October 19, 1881, ibid, Bd. 2, Bl. 30, passim.

62. Landrat Obernik, August 22, 1881, GStAPK, Rep. 76 III, Sekt. 1, Abt. XIIIa, Nr. 56, Bd. 1, Bl. 335.

zation of the disturbances. Yet closer investigation of the substance and language of the "notices," which were signed by, for example, "the executive for Jew-baiting" or "the Committee of the Ku Klux Association [*Kucklucks Verbindung*]," suggests the mischief typical of youthful perpetrators rather than seasoned conspirators.[63] To what extent these notices were inspired by the Russian pogroms, which were occurring at the time and in which anti-Jewish posters played an important preparatory role, is difficult to say with certainty.[64] But it appears possible, in light of the fact that some newspapers reported the Russian case in relative detail.[65]

After the phase of preparation, resulting in a general mobilization of the population through regular demonstrations and the setting of a date, the escalation phase ensued if state authority remained passive.[66] But even when government agencies became active, further escalation was often the result. Measures such as the arrest of a demonstrator, the declaration of a curfew, or the banning of a festival provoked the mob. In some towns, at this critical juncture, self-proclaimed leaders—often shady characters of unsound mind—appeared on the scene and greatly heightened the tension. In Hammerstein, for example, a shabby aristocrat, easily identifiable by his turbanlike headwear, placed himself before the crowd, distributed herring and drinks, toasted Bismarck and Henrici, and called for the driving off of the Jews. When he was arrested, the crowd forced the outmanned police to release him. Then violence and destruction ruled the streets.[67]

Most of the disturbances took place on weekends, when many people were on the streets and in a boisterous mood after visiting the taverns. Egged on by onlookers and sympathizers, the anonymous crowd would smash the windows of the synagogues, shops, and residences. Such action was accompanied by the chanting of antisemitic slogans ("Hep! Hep! and Hurra!" "Jew out!") and sometimes the singing of patriotic songs ("I am a Prussian"). The perpetrators were mostly youths (apprentices or high school students) and journeymen. Individuals who were especially hated—such as, in Hammerstein, a Jewish judge, the owner of a confectionery, and the owner of a shoe store—were subjected to more intensive attacks, in which adults (master craftsmen, workers, and peasants) took part. Many witnesses' reports emphasize the active participation of women in

---

63. *Allgemeine Zeitung des Judenthums* 45 (1881): 846; Police headquarters, Stettin, August 17, 1881, GStAPK, Rep. 76 III, Sekt. 1, Abt. XIIIa, Nr. 56, Bd. 1, Bl. 288.

64. Aronson, *Troubled Waters,* 82–100.

65. Dubnow, *Weltgeschichte,* 10:39.

66. In Lauenburg and Rogasen, for example, the immediate intervention of the police and military after the appearance of antisemitic posters prevented an escalation of the situation.

67. Regierungspräsident Marienwerder, January 1, 1882, GStAPK, Rep. 76 III, Sekt. 1, Abt. XIIIa, Nr. 56, Bd. 3, Bl. 107; Indictment from the public prosecutor at the Konitz court against von Schmeling, ibid., Bd. 2, Bl. 90, passim.

the riots, particularly in instigating the crowds and in looting.[68] The attacks were almost everywhere directed exclusively against property rather than persons. Where windows were shattered, the crowd would often disperse on its own or would be scattered by the now reinforced police or by the soldiers that had been summoned. Some towns were exceptions to this pattern. In Schivelbein, where "bands of 10–12 men" with blackened faces and armed with crowbars and hatchets were observed, the excesses, contrary to the usual practice, were associated with substantial plundering, destruction, and cases of personal injury.[69] The action appears to have been planned well in advance, although the obvious ringleader—a former property owner, now a drunkard and notorious antisemite—was set free for lack of clear evidence in the ensuing court case.[70] In Pollnow, the shop of the only Jewish merchant was totally destroyed and plundered.[71] The three-day riot in Stettin was limited to serious conflicts between the demonstrators and state officials. Even though the rioters chanted the antisemitic slogans, no Jewish property was damaged.[72]

If one looks beyond Schivelbein and Pollnow, the incidence of violence in riots in Pomerania and West Prussia was relatively limited. Unlike in the Russian pogroms, persons were mostly not directly attacked.[73] Even in Schivelbein, it was possible to convince the rioters not to vandalize two houses where women were recovering after childbirth or where an invalid lived, although they threatened to return at a later time.[74] The tumults were often processionlike and characterized by ritualized forms.[75] They largely followed the traditional pattern of Jew-baiting, with mass rallies on the streets, "Hep hep!" chants, and stone-throwing, and they generally ended when it was somehow determined that all Jews had been "taught their lesson." This behavior suggests that the riots were rituals of collective humiliation and submission by which a majority tries to reestablish its superiority over a socially rising minority perceived as a threat. In the case of the Pomeranian riots, these submission rituals took the form of symbolic expulsions ("the Jews must leave for Palestine").[76] The actions

---

68. *Allgemeine Zeitung des Judentums* 45 (1881): 554; *Der Israelit* 22 (1881): 826.

69. *Der Israelit* 22 (1881): 853, passim.

70. *Allgemeine Zeitung des Judentums* 45 (1881): 828–29.

71. Oberpräsident Pomerania, September 20, 1881, GStAPK, Rep. 76 III, Sekt. 1, Abt. XIIIa, Nr. 56, Bd. 3, Bl. 23.

72. Ibid., Bl. 24–28.

73. Philippson, *Neueste Geschichte des jüdischen Volkes,* 2:26.

74. *Der Israelit* 22 (1881): 853–54.

75. On this subject, cf. Rohrbacher, *Gewalt im Biedermeier,* 50–53.

76. On the function of pogroms as rituals of public degradation, see Peter Loewenberg, "The Kristallnacht as a Public Degradation Ritual," *Leo Baeck Institute Year Book* 33 (1987): 309–23.

were especially aimed at those Jews who had achieved some official status, public influence, or economic leadership (such as judges, deputy mayors, and editors) and who were seen as representatives of alleged "Jewish domination."

Because of the convergence of the political aims of organized antisemitism and the thrust of the excesses, most of the rioting youths could count on the understanding or clandestine support of the population.[77] They merely acted out what the antisemitic associations and sections of "good society" believed.[78] That the violence was strategically inappropriate and anachronistic in the political and legal circumstances of the *Kaiserreich,* and that it would ultimately discredit the antisemitic movement in the eyes of the public, exceeded the political horizon of the rioters. Many were deeply shocked when they had to realize that instead of being rewarded for their "loyal" actions, they were treated and punished as criminals. After the Schivelbein riots, the authorities staged a very public warning for the local people. They forced the twenty-one perpetrators of the riots, handcuffed and tied together in groups of five, to march through town to the Köslin prison accompanied by an imposing military force. The public spectacle made a strong impression on the locals and signified a major setback for the antisemitic cause. Thereafter, the "respectable" antisemites of Schivelbein officially condemned the violent excess, while still defending the motives of the perpetrators and presenting them as victims of "Jewish provocation." In a sermon, the Lutheran superintendent Henske added fuel to the flames and accused the Jews of Schivelbein of gloating and sneering at the sight of the arrested rioters. The situation in the town remained explosive after that. Rumors spread that the wives of those arrested would set fire to the whole town. It is indicative of the critical and weak position of the Schivelbein Jews that they found it necessary to declare their sincere sympathy with the arrested rioters despite the fact that they had been harmed considerably by them.[79]

The Reaction of the Authorities

Soon after the outbreak of the unrest in Pomerania, the Prussian government found itself accused by the liberals of having indirectly caused the eruption and spread of the riots by its benevolent toleration of the antise-

77. A decisive condition for the tumults was the fact that the Christian master craftsmen and shopkeepers mostly tolerated the riotous behavior of their apprentices and journeymen. Regierungspräsident Marienwerder, January 1, 1882, GStAPK, Rep. 76 III, Sekt. 1, Abt. XIIIa, Nr. 56, Bd. 3, Bl. 116; *Allgemeine Zeitung des Judentums* 45 (1881): 559.

78. *Allgemeine Zeitung des Judentums* 45 (1881): 509, 543.

79. Ibid., 625–26.

Fig. 2. "Seed and Harvest." The agitator is probably Adolf Stoecker.
(© Staats- und Universitäts bibliothek Hamburg.)

mitic agitation and by the hesitancy of the police intervention. In particular, the new minister of the interior, Robert von Puttkamer—whose sympathy for Stoecker's socially conservative efforts was well known—was charged with moving with insufficient energy against the antisemitic disturbers of the peace.

The government authorities originally attempted to present the disturbances as the work of "foolish youths" and antisocial elements, or to stress the significance of the "Jewish usurer" in the provocation of the people's "violent emotions." The riots were seen solely as a criminal problem and therefore as the responsibility of the police and justice departments. On the whole, the only measures for the prevention of further outbreaks were the strengthening of the police and the forceful reminder of the relevant sections of the penal code—breach of the public peace (*Landfriedensbruch*). The political connection between the antisemitic propaganda and the violence was denied or downplayed. When the representative of the Köslin *Regierungspräsident* (district president) traveled to Neustettin to suggest the establishment of a security committee, a town alderman advised him that the problem could be solved only by addressing the agitation of the *Norddeutsche Presse* and the demagoguery of Henrici. But the *Oberregierungsrat* replied that he could "not follow the previous speaker in the political field."[80] Simultaneously, however, he energetically advocated the closing of the liberal *Neustettiner Zeitung,* "because the articles of this newspaper had substantially upset the public atmosphere, and the common man had been provoked into the excesses."[81] How partial the individual civil servants were can also be shown by the fact that the police headquarters of Neustettin demanded the correction of a report about the incidents from a liberal newspaper and presented the antisemitically skewed presentation of the *Norddeutsche Presse* as a model of veracity.[82]

But the attempt by individual government politicians and civil servants to exploit the popular mood in their struggle against liberalism became less effective with the spread and radicalization of the riots. After the plundering in Schivelbein, it became apparent "that these are not simply riots and outbreaks of hate against the Jews, but the consequences of a regular agitation."[83] Accordingly, the Prussian minister of the interior issued a decree to the district governments in Köslin and Marienwerder on August 9, 1881, that in order to avoid renewed disturbances, the "agita-

---

80. Ibid., 510.
81. Regierungspräsident Köslin (represented by Count d'Haussonville), July 21, 1881, GStAPK, Rep. 76 III, Sekt. 1, Abt. XIIIa, Nr. 56, Bd. 2, Bl. 231.
82. *Allgemeine Zeitung des Judentums* 45 (1881): 526–27.
83. Regierungspräsident Köslin (represented by Count d'Haussonville), August 10, 1881, GStAPK, Rep. 76 III, Sekt. 1, Abt. XIIIa, Nr. 56, Bd. 2, Bl. 271.

tional efforts of antisemitic leaders" should be thwarted by the strict implementation of laws governing associations and meetings.[84] As the unrest continued nonetheless, and the kaiser himself was moved to remark critically that "in Stettin, where the excesses could go on for three days, the responsible authorities had acted with a great lack of energy," von Putt-kamer issued a new decree on August 30, 1881, for stronger measures and a more detailed investigation of the incidents.[85] He thereby made it finally and unmistakably clear to the public that the government would no longer tolerate the tumults.[86] The subordinate civil servants acted to "counter in no uncertain terms the possible assumption among the public that the government supported or did not view unfavorably the incriminated movement and riots."[87] By clarifying the matter, the government withdrew the legitimation and substantial precondition for the "loyalist pogroms." With the exception of the riots in Stolp, which were ended only after a massive and bloody military intervention, there were no further incidents in the region. The direct perpetrators were severely punished, and the local community councils were required to pay for the damage sustained. Forced by the series of violent outbreaks, the government finally defined the limits of its support for the antisemitic movement.

IV.   Implications and Consequences of the Riots

The anti-Jewish riots of the summer of 1881 are only one episode in the history of German antisemitism. Still, one should not underestimate their significance. At the regional level, the formerly peaceful relations between Jews and Christians in many Pomeranian and West Prussian towns deteriorated markedly. In March 1884, renewed antisemitic violence erupted in Neustettin after the Jewish defendants in the synagogue-fire appeal trial were found not guilty and returned to town.[88] Ten years later, the anti-semites of Neustettin were able to mobilize a large number of supporters. During the Reichstag election of 1893, the radical antisemitic demagogue Hermann Ahlwardt defeated the less radically antisemitic agitator Adolf Stoecker. The virulent antisemitism of the region, along with lingering

---

84. Prussian minister of the interior, August 21, 1881, BA, Abtl. Potsdam, Reichskan-zlei, Nr. 679, Bl. 203.

85. Secret civil cabinet, August 23, 1881, GStAPK, Rep. 76 III, Sekt. 1, Abt. XIIIa, Nr. 56, Bd. 1, Bl. 328.

86. *Vossische Zeitung,* September 2, 1881.

87. Oberpräsident Pomerania, September 20, 1881, GStAPK, Rep. 76 III, Sekt. 1, Abt. XIIIa, Nr. 56, Bd. 2, Bl. 19.

88. See also the various reports of the Prussian minister of the interior, ibid, Bd. 3, Bl. 12–127.

economic troubles, prompted many Jews to leave both provinces for larger towns in the Ruhr and the more hospitable Berlin.[89]

As for the government, its reaction to the anti-Jewish riots in Pomerania and West Prussia did not signal that there had been a fundamental change in its assessment of antisemitism. As in the past, many conservative politicians viewed antisemitism as a possible ally in their struggle with liberalism and as a means by which to furnish their own party with a mass basis. Accordingly, they limited their disciplining of the movement to police intervention against the movement's radical fringe, while signaling their approval "between the lines" and, as in the past, satisfying some antisemitic demands with administrative practice. The access of Jews to the civil service or military careers, for example, continued to be substantially difficult, if not impossible. Eastern European Jewish immigrants were treated vexatiously and deported en masse with Polish workers in 1885–86.[90] With such measures, the government attempted to utilize the potential of antisemitic protest and bind it to the government—without, however, letting it get out of hand. It was prepared to pay the price that in some areas Jews were reduced to the status of second-class citizens and that laws were thereby broken.

Within the antisemitic movement itself, the riots of 1881 led to a split between the politically conservative antisemites, such as Stoecker, and radicals such as Henrici and Ahlwardt who called into question the prevailing order. To protect his wing of the "movement" from official reprisal, Stoecker, whom liberals also held responsible for the riots, distanced himself from the violence and the militant Henrici.[91] In the long term, the government's firm though belated stand against agitation and open violence worked to "domesticate" antisemitism in Germany. To be sure, a few major antisemitic riots still occurred, in particular related to ritual murder accusations.[92] The Konitz riots of 1900 affected almost exactly

---

89. Rautenberg, "Geschichte des Judenthums," 62.

90. On this point, see Helmut Neubach, *Die Ausweisungen von Polen und Juden aus Preussen, 1885/86* (Wiesbaden, 1967); and Jack Wertheimer, *Unwelcome Strangers: East European Jews in Imperial Germany* (New York, 1987).

91. See, for example, *Der Reichsbote,* August 30, 1881: "[The hatred of Jews] is there and will find a solution: the question is only whether it will be solved by the quieter, legal way of Stoecker and the conservatives, or by the liberal rabble on the path to naked violence."

92. On the riots caused by ritual murder accusations—as in Xanten in 1891 and Konitz in 1900—see Rohrbacher and Schmidt, *Judenbilder,* 336–41; Christoph Nonn, "Zwischenfall in Konitz: Antisemitismus und Nationalismus im preußischen Osten um 1900," *Historische Zeitschrift* 266, no. 2 (1998): 387–418; Bernhard Vogt, "Die 'Atmosphäre eines Narrenhauses': Eine Ritualmordlegende um die Ermordung des Schülers Ernst Winter in Konitz," in *Zur Geschichte und Kultur der Juden in Ost- und Westpreußen,* edited by Michael Brocke et al. (Hildesheim, 2000), 546–77; and Helmut Walser Smith's article in this volume.

the same region as did the 1881 pogroms. The disturbances in Xanten in 1891–92 (the "Buschhoff affair") occurred in the Niederrhein (Lower Rhine) region, which had a long tradition of anti-Jewish riots in connection with ritual murder accusations.[93] What is distinctive about these events is their regional concentration. In this, they differed from the pogroms of 1819, 1848, and 1938 in Germany, and also from the Russian pogroms of the same time. These riots cannot be satisfactorily explained as "normal" phenomena concomitant with the development of the antisemitic movement in Germany; they were the exceptions rather than the rule. Antisemitism in the Second Empire limited itself more and more to a worldview expressed in various publications, while Henrici's brand of activist rhetoric found an echo with the masses only some decades later, in the efforts of National Socialism.[94]

This apparent moderation was of considerable import for German antisemitism. A "respectable," middle-class antipathy toward Jews developed, one that distanced itself from the "mob" antisemitism of the street, distinguished in good conscience between "good" and "bad" Jews, and through such a "civilized" approach morally anesthetized itself. This "tamed," or "domesticated," antisemitism did not pursue any direct political goals, detached itself from real conflicts between Jews and non-Jews, and evolved into a cultural code and ideological shibboleth of the antiliberal, "nationalistic" milieu.[95] Paradoxically, however, comparatively benign as it might have been, the detachment of this antisemitism from the real object of disdain and its apparent inconsequence only served to spread and radicalize anti-Jewish thinking in Germany, whose destructive potential became apparent only in the years of crisis after 1918.

93. Rohrbacher and Schmidt, *Judenbilder,* 304–68.

94. On the differentiation between the "written word" and the "spoken word" in the history of German antisemitism, see Shulamit Volkov, *Jüdisches Leben und Antisemitismus im 19. und 20. Jahrhundert* (Munich, 1990), 54–75.

95. Ibid., 35–36.

Konitz, 1900: Ritual Murder and Antisemitic Violence

Helmut Walser Smith

Ernst Winter, an eighteen-year-old high school student, was seen in the West Prussian town of Konitz for the last time on Sunday afternoon, March 11, 1900. When apprised by telegraph of the boy's absence, his father took the next train into the town to look for him. Probably, the father was not expecting anything out of the ordinary. But on the next day, Tuesday, he went to the Mönchsee, a small lake in the center of town. His son was an avid skater, and the father was worried that perhaps he had fallen through the ice, which in early March was increasingly thin. There in the lake he found the body of his son, but the body was not whole, and an ice-skating accident this was not. Rather, the father found the boy's upper torso cut off at the bottom of the ribs and wrapped in brown pack paper. Later in the day, he found the lower torso—disemboweled, but with the boy's buttocks and penis still attached. Two days after that, a fourteen-year-old child stumbled upon the right arm, which had been placed on the freshly fallen snow in back of the small door flanking the main portal of the Protestant cemetery. And five days later, on March 20, another person found the left thigh, again in the Mönchsee.[1]

The murder of Ernst Winter drew a great deal of attention from townspeople, from the sensation-hungry press, and from the Prussian police. But the police had few substantial clues, and by the end of March, two weeks after the murder, many of the body parts had still not been found. The boy's head, for example, was still missing. As the search for the killer dragged on, speculation among the townspeople spread and focused

---

1. Bruno Borowka, *Aus Sage und Geschichte von Konitz* (Konitz, 1919), 101–2.

increasingly on the Jews. "Nearly the whole population of the town of Konitz as well as its hinterlands," a county official wrote, "is convinced that Winter was a victim of a Jewish ritual murder."[2]

It was of course sheer superstition, the kind of thinking that supposedly belonged to more distant, darker eras. But at the turn of the last century, the accusation that Jews killed Christian boys in order to use their blood in Passover rituals proved disturbingly common. Indeed, Christian accusations that Jews had committed ritual murder had never been so numerous nor so persistent. According to one organization, 120 such accusations had been made public between 1891 and 1900.[3] They centered in eastern Europe, but they also spilled into the German Empire. In 1891, for example, German Catholics in the town of Xanten in the Rhineland accused a German Jew, Adolf Buschhoff, of murdering a five-year-old Christian boy for ritual purposes. The charges were groundless. But a trial ensued, as did a spate of antisemitic violence.[4]

In Konitz, accusations escalated into popular violence as well, first sporadic, then increasing in intensity, and finally culminating in the worst outbreak of antisemitic violence in the history of Wilhelmine Germany.[5]

---

2. Geheimes Staatsarchiv Preußischer Kulturbesitz (hereafter, GStAPK), Rep. 77, Tit. 500, Nr. 50, Bd. 1, bl. 8, Landratsamt (hereafter, LA) Konitz, March 31, 1900.

3. *Mitteilungen aus dem Verein zur Abwehr des Antisemitismus* 10, no. 31 (August 1, 1900), 1. See also Hillel J. Kieval, "The Importance of Place: Comparative Aspects of the Ritual Murder Trial in Modern Central Europe," in *Comparing Jewish Societies,* edited by Todd M. Endelman (Ann Arbor, 1997), 136.

4. See Stefan Rohrbacher, "Volksfrömmigkeit und Judenfeindschaft: Zur Vorgeschichte des politischen Antisemitismus im katholischen Rheinland," *Annalen des Historischen Vereins für den Niederrhein* 192/193 (1990): 125–44; and Julius Schoeps, "Ritualmordbeschuldigung und Blutaberglaube: Die Affäre Buschoff im niederrheinischen Xanten," in *Köln und das rheinische Judentum,* edited by Jutta Bohnke-Kollwitz et al. (Köln, 1984), 286–99.

5. Despite the prominence of the Konitz affair, it has until recently escaped the scrutiny of modern historians of antisemitism. But see now Christoph Nonn, "Zwischenfall in Konitz: Antisemitismus und Nationalismus im preußischen Osten um 1900," *Historische Zeitschrift* 266, no. 2 (1998): 387–418. Nonn uses the Konitz affair to argue (1) that the state opposed antisemitic violence when it perceived its own monopoly on violence to be challenged (and not, in the first order, to protect Jews); (2) that religious denomination, whether Protestant or Catholic, seems not to have determined antisemitic attitudes and practices; (3) that oral communication was significantly more important than written communication for the spread of antisemitic prejudice in the region; (4) that actual violence proved sporadic and did not find a large and constant echo; and (5) that in any case, antisemitic prejudice and violence constituted a marginal phenomenon over against the significantly more central conflict between Germans and Poles, in which everyday violence was a normal part of life in the Prussian east. Beyond these specific conclusions, Nonn also argued that the Konitz affair demonstrates the utility of "older" economic approaches for understanding antisemitic violence (antisemitism as a reaction to economic crisis), as opposed to "newer" approaches that emphasize ideology and political culture. In the essay that follows, I will take issue with some of Nonn's conclu-

Important unto itself, the Konitz affair also serves as a lens onto themes in the history of German antisemitism. Looking through this lens, we can see a pattern of antisemitic violence in sharp relief; we can observe how antisemitic ideology spread throughout a region and can discern who its carriers were; and we can enter into a set of beliefs that served as the spur for violence. At the local level, we can see these things more clearly and with greater precision than is often possible in a general study. And we can see the truth and the past, in the words of the Polish American writer Eva Hoffmann, as "more striated, textured, and many-sided."[6] When we do this, so I will argue in what follows, the importance of a process, not reducible to one factor, of making neighbors into strangers becomes increasingly visible.

I

In 1900, Konitz was in many ways an unremarkable place, its small claims to fame epitomizing turn-of-the-century German homeliness. The town boasted a handsome county office building, a modest but centrally located monument to Kaiser Wilhelm I, and a marketplace newly paved with stone. Konitz was also situated on two important railways, one running from eastern Pomerania southeast in the direction of Graudenz, the other from Berlin to Danzig. The railroad junction, according to a 1906 travel guide, constituted the town's only point of interest.[7] But the railroads, and the industry they brought in their wake, also provided Konitz with a measure of well-being, which set it apart from its poverty-stricken, ethnically mixed hinterlands. These were made up of Germans, Poles, and, further north and east, of Kashubians. By contrast, mainly Germans peopled the town itself, with Poles counting for less than 10 percent of the population. Among the German and Christian population of Konitz, rough denominational parity existed, Protestants and Catholics each constituting just under 50 percent of local inhabitants. Served by a modest synagogue nestled in a side street, a small Jewish community also existed here.[8]

---

sions (particularly 3, 4, and 5). More importantly, the general emphasis is different. Serious readers should, however, also consult Nonn's fine article.

6. Eva Hoffmann, *Shtetl: The Life and Death of a Small Town and the World of the Polish Jews* (London, 1998), 16.

7. Karl Baedecker, *Deutschland in einem Bande: Handbuch für Reisende* (Leipzig, 1906), 60.

8. On the history of the Jewish community in Konitz, see Peter Letkemann, "Zur Geschichte der Juden in Konitz im 19. Jahrhundert," *Beiträge zur Geschichte Westpreußens* 9 (1985): 99–116. On the wider community of Jews in West Prussia, see Max Aschkewitz, *Die Juden in Westpreußen* (Marburg, 1967).

If Konitz seemed an unremarkable town, the murder that took place here struck people as anything but ordinary. The fact that Winter had been consciously sliced to pieces, that he seemed to be bloodless, and that his body parts and clothing were spread around the town all encouraged rumor and suspicion. Hardly a week had gone by when the first bits of public antisemitism hit the streets. Mainly, this consisted of youngsters yelling antisemitic slogans. By the end of March, however, the situation had become sufficiently disconcerting that the mayor of Konitz, Georg Deditius, issued a public warning in the local newspaper, the *Konitzer Tageblatt.* "It is not to be condoned," he admonished, "that a great number of people are as a result [of the murder] being misguided into harassing Jewish citizens and their religious authorities."[9] Deditius referred specifically to "gatherings of teenage boys, namely from the evening school," who had yelled insults and threats against the Jews and who had damaged shop windows and doors. The evening school got out at 9:00 P.M., when it was already dark. Students would start their night by tearing through the streets in great numbers, smashing windows with stones and calling "Hep hep!" (a popular antisemitic catchword) whenever they saw Jews.[10]

In ordinary circumstances, the problem might have remained one of juvenile discipline. But it did not, in part because of the widespread suspicion that "the Jews" had killed Ernst Winter and that the killing was a ritual murder. In a letter to the Prussian minister of the interior, county official Baron von Zedlitz outlined the principal "facts" leading people to this belief: the body parts that had been found were bloodless; the murder took place shortly before Passover; credible witnesses had evidently heard a scream not far from the synagogue at 7:30 P.M. on the night of the murder; and others had claimed that a foul smell, as if something were burning, emanated an hour later from the same area. Baron von Zedlitz also pointed out that nothing suggested a murder of a more ordinary kind, whether a crime of passion or one connected to robbery. Moreover, the town of Konitz had become a trading place for "a daily increasing amount of all possible rumors, partly of the most ridiculous kind." All of these things, von Zedlitz reported, "sustain people in their conviction that this must be a ritual murder case."[11]

This conviction was not confined to the town; it spread throughout the region, as did violence against Jews. Between late March, when the daily harassment of Jewish citizens in Konitz began, and the twelfth of

---

9. GStAPK, Rep. 77, Tit. 500, no. 50, Bd. 1, bl.12, *Konitzer Tageblatt,* March 29, 1900 (the warning was dated March 27).

10. Ibid., bl. 9, LA Konitz, March 31, 1900.

11. Ibid.

June, when a battalion of Prussian soldiers moved in to quell the violence, there were thirty separate cases of antisemitic rioting in the area. Roughly speaking, the area in which violence against Jews occurred constituted a circle approximately a hundred miles in diameter, with Konitz at its center and with the lion's share of the rioting occurring to the west of Konitz in the direction of Pomerania.

The riots occurred in clusters. In the spring of 1900, there were three such clusters, the first on the third weekend of April, the second at the end of May, and the third on the second weekend in June, with only a small number of riots not conforming to this pattern. The timing of the riots therefore betrayed highly specific proximate causes. They cannot be explained by appeal to special economic factors nor to a generalized antipathy. Rather, the riots were ignited by symbolic events, mainly having to do with the murder investigation and the climate of denunciation it created. Put differently, it was the conviction that "the Jews" killed Ernst Winter that led directly to antisemitic violence.

The first series of riots occurred on the weekend of April 20–22, Friday to Sunday. On the preceding Sunday, April 15—the first day of the Easter holiday—some children who were playing had stumbled upon Winter's head, which was half-buried in a ditch behind the lodge of the shooting club. In the days that followed, rumor and denunciation became the daily fare of street talk and discussions in the pubs. One person allegedly overheard a Jewish merchant, Selig Zander, admit that ritual murder did in fact exist. Another person, the painter Schönberg, eavesdropped on a conversation between a Jewish merchant and a Jewish grain dealer in which one of them allegedly speculated that the punishment for the Jew who had committed the crime would not be more than eight months in jail. A finger was also pointed at the Jewish cantor Heymann, who had suddenly left town on a trip, thus raising suspicion.[12] One denunciation of a local Jew even stuck, leading to an arrest, not for the murder of Ernst Winter, but for aiding in the dispersal of the body parts. The civil servant Friedrich Fiedler insisted that on Good Friday he had seen Wolf Israelski, a down-and-out, often inebriated Jewish skinner, walking with a sack in his hand near the lodge of the shooting club.[13] Because the sack had something round in it, Fiedler swore that Israelski must have been carrying Winter's head. Though dubious at best, the accusation sufficed for the

---

12. These rumors are reported in *Im deutschen Reich* 6, no. 4 (1900): 214.

13. GStAPK, Rep. 77, Tit. 500, no. 50, Bd. 1, bl. 90, LA Konitz, April 18, 1900; *Im deutschen Reich* 6, no. 4 (1900): 214–15. The provincial court (*Landgericht*) found the evidence against Israelski insufficient. See GStAPK, I/84a 16775 Staatsanwaltschaft Konitz, September 10, 1900.

Am Mönchsee

Spüle

Hinter'm Schützenhaus

Gruss aus Konitz W.-Pr.

7768

Fig. 1. Postcard: Greetings from Konitz, West Prussia. *Top left:* fishing Winter's torso out of the lake; *bottom left:* unearthing
Winter's head from a ditch behind the shooting lodge. (GStA PK IX. HA Bilder, Post-arten Konitz. Courtesy Geheimes Staatsarchiv

police to proceed with a preliminary arrest. For excited crowds through-out the region, the arrest gave sufficient cause to go after the Jews.[14]

The antisemitic riots, which took place in a number of towns through-out the region, began on Saturday evening. In the town of Baldenburg, in the county of Flatow, antisemitic rioters prevented Jews from attending holy services and, in the course of the evening, damaged the synagogue. The president of the Central Association of German Citizens of the Jewish Faith, the largest Jewish organization in Germany, complained to the Prussian minister of the interior that in Baldenburg "the small number of Jews living there see their lives in danger."[15] The county official in Flatow also received "complaints from the Jews about riots in Preussisch-Fried-land, Stegers, and Hammerstein."[16] This official reported that the com-plaints and the newspaper reports were "usually exaggerated."[17] But the actions of the local police told a different story. In Hammerstein, antise-mitic excesses got so out of hand that the police called in the army for help, and the local commander sent eighty troops to restore order in a town of less than three thousand people and with a Jewish population of under one hundred.[18] Similarly, in Konitz the antisemitic tumult on Saturday evening became so raucous that, according to the *Danziger Zeitung,* many people "fear going out in the evening, and not only Jews, but also Chris-tians, especially women."[19]

The distinct dynamics of these riots are often more difficult to discern. Some cases suggest if not conscious organization, at least a tight network of news and information. Put simply, word got around quickly. In Vands-burg, for instance, the riots only began late in the evening when, according to the Flatow county official, "large crowds gathered and were reinforced by a significant influx of peasant sons and farmhands who swarmed in from the neighboring rural villages."[20] In Czersk, a German-Polish indus-trial town, the riots suggested more spontaneity. Shortly before seven in the evening, a drunkard was thrown out of Jendryczka's pub, "a Polish-Catholic tavern." When the drunkard started smashing the tavern win-dows, someone yelled, "Let's go after the synagogue." One person tried to

---

14. *Im deutschen Reich* 6, no. 4 (1900): 214–15.

15. GStAPK, Rep. 77, Tit. 500, no. 50, Bd. 1, bl. 96, General Secretary of the CVdSjG, Alphonse Lewy, to the Prussian Minister of the Interior, April 21, 1900.

16. Ibid., bl. 31, telegram from Schlochau, April 23, 1900.

17. Ibid. Compare also the official's report about the village of Prechlau, in which he wrote that newspaper reports were "greatly exaggerated" and, as evidence, pointed out that "also here in Prechlau only some of the windows of Jewish houses were shattered by stones." Ibid., telegram from Prechlau, April 21, 1900. In 1905, only six Jews lived in Prechlau.

18. Ibid., bl. 33, telegram from Schlochau, April 24, 1900.

19. Ibid., bl. 25, *Danziger Zeitung,* April 23, 1900.

20. Ibid., bl. 94, LA Flatow, April 23, 1900.

climb the fence around the synagogue and was arrested. As the police took him away, the crowd swelled "to a mob of several hundred." Soon stones flew from the crowd, then shots; first the stones were hurled at Jewish houses, then at the gendarmes as well. It was not until the latter drew their pistols that the crowd was disbanded.[21] More or less the same thing happened the next day in Neustettin. Here, as in Baldenburg, Hammerstein, and Czersk, the synagogue constituted the symbolic focus of popular anger. And here, too, the crowd could not be dispersed until the forces of order drew their weapons.

The second wave, at the end of May, was touched off by the convergence of two highly symbolic events. The first was Winter's funeral, which took place on May 27 and had already worried local officials. As they expected, the funeral proved far from a solemn affair. Rather, it seemed more like a "stage play for the many thousands of onlookers" who had streamed into Konitz from the outlying villages and towns.[22] According to the police, many of the onlookers were "antisemites," and not a few accompanied the funeral procession by shouting antisemitic slogans while beating on the doors and windows of Jewish stores as the procession marched down the main street, the Danziger Strasse. When the procession reached the cemetery, Pastor Hammer of the Protestant church in Konitz delivered the funeral oration, which, while it did not mention the Jews, did suggest that the murder must have been planned.[23]

This funeral certainly fanned the flames of antagonism. But a second event made matters much worse. On May 14, the Prussian police had sent a special investigator, Inspector Braun, to Konitz in order to solve the murder case posthaste.[24] Like many people, Braun was impressed by the precision of the cuts and concluded that it was at least conceivable that they had been made by a trained hand: a butcher. In Konitz, there were two butchers, their properties nearly adjacent, who lived near the Mönch-see, where many of the body parts had been found: one, Adolf Lewy, was Jewish; the other, Gustav Hoffmann, was Christian. On May 29, Braun summoned and interrogated Hoffmann, "the devout Lutheran," the former town councillor, the president of the butchers' guild, and a man locally respected and even revered. The police also interrogated his fifteen-year-old daughter, Anna.[25] Braun suspected that Winter had tried to

21. Ibid., bl. 87, LA Konitz, April 23, 1900.

22. Ibid., bl. 251, Regierungspräsident Marienwerder, May 31, 1900.

23. Ibid., bl. 148, *Danziger Zeitung,* June 3, 1900.

24. Ibid., bl. 159, Chief of Police in Berlin to Prussian Minister of the Interior, May 18, 1900.

25. Ibid., bl. 78, *Berliner Zeitung,* May 30, 1900; Borowka, *Aus Sage und Geschichte von Konitz,* 104.

seduce Anna (she denied it) and that the father had discovered him in the act. Enraged, so Braun's theory went, Hoffmann had murdered Winter and disposed of his body piece by piece. It was pure conjecture, and it was only an indictment, from which Hoffmann as well as his daughter would be released in the course of the afternoon.[26] But to the popular imagination, it looked like an arrest. And news of it, reported county official Baron von Zedlitz, "spread throughout the town like wildfire."[27]

The riots ignited soon thereafter, in Konitz as well as in Bütow and Stolp in Pomerania. Since the funeral, there had been daily antisemitic gatherings in Konitz late into the evening, though they had ended without serious incident. That afternoon, on Tuesday, May 29, there had also been a small riot at the annual fair in Krojanke, when shoemakers from the town of Jastrow came into conflict with Jewish traders, each insulting the other about who must have committed the murder. When a shoemaker started a fight, a gendarme drew his sword in order to disperse the combatants and the crowd. After the incident, "in which the public was without exception against the Jews," rowdies ran through the streets. "Only eight windows in the synagogue," the county official of Flatow reported, "and one shop window of a Jewish merchant were smashed."[28]

In Konitz, events took a more threatening turn. The summons of Hoffmann and his daughter galvanized the antisemites. Some of these were local, such as Albert Hoffrichter, a high school teacher, and Julius Lehmann, the publisher of the *Konitzer Tageblatt.* Others were journalists for antisemitic newspapers, who, coming from Berlin, took up quarters in Konitz, partly to report on the affair, partly to drive events forward. They had also worked with an unofficial citizens' committee to find the killer. When Inspector Braun summoned Hoffmann, the committee called its own witness, Bernhard Masloff, whom Wilhelm Bruhn, the publisher of the antisemitic newspaper *Die Staatsbürgerzeitung,* had convinced to testify. A crude, barely literate worker, Masloff told the citizens' committee that on the night of the murder, he had been lying in wait outside Adolf Lewy's basement wanting to steal a slab of meat. While there, he had observed Lewy and two other men walking (two in front, one in back) to the Mönchsee carrying a heavy package, presumably containing Winter's upper torso.[29] This improbable story would later lead to Masloff's being

26. GStAPK, I Rep. 77, Tit. 500, no. 50, Bd. 1, bl. 206, LA Konitz, May 29, 1900; ibid., bl. 78, *Berliner Zeitung,* May 30, 1900; ibid., bl. 90, *Berliner Neuste Nachrichten,* May 31, 1900.

27. Ibid., bl. 206, LA Konitz, May 29, 1900.

28. Ibid., bl. 199, LA Flatow, May 30, 1900.

29. Ibid., bl. 9, 206, LA Konitz, May 29, 1900; *Der Prozeß gegen Masloff und Genossen (Konitz, 25.10–10.11.1900) nach stenographischer Aufnahme* (Berlin, 1900), 591–92.

tried and found guilty of perjury. But on that Tuesday afternoon, his testimony polarized the population and sharpened local enmity against the
police inspectors from Berlin, who, antisemitic voices claimed, were protecting the Jews.

There were demonstrations without incident that evening. But the situation deteriorated around 10:30 at night, when cartloads of people rode
into the town. Though he could not prove it, the county official believed
that the "reinforcements" betrayed a certain degree of organization.[30]
Within the crowd, a rumor spread (or was strategically planted) that Hoffmann would be arrested again at 1:00 in the morning. This roused the
crowd, which now numbered more than a thousand people, to riotous
action.[31] Some tried to storm Lewy's house; others tried to break into Jewish houses along the side streets. Most contented themselves with yelling
antisemitic epithets and tossing stones, now at Jewish houses and shops,
now at local officials. The mayor, whom the antisemites decried as pro-
Jewish, tried to calm the crowd. When he could not, the gendarmes—eight
men on horses, two on foot—drew their swords and, around 3:00 A.M.,
dispersed the crowd.

From the perspective of the forces of order, the riots had taken on a
"dangerous character." The county official, Baron von Zedlitz, later
learned that a group of antisemites had banded together and, armed with
sticks and clubs, were ready to liberate Hoffmann in the event of an arrest.
"No one doubts," von Zedlitz reported, that "lynch justice against the
Lewy family would have followed."[32] And this, he added, had to be prevented at all costs and in such a way that "a defeat of state authority was
precluded from the start."[33]

The riots of Tuesday evening unsettled town and county officials.
When it appeared that the whole business would begin again the next
morning, a market day in Konitz, the county official no longer felt secure
in relying on his gendarmes. He requested that the Thirty-fifth Division of
the Prussian Army, stationed in nearby Graudenz, send a company
(roughly 150 men) to ensure order. The army complied, sending the
Eleventh Company of the Fourteenth Infantry Regiment. Meanwhile, the
mayor and the city council issued a plea to the citizens of Konitz, urging
them to stay at home after sunset.[34] The police made a similar plea and

---

30. GStAPK, Rep. 77, Tit. 500, no. 50, Bd. 1, bl. 210, LA Konitz, May 30, 1900.

31. Ibid., bl. 222, LA Konitz, June 4, 1900.

32. Ibid. See also GStAPK, Rep. 77, Tit. 500, no. 50, Bd. 2, bl. 30, Advocate Appelbaum to CVdSjG, June 10, 1900.

33. Ibid., Bd. 1, bl. 222, LA Konitz, June 4, 1900.

34. Ibid., bl. 214, "An unsere Mitbürger," June 1, 1900.

added that further riotous actions would, on the orders of the company commander, be met with the use of firearms.[35]

A threshold of violence had been crossed. A local Jewish lawyer reported, "The threats to beat the Jews to death and to set fire to all four corners of the town are to be taken very seriously."[36] Clearly, the social fabric was unraveling. Increasingly anxious, Baron von Zedlitz provided the Prussian minister of the interior with a résumé of the situation in Konitz: "For three months the population has been roused against the Jews with all the weapons of fanaticism. Many really believe that they do a good deed and protect their children from the fate of Winter if they beat a Jew to death."[37] The soldiers of the Eleventh Company stayed in Konitz for four days, until Tuesday. When they withdrew, there was a brief respite from violence. But a few days later, rioting started anew.

The third wave of violence began in an atmosphere thick with anticipation. Zedlitz feared that any new and unsuspected turn in the murder investigation would incite local riots all over again.[38] One such turn came when Inspector Braun arrested Bernhard Masloff and his mother-in-law for perjury. Both had been key witnesses for the accusations of the citizens' committee against Adolf Lewy. Now the antisemites, and their increasingly large following, became ever more convinced that the Prussian police were in the pay of the Jews, local or otherwise. But there was more to come: as had been the case with rumors of Hoffmann's rather unlikely arrest at 1:00 in the morning on May 30, the antisemites fabricated a further pretext to instigate local ire. On Thursday, June 7, the *Konitzer Tageblatt* falsely reported that the police intended to pursue the investigation against Hoffmann with renewed vigor.[39] This sufficed.

By eight o'clock on Thursday evening, there was already talk in the pubs that the synagogue would be burned later that night.[40] Around nine o'clock, women "who knew that something was up" gathered in the center of town.[41] And at 10:30 P.M., antisemites began to set fires to the fence that sealed off the synagogue, as well as to a number of nearby sheds. Because the sheds were extremely dry, the fires caught quickly, and it took the fire department until midnight to douse the flames and dampen the synagogue, the real target of the arsonists.[42] The next day, the newspapers

---

35. Ibid., bl. 216, Die Polizeiverwaltung Konitz, "Warnung," June 1, 1900.

36. GStAPK, I Rep. 77, Tit. 500, no. 50, Bd. 2, bl. 30, Advocate Appelbaum to CVd-SjG, June 10, 1900.

37. Ibid., bl. 105, LA Konitz, June 11, 1900.

38. Ibid.

39. Ibid., Bd. 1, bl. 254, LA Konitz, June 8, 1900.

40. Ibid., bl. 270, LA Konitz, June 9, 1900.

41. Ibid.

42. Ibid., bl. 254, LA Konitz, June 8, 1900.

reported that the Jews had started the fires in order to expunge evidence against them. They also reported that two Christian boys were missing. The next night, on Saturday, June 9, the rioting started once again.[43]

The pattern was familiar. After dusk on Saturday night, a crowd gathered in the Danziger Strasse, where Lewy and Hoffmann lived. After shouting epithets and insisting that Masloff and his mother-in-law be released, they hurled stones and bricks at the houses of the Jews. Wishing to forestall further trouble, the police and the gendarmes charged through the streets, six men abreast, and dispersed the crowds.

But the clash had only just begun. The next morning, on the tenth, antisemites rode their bicycles to neighboring towns and villages to round up farmers and rural laborers and anyone else who wanted to join the protest. By 11:00 A.M., thousands of people, according to the liberal *Danziger Zeitung,* had assembled in the marketplace to demand the release of Masloff and his mother-in-law, Frau Roß. The police arrested one of the troublemakers among them, Theodor Knievel, but the rumor spread (or was planted) that Hoffmann had been arrested. Irate, the throng pressed on to the town hall, demanding now Hoffmann's, now Knievel's, release and threatening mayor Deditius, whom they decried as philosemitic. Fearful of the crowd, Deditius barricaded himself inside the building. The police and the gendarmes, alarmed by what they saw, now drew their swords. In the hope of breaking things up, the town's fire alarm was also sounded. But the crowd seemed unimpressed. They attacked Inspector Wehn from Berlin, throwing him to the ground, and wounded Commissar Block, whom they also thought to be overly protective of the Jews.[44] Demonstrators then marched to Lewy's house and pummeled it with rocks. They also damaged the shop of a Jewish merchant who had not shut his storefront grate in time. Then the vandals marched down the Rähmstrasse and to the synagogue. Breaking inside, they smashed the wooden pews, yanked down the lamps, ripped apart the drapes, and tore pages out of the holy books. Fortunately, the Torah rolls had already been placed in safety, a precautionary measure taken after the attempt to burn down the synagogue on Thursday night. But the temple, the *Danziger Zeitung* reported, now "resembled a ruin."

Konitz, a Jewish denizen wrote, is "in a state of revolt."[45] Local officials saw the situation like this as well. When the crowd could no longer be controlled, Baron von Zedlitz, "obviously shaken and as pale as a

43. Ibid., bl. 270, LA Konitz, June 9, 1900; ibid., bl. 263, LA Konitz, June 7, 1900.

44. Ibid., Bd. 2, bl. 30, Advocate Appelbaum to CVdSjG, June 10, 1900; ibid., Rep. 181a, No. 16775, bl. 136, August 21, 1900.

45. Ibid., Rep. 77, Tit. 500, no. 50, Bd. 2, bl. 30, Advocate Appelbaum to CVdSjG, June 10, 1900.

chalkboard," called the Prussian minister of the interior, who in turn ordered once again that the garrison in Graudenz send the Eleventh Company. As the train carrying the troops passed through the neighboring town of Tuchel, a parallel demonstration that had gathered at the railway station reviled them for protecting the Jews.[46] When the soldiers arrived in Konitz at 9:30 in the evening, Zedlitz read the riot act, and the infantry marched into town, their rifles loaded, their bayonets fixed. Although no shots were fired, there were injuries in the clash, mainly when people were struck by rifle butts or cut by bayonets.[47] As this was going on in Konitz, the Prussian minister of the interior, Baron von Rheinbaben, met with Kaiser Wilhelm II in Berlin to apprise him of the situation. The Kaiser, who no doubt sensed a revolt against state authority, ordered that not just a company but a battalion be sent to Konitz. The battalion arrived on Tuesday, June 12, stationing a soldier every sixty paces, as well as a cordon of infantrymen around the synagogue and a special guard around Lewy's house.[48] There they would stay until January of the following year, when the county official finally felt that they could be safely withdrawn.

This put an end to the major incidents of antisemitic violence in Konitz, though isolated instances of antisemitic rioting continued to occur on the periphery of the region throughout the month of June: in Berent, north of Konitz, where there had already been a case of alleged ritual murder in 1894; in Mrotschen in the province of Posen; and in Schlawe in Pomerania.[49] In addition, antisemites again demolished the Jewish cemetery in Hammerstein, while in Janowitz, in the district of Bromberg, two men broke into the synagogue through the side window and vandalized the temple.[50] There were also instances of serious violence. On a country road leading out of Kamin, a village to the south of Konitz, a worker named Josef Krajetski attacked a sixty-four-year-old Jewish trader with a pitchfork, beating him senseless. As Krajetski struck blows, his wife encouraged him, shouting "Hep Hep!" Had the lord of the local manor not come to the trader's aid, Krajetski would presumably have left him for dead.[51] Similarly, in Prechlau, Ernst Winter's village, young rowdies

46. On the parallel demonstration, which also included the usual assaults on Jewish property, see GStAPK, Rep. 77, Tit. 500, no. 50, Bd. 2, bl. 74, LA Tuchel, June 11, 1900.

47. *Berliner Neueste Nachrichten,* June 12, 1900.

48. *Die jüdische Presse* 31, no. 24 (1900): 243–44.

49. GStAPK, Rep. 77, Tit. 500, no. 50, Bd. 2, bl. 116, LA Berent, June 12, 1900; ibid., bl. 121, Regierungspräsident Bromberg, June 18, 1900.

50. On Hammerstein, see GStAPK, Rep. 77, Tit. 500, no. 50, Bd. 2, bl. 63, Regierungspräsident Marienwerder, June 12, 1900; and *Die jüdische Presse* 31, no. 26 (1900): 264–65. On Janowitz, see *Die jüdische Presse* 31, no. 25 (1900): 258.

51. *Im deutschen Reich* 6, no. 9 (1900): 461, 471. Krajetski received four years in jail for assault.

attacked a Jewish cantor and his seventy-year-old father, who had come to the town to perform a circumcision. The father had to be admitted to a hospital with serious head wounds.[52]

Despite these incidents, the wave of antisemitic rioting and violence had substantially come to a close. This did not signal a change in sentiment. "Despite the surface calm," the county official reported two days after the military occupation, "I judge the situation as more serious than ever before."[53] Yet the violence had been contained. How far it would have gone had the Prussian Army not intervened is difficult to say. Local officials certainly believed that without a substantial military presence, they could not have controlled the escalating violence. This was true of Konitz; it was also true of the surrounding area. Throughout the region, local police received reinforcements, so that every evening, in almost every town, gendarmes on horseback patrolled the streets. Fifty troops had been sent to the tiny but violent town of Hammerstein; sixteen to the proletarian village of Czersk. Indeed, there were so many gendarmes working overtime, as well as gendarmes who had been ordered to the area from East Prussia, Posen, and Brandenburg, that when a labor strike broke out in Gotzlow and Frauendorf in western Pomerania, there were hardly enough men to maintain order there.[54] From the perspective of the government, and, I would argue, from a wider historical perspective as well, Konitz represented a major uprising—against the Jews, and against a government perceived (ironically) as protecting the Jews. It was, as a reporter for a conservative Jewish newspaper put it, "nearly revolutionary."[55]

II

How did this "nearly revolutionary" situation come about? This is a harder question to answer, and one that has to be addressed at a number of levels and with a sense for complexity. For, at first glance, it would seem that Konitz shows us a nearly monolithic image of late-nineteenth-century German antisemitism. "Nearly the whole population of the town of Konitz as well as its hinterlands," one may recall the county official Baron von Zedlitz as having written, "is convinced that Winter was a victim of a Jewish ritual murder."[56] Moreover, in the eye of the storm, in the counties of Konitz and Schlochau, antisemitic demonstrations and violence took place

52. *Die jüdische Presse* 31, no. 26 (1900): 265.

53. GStAPK, Rep. 77, Tit. 500, no. 50, Bd. 2, bl. 42, LA Konitz, June 14, 1900. The same statement was made a week later; ibid., bl. 150, LA Konitz, June 22, 1900.

54. Ibid., Bd. 1, bl. 251, Regierungspräsident Stettin, July 17, 1900.

55. *Die jüdische Presse* 31, no. 37 (1900): 381.

56. GStAPK, Rep. 77, Tit. 500, no. 50, Bd. 1, bl. 8, LA Konitz, March 31, 1900.

in every town with a Jewish population of more than twenty inhabitants, as well as in some places with fewer. And these demonstrations, one may also recall, often involved a great many people, more than a thousand in the major demonstrations in Konitz, and hundreds of people in smaller places such as Baldenburg and Hammerstein. On the face of it, then, Konitz suggests a great degree of consensus, with a large, angry Christian population directing its collective enmity at a small, vulnerable Jewish minority.

There is a good deal of truth in this view. But it does not help us see how this violence came about, who was responsible, or why it enjoyed support. To get at these questions, we must consider the relative involvement of social groups, for, especially in this part of Germany, deep divisions ran through Christian society—of ethnicity, of religion, of class, and of gender—each in its own way structuring social processes. Also, an important dynamic existed between outside agitators (journalists who in some cases were also professional politicians) and local antisemites. This dynamic gave the Konitz uprisings their persistence, their doggedness, through the late spring of 1900. Finally, and I think decisively, a certain kind of public culture was created in Konitz, a culture marked by fear, by mistrust, by daily denunciation, and by a disturbing degree of ill will.

In West Prussia, the line that most obviously divided the population was ethnic—between Germans (including the Jews) and Poles. Reinforced by sharp linguistic differences, class cleavages, and decades of political conflict, this line of division, as Christoph Nonn has pointed out, marked the area around Konitz more than any other. Yet how did it shape antisemitic violence? Here the evidence is not so clear, in part because local reports rarely differentiated between Germans and Poles. We can say with a great deal of certainty that the force behind the antisemitic agitation was German, and that in Konitz itself Germans, not Poles, propagated the antisemitism and instigated the riots. Moreover, most of the other towns and villages in which riots took place were German: this certainly holds for the towns of eastern Pomerania, which were ethnically homogeneous, and for the predominantly German towns of the counties of Schlochau, Flatow, and Deutsch Krone.

But as one traveled east, north, or south of Konitz, the ethnic complexion of the area became markedly more mixed, especially in the villages. Thus in the town of Czersk, where a significant antisemitic "excess" took place on the evening of April 22, Poles outnumbered Germans by two to one. Conceivably, the Germans instigated the rioting in Czersk nevertheless, though police reports state that the tumult started in a "Polish-Catholic tavern."[57] The antisemitic riots in the small towns of Bruss,

---

57. Ibid., bl. 87, LA Konitz, April 23, 1900.

Wielle, and Karschin, on the other hand, almost certainly drew their élan from angry and antagonistic Polish peasants, as for the most part only Poles lived there. Impressionistic evidence also supports Polish participation in the antisemitic rioting unleashed by the murder of Ernst Winter. In his account of the riot that took place in Berent on June 12, the Berent county official reported that "for a longer period of time the people here have been secretly propagandized, mainly from the Polish side, but partly also from fanatical antisemites of German background."[58] The *Danziger Zeitung,* perhaps the newspaper best informed about events in Konitz, also focused on the role of the Polish population in propagating antisemitism throughout the region. "In the series of assaults on the Jewish population and in the demolition of Jewish houses and synagogues," the paper reported, "the Polish population has participated to a significant degree."[59] Indeed, major Polish newspapers, including the *Gazeta Grudzionska,* spewed forth a steady stream of antisemitic venom (though a venom that typically drew its poison from articles that had already appeared in German newspapers).[60] Published in nearby Graudenz, the *Gazeta* was at the time among the most widely read Polish newspapers, and its coverage of the murder in Konitz made its way to many Polish households, both within and beyond the boundaries of West Prussia.[61]

Thus while the impetus for the riots came from the German side, the Poles also waxed antisemitic, sometimes joining in the violence. In the area around Konitz, ethnic divisions between Germans and Poles mattered a great deal, but they were not unbreachable. And for a time, as rocks were thrown, as aspersions were cast against the Jews, German-Polish antagonism may even have been suspended. But about this we can only speculate. What is certain is that for several months in the spring of 1900, Germans as well as many Poles directed their enmity against a small and ever decreasing Jewish minority.

Religious denomination constituted a second line of division, separating Christians from one another, structuring mentalities, and in some areas powerfully influencing politics. Again, the story becomes more complex as one moves from west to east, from the purely Protestant areas of Pomerania to the religiously mixed areas of the Tucheler Heide. How, as

---

58. Ibid., Bd. 2, bl. 116, LA Berent, June 12, 1900.

59. Ibid., Bd. 1, bl. 170, *Danziger Zeitung,* June 12, 1900.

60. See, for example, the story in *Gazeta Grudzionska* 7, no. 83 (July 12, 1900), which is based on an article in the *Danziger Allgemeine Zeitung.* A copy of the *Gazeta* can be found in the main library of the University of Torun, Poland.

61. On antisemitism in other Polish newspapers, see GStAPK, Rep. 77, Tit. 500, no. 50, Bd. 1, bl. 236, *Vorwärts,* June 21, 1900. For the circulation of the *Gazetta Grudziadzka,* see Fritz Schultz, *Die politische Tagespresse Westpreußens* (Deutsch-Krone, 1913), 27.

one traveled in this direction, did the changing religious composition affect the course of the antisemitic violence?

The majority of antisemitic riots occurred in predominantly Protestant communities. This does not surprise. Already in the 1880s, Protestant artisans and peasants in Pomerania had shown their willingness to support antisemitic movements and to participate in the violence that followed in their wake.[62] Conversely, antisemitic "excesses" took place in only one predominantly German Catholic village in the spring of 1900, Stegers. Still, the best evidence, especially from the mixed communities, points to Catholic as well as Protestant participation in antisemitic violence.

Konitz may serve as an example. As a result of the balance of forces between Reformation and Counter-Reformation, Protestants and Catholics had achieved rough parity over the years, with the Protestants somewhat more dominant in local society and politics.[63] Here, too, the major conduits for the antisemitic movement were local Protestants. Nevertheless, Catholics supported the discourse of ritual murder and the public displays of anger with a good measure of enthusiasm. This can be deduced partly from the belated efforts of the clergy to dampen antisemitic passions. Father Boenig, the priest of the Catholic church in Konitz, declined to take a public stand against the antisemitic movement until mid-June, when in his Corpus Christi day sermon he admonished his parishioners, especially those from the countryside, to calm down. Until that point, his position had been one of "benevolent neutrality."[64] But local Catholics did not need to turn to their priests in these matters; they could also read the Catholic press. In Konitz and its hinterlands, most Catholics read the *Westpreussisches Volksblatt,* a Catholic newspaper that, according to Zedlitz, fed antisemitic sentiments with "sensational stories" and "unbelievable idiocies."[65]

Thus, neither the walls of ethnicity nor of religious denomination dammed-in the spread of antisemitic convictions. What of class and gender? Two kinds of evidence help us answer this question: prosecution records, which tell us something about the most active element in the riots of 1900; and descriptions of the crowd in the reports of county officials. According to one count, state prosecutors successfully brought ninety-two cases before the courts, the charges including disturbing the peace, rebel-

---

62. See the previous essay in this volume: Christhard Hoffmann, "Political Culture and Violence against Minorities: The Antisemitic Riots in Pomerania and West Prussia."

63. Borowka, *Aus Sage und Geschichte von Konitz,* 43–47.

64. GStAPK, Rep. 77, Tit. 500, no. 50, Bd. 2, bl. 60, LA Konitz, June 15, 1900.

65. Ibid., Bd. 1, bl. 42, LA Konitz, April 25, 1900. Zedlitz was not alone in this view. According to an article of June 21 in the Socialist newspaper, *Vorwärts,* the *Westpreussisches Volksblatt* "often outbid the antisemitic papers in rabble-rousing."

lion, property damage, and assault and battery.[66] The geographical distribution of these cases and the range of sentences were as follows:

Town	Number of cases	Minimum sentence	Maximum sentence
Stolp	33	4 weeks	3 years
Bütow	10	fine	10 months
Konitz	24	fine	1 year
Czersk	10	fine	8 months
Berent	9	fine	12 months
Rummelsburg	4	4 weeks	1 year
Hammerstein	2	1 month	2 months

Of these cases, prosecution lists are still extant for twenty-three people convicted in the riots in Stolp on May 30 and for twenty-eight in Konitz.

These documents suggest sharp social and demographic contours. In Stolp, the most active rioters were young men, twenty-two years of age on average, nearly a third of whom had been arrested before. Their occupations reflected their youth: there were sixteen apprentices, two artisans, four workers, and one without an occupational designation. Also, the majority (thirteen) of them had been born elsewhere, typically in the Pomeranian hinterlands around Stolp. And all were Protestant.[67] The arrests in Konitz show a similar profile. Here, the group consisted of ten apprentices, eight workers (and two "sons of workers"), a bartender, a coachman, a butcher, a musician, a hired farmhand, a "property owner," and two school students, one of them, Katharina Grabowski, a girl. For nine of the rioters, the documents provide more detailed information: their average age was twenty-four (higher than in Stolp because of the arrest of August Kath, a forty-year-old property owner). There were six Catholics and three Protestants, reflecting the mixed composition of the area; four of them lived in Konitz, the others in the countryside around it; and only

---

66. M. Horwitz, "Konitz," *Im deutschen Reich* 7, no. 1 (1901): 571–605, here p. 601. Horowitz's numbers represent cases in which the prosecution obtained convictions. This was not always possible. In the aftermath of the riot in Berent, for example, state prosecutors in Danzig tried thirteen people. But after six hours of testimony from forty-three witnesses, the accounts became so confused and confounded that only nine convictions could be obtained. In a number of other cases, the courts released the accused because they were too young to be tried—a sixteen-year-old girl who took part in the riot in Czersk on April 22, for example, or the five Konitz boys, the eldest of whom was eleven, who were caught throwing stones through the synagogue windows. See *Die jüdische Presse* 31, no. 42 (1900): 433; and *Im deutschen Reich* 7, no. 5 (1901): 285.

67. GStAPK, Rep. 77, Tit. 500, no. 50, Bd. 2, bl. 231, Schwurgericht Stolp, July 10, 1900.

three had been born in Konitz. In addition, three had previous arrests—one, the "ringleader" Theodor Knievel, for theft and beggary; another, Karl Pikarski, for aiding in a prison break.[68]

Court records thus present a less than flattering picture of the crowd. Far from being solid citizens of a German town, the rioters tended to be restless young men, many of them still students and apprentices (and therefore probably not married), who, after spending time in the local bar, stirred up trouble. The reports of county officials confirm this image. Baron von Zedlitz believed that "the smallest part [of the rioters] are to be found among the taxpayers." Rather, he observed, "loaf-abouts, half-grown boys who have temporary jobs here, servants who are roaming around the streets without the permission of their masters—these are the elements that make up the rabble in Konitz."[69] While Zedlitz in his reports no doubt betrayed upper-class projections and fears about the crowd, he was not alone in emphasizing its sharp class contours. The county official of Tuchel also wrote about the "hordes of people made up of journeymen, apprentices, and workers who noisily marched through town and damaged Jewish houses."[70]

At first glance, then, the riots seem to have had a strong class dimension. But the rioters themselves rarely made economic demands. Nor did their shouting reflect anger that the Jews tended to be better off. What galvanized the crowd, time and again, was something else: their perception that the Jews were getting away with murder. The Jews, so ran the tenor on the street, had the justice system in their hands. The Jews, the rioters believed, were privileged and protected. For this reason, rumors of Hoffmann's arrest repeatedly touched a nerve.

The crux of the matter is a different one, then: not the specific class dimension of the riots, but their wider appeal. One must remember the sheer dimension of the disturbances, especially in Konitz, a town of ten thousand. Behind the rioters throwing rocks and storming the synagogue was a wider crowd—of "more than a thousand people," according to Baron von Zedlitz. Who made up this wider crowd? Were they merely there for the spectacle? Did they also scream antisemitic epithets? What did they think as the rioters smashed the windows of their Jewish neighbors? On these questions, the documents are largely silent. But from the

---

68. Ibid., Rep. I/81a, Nr. 16775, bl. 85, August 21, 1900.

69. Ibid., Rep. 77, Tit. 500, no. 50, Bd. 2, bl. 105, LA Konitz, June 11, 1900.

70. Ibid., Bd. 1, bl. 268, LA Tuchel, June 11, 1900. The county official in Berent also reported that in his town, the "rioters were young people, workers, apprentices, and a few students." Ibid., Bd. 2, bl. 116, LA Berent, June 12, 1900. For a similar description for Mrotschen, see GStAPK, Rep. 77, Tit. 500, no. 50, Bd. 1, bl. 121, Regierungspräsident Bromberg, June 8, 1900.

sources, we can cull bits of evidence telling us who these people were and whether they shared a hatred of the Jews with the rioters tossing rocks and vandalizing Jewish holy sites.

The larger crowd was made up of women as well as men. Zedlitz often remarked on this. Before rioters tried to set the synagogue afire on Thursday, June 7, women had gathered in the marketplace to discuss what was happening that evening.[71] Did they approve? Some evidence suggests that they did. By manipulating maternal anxieties, the antisemites had, according to Zedlitz, "won over the women" so that the women "had become the main proponents of a wild hatred of the Jews."[72] Whether they were really the main proponents or the county official merely imagined it this way is an open question. It does seem certain that women figured importantly in the wider crowd, in Konitz and elsewhere. According to the county official in Berent, a crowd had gathered there around ten o'clock at night on Sunday, June 12, some yelling antisemitic slogans. "Many people, predominantly pedestrians and the curious, also many women, were moving around the marketplace and along the main streets, without, however, forming compact groups."[73] This crowd constituted the background to a festival of rock-throwing and riotous behavior.

Were the "polite" classes—businessmen, lawyers, doctors, schoolteachers—also in this crowd? They are rarely mentioned in the official reports. In his three months of daily reports, Zedlitz mentions them only once, writing that "a relatively small proportion" could be held responsible "for positive participation in the riots."[74] In this sense, class delimited antisemitic violence, defining who participated in it and who supported the rioters vocally and with their physical presence in the streets. Yet there is another dimension to consider. For, although few business and professional people took to the streets, some supported the antisemitic movement nevertheless. Thus the town councillor Carl Gebauer, who was butcher Hoffmann's lawyer, counted as one of the "rabid antisemites," as did the editor of the local newspaper, Julius Lehmann. The same may be said of at least three schoolteachers (Josef Thiel, Albert Hoffrichter, and Maximillian Meyer, who was also a town councillor) as well as Auguste Rhode, the wife of the superintendent of schools.[75] Moreover, the social

---

71. GStAPK, Rep. 77, Tit. 500, no. 50, Bd. 1, bl. 270, LA Konitz, June 9, 1900.

72. Ibid., bl. 214, LA Konitz, May 30, 1900.

73. Ibid., Bd. 2, bl. 116, LA Berent, June 12, 1900.

74. Ibid., bl. 105, LA Konitz, June 11, 1900.

75. On Gebauer, see GStAPK, I Rep. 77, Tit. 500, no. 50, Bd. 2, bl. 163, LA Konitz, June 30, 1900. On Hoffrichter and Thiel, see GStAPK, Rep. 77, Tit. 500, no. 50, Bd. 2, Oberpräsident Provinz Westpreußen, June 14, 1900. On Rhode—who, when asked why she didn't turn over a piece of evidence, replied, "The murderers are the Jews"—see *Im deutschen Reich* 6, no. 5 (1900): 275.

circles to which these people belonged constituted a tight network within the town, allowing many of them to come together in meetings of the *Bürgerverein* (the club of the local notables), at the Masonic lodge, and at pubs and restaurants. Through marriage, some even had familial ties. For example, Hoffmann's other daughter, Martha, would in this year become engaged to marry Julius Lehmann, the newspaper editor.[76] These circles had also set up the unofficial citizens' committee to investigate the murder, a committee that constituted a source of continued frustration to the inspectors from Berlin, in no small measure because it encouraged an atmosphere of rumor and denunciation.

The outstanding impression, then, is that antisemitic sentiment, focusing on the suspicion that "the Jews" had committed and were getting away with murder, cut across lines of class and gender, religion and ethnicity. This does not, however, imply that everyone in Konitz and the surrounding area participated in this prejudice or took part in the violence it engendered. Some resisted: for example, the mayor, Georg Deditius; the county official, Baron von Zedlitz, who publicly declared "as superstition the idea that the Jewish religious community carried out a ritual murder"; the two non-Jewish liberals on the town council, merchant Friedrich Paetzold and high school teacher Dr. Ignatz Praetorius; Dr. Paul Petras, a local publisher who founded a left liberal newspaper intended to combat the infamies of the *Konitzer Zeitung* and who would pen an incisive critique of the events in Konitz; some members of the clergy, such as Pastor Böttcher in Schlochau, who on Whitsuntide admonished his Protestant parishioners to desist from further violence against the Jews; and some members of the police, who in time became the object of popular enmity.[77]

Perhaps there were others. But the balance of forces weighed against them. A sense of how this looked in the area can be gleaned from the elections to the Reichstag in 1903. Although the antisemites did not put up a candidate in the district of Konitz (because its ethnic composition always ensured a Polish victory), they did run in the neighboring district of Schlochau-Flatow, where there had been plenty of antisemitic violence. In the first election, the antisemites received a third of the vote; in the second, when they ran against the Polish Party, two-thirds.[78] What do these results

76. *Im deutschen Reich* 6, nos. 6–7 (1900): 399.

77. Zedlitz's statement is in GStAPK, Rep. 77, Tit. 500, no. 50, Bd. 1, bl. 261, *Danziger Zeitung,* June 29, 1900. On members of the town council and on a meeting on June 27 of "citizens who enjoy general trust in our town," see GStAPK, Rep. 77, Tit. 500, no. 50, Bd. 2, bl. 163, LA Konitz, June 30, 1900. On Dr. Praetorius, see *Mitteilungen aus dem Verein zur Abwehr des Antisemitismus* 40 (1900): 316. On Pastor Böttcher, see *Im deutschen Reich* 6, nos. 6–7 (1900): 354.

78. The election returns are in *Vierteljahreshefte zur Statistik des deutschen Reichs* 12, no. 1 (1903): III, 44–45. In the first ballot, the antisemites ran against candidates from the

tell us? When competing in the first election against other German parties, the antisemites could not attain a majority. Among German Protestants, roughly 44 percent supported the antisemites in the first ballot; in the second, almost all German Protestants cast their ballots for the antisemitic candidate. For their part, German Catholics supported the Catholic Center in the first round; in the second, they supported the Poles, with whom they shared a common religious denomination. Thus in voting behavior (though not in antisemitic sentiment), lines of religion and ethnicity still counted.

For Konitz itself, other kinds of evidence must suffice to determine where the balance of forces rested. The evidence is not reassuring. In December 1900, Dr. Paul Petras and other left liberals attempted to publish a new local paper, the *Ostdeutsche Zeitung* (also known as the *Konitzer Anzeiger*), which promised to be "impartial," "free of hatred," and "loyal to Kaiser and Reich."[79] Its editors insisted that "there are in fact many upstanding people (who are not antisemites) in our area." But in the next sentence, they conceded that "of course, they are silent now."[80]

The fate of Gustav Hoffmann, the Christian butcher, provides another index of the balance of forces. In early June, he had helped author a pamphlet that falsely accused Adolf Lewy, the Jewish butcher, of murdering Ernst Winter. It was an immensely popular pamphlet that further polarized an already divided town.[81] Then, in late July, Hoffmann demanded a reparation of honor (*Ehrenerklärung*) from the town council, which he received. When he addressed the assembly, he repeated his denunciations of his Jewish neighbor. Tellingly, no one on the town council dared raise a public objection against Hoffmann's vituperations, despite any private misgivings they might have had.[82]

National Liberal Party, the Center, the Polish Party, and the Agrarian League. In this round, the antisemites received 33 percent of the vote and were forced into a runoff with the Polish Party, which captured 25 percent of the ballots. In the second election, the antisemites won 64 percent, the Polish Party 36 percent.

79. GStAPK, Rep. 77, Tit. 500, no. 50, Bd. 3, bl. 161, *Konitzer Anzeiger,* December 5, 1900.

80. The passage from the *Ostdeutsche Zeitung* is quoted in *Im deutschen Reich* 7, no. 5 (1901): 286. As the advertisements in the back of the *Ostdeutsche Zeitung* clearly showed, the new newspaper received most of its support from the Jewish community. Julius Lehmann referred to the paper as the "Konitzer Judenblatt." GStAPK, Rep. 77, Tit. 500, no. 50, Bd. 3, bl. 155, *Konitzer Tageblatt,* December 7, 1900.

81. See *Staatsbürgerzeitung* 36, no. 270 (June 13, 1900). This accusation, colloquially called "Hoffmann's Defense," was officially titled "Petition of the Butcher Gustav Hoffmann in Konitz Pertaining to the Matter of Winter's Murder." It was reprinted in its entirety in *Antisemitische Correspondenz* 15 (June 14, 1900): 277–81. As a pamphlet, it was printed in a run of fifty thousand copies, making it perhaps the most widely read piece of writing in all of West Prussia that summer.

82. *Danziger Zeitung,* July 28, 1900.

Indeed, the local notables who tried to stem the tide of antisemitic violence were deeply affected by the events of the summer of 1900. Dr. Praetorius, who had been one of the founders of the Konitz *Bürgerverein* in the 1870s, was forced to resign his position, both in the club and as a teacher in the local high school.[83] Dr. Lemm, the assistant mayor, applied for a position on the city council of Fürstenwalde. And Georg Deditius, the sensible, dutiful mayor of Konitz and a man who had opposed the antisemitic violence from the start, applied for a lesser post in the town of Landshut in Silesia.[84] Deditius ended up staying in Konitz, but the atmosphere there remained vengeful, marked by ongoing libel suits (including suits by Christians against other Christians) and a heavy dose of ill will toward the Jewish population. There were portentous signs. A local inn, the Golden Lion, advertised itself as a place where you could get "good home-cooked meals, refreshing drinks, comfortable beds, and lodging free of Jews."[85]

III

Konitz was not a world unto itself. When news of the murder spread, people scrambled to their maps and atlases to figure out exactly where the town was. Among the most interested were journalists drawn to sensation.[86] But if Konitz offered sensation, this was not exactly the big city: work on a sewage system was still a decade away, all but one of the streets were unpaved, and it was not until 1900 that a telephone was installed in the post office.[87] Newspapers in Berlin and Frankfurt reported on the murder, but they could not expect their correspondents to actually go there to stay for any length of time. For the antisemites, it was very different. Konitz was not just a story to be reported, it was a spectacle to be made. The journalists for antisemitic newspapers traveled to Konitz and stayed there for weeks on end; they ingratiated themselves with the people involved, such as Ernst Winter's father, and they made local connections.

Although there were others, three antisemitic journalists were espe-

---

83. *Mitteilungen aus dem Verein zur Abwehr des Antisemitismus* 40 (1900): 316.

84. *Im deutschen Reich* 6, no. 10 (1900): 537.

85. GStAPK, Rep. 77, Tit. 500, no. 50, Bd. 3, bl. 157, *Konitzer Tageblatt,* December 7, 1900.

86. On the press generally, see Peter Fritzsche, *Reading Berlin, 1900* (Cambridge, Mass., 1996), 53–59. On ritual murder cases and the newspapers, see the remarks in Albert Lichtblau, "Die Debatten über die Ritualmordbeschuldigungen im österreichischen Abgeordnetenhaus am Ende des 19. Jahrhunderts," in *Die Legende vom Ritualmord,* edited by Rainer Erb (Berlin, 1993), 291. See also Hillel J. Kieval, "Antisémitisme ou savoir social? Sur la genèse du procès moderne pour meurtre rituel," *Annales HSS* 5 (1994): 1091–1105.

87. Borowka, *Aus Sage und Geschichte von Konitz,* 94–95.

cially prominent: Max Wieneke, Wilhelm Bruhn, and Georg Zimmer. All three were roughly thirty years old, lived on a shoestring, and hailed from Berlin; and all three wrote for the antisemitic *Staatsbürgerzeitung.* But they did not write only for this newspaper. Wieneke, for example, sent his stories to a "large number" of papers, including the *Leipziger-Tageblatt* and the *Danziger Neueste Nachrichten.*[88] For his part, Georg Zimmer would soon be employed by Julius Lehmann, writing about the murder investigation for the *Konitzer Tageblatt.* Nor did these journalists just write. They traveled, now by bicycle, now by train, to nearby towns and villages, informing people of the newest events, making more contacts, conducting their own investigations, selling their newspapers, and telling people what was happening. They were, then, not just reporting; they were also making politics. And they were living from it.[89]

These journalists drove events forward. Zedlitz constantly assumed that the crowds had been organized beforehand and that "the riots were staged by outsiders."[90] It is difficult to establish the veracity of his assumption. The first wave of riots in the third week of April seems to have been a direct response to an escalation of events having to do with the murder—namely, the discovery of Winter's head and the arrest of Israelski. These events were real; mendacious journalists did not simply invent them. But subsequent riots increasingly suggested conscious intervention. Wilhelm Bruhn had, for example, come to Konitz late in May in order to report on Winter's funeral. When he decided to stay, he worked closely with the unofficial citizens' committee, which created a constant counter-spectacle to the official investigation. He also helped focus the agitation on two personalities, Hoffmann and Lewy: the one Christian, well known, and well liked; the other Jewish, of quiet demeanor, and held to be secretive. The antisemitic journalists thus fastened onto an explosive formula focused on personalities symbolizing larger affinities and antagonisms, as well as a range of fears and projections.

From late May onward, these antisemites took up quarters in Konitz and gave their full being to their cause. In this context, historians' debates about the relative prominence of print versus oral culture in the propagation of antisemitic ideas and sentiments may well be based on a false

88. *Der Prozeß gegen Masloff und Genossen,* 703.

89. For the classic distinction between "living for" and "living from" politics, see Max Weber, *Wirtschaft und Gesellschaft,* ed. Johannes Winckelmann, 5th ed. (Tübingen, 1976), 829–30. On the role of antisemitic journalists in another context, see Helmut Walser Smith, "Alltag und politischer Antisemitismus in Baden, 1890–1900," *Zeitschrift für die Geschichte des Oberrheins* 141 (1993): 282–83.

90. GStAPK, Rep. 77, Tit. 500, no. 50, Bd. 2, bl. 105, LA Konitz, June 11, 1900.

dichotomy.[91] The men who penned the stories for the papers also spent their evenings in the pubs and on the streets. The journalists lived from rumors and at the same time replenished them, sometimes even outright fabricated them, or the documents on which they were based.[92] For the course of events in Konitz, all of this had an extremely deleterious influence. "Hardly a day goes by," Baron von Zedlitz complained, "that the news does not throw oil onto the fire anew." Much of this news, according to Zedlitz, was made up of "fantastic and twisted information" fed to a sensation-hungry public.[93]

But there was a still deeper context. The investigation had dragged on since mid-March, and by mid-June the police had not come any closer to apprehending the person who killed Ernst Winter. This opened a space for fears, for suspicions, for projections, even for settling scores. This was the space that antisemitism filled. An eminently public space, it created a theater for daily spectacle, with the people of Konitz providing the script and constituting the primary audience. People's fears and suspicions became public partly because the newspapers printed them, regardless of how absurd. Once in print, they assumed legitimacy, becoming the subject of public discussion. In this way, everyone from servant to schoolmaster could cut themselves a piece of public attention. Partly, however, the space was also opened by the investigation. As the police had few leads, they had to pursue every shred of evidence, no matter how tenuous. This forced them to search people's homes on eighty separate occasions.[94] It also meant that the police had to take every story, every denunciation, seriously. And in Konitz, there was no shortage of denunciations, especially since the Prussian police, not altogether wisely, put up a reward of twenty thousand marks for information leading directly to the arrest of the killer.[95] By July, according to one report, there had already been four hundred separate denunciations—people coming to the police and to the newspapers with stories of what they had seen, heard, smelled, even dreamed.[96]

---

91. A similar point is made with respect to elite and popular culture by Rainer Erb in the introduction to *Die Legende vom Ritualmord,* 15.

92. On June 9, for example, one of the journalists sent Winter's father a handwritten letter saying that the Jews would give him fifty thousand marks if he would remain quiet. The letter was, of course, forged. A picture of the original forgery is in *Der Blutmord in Konitz,* 4th ed. (Berlin, 1901).

93. GStAPK, Rep. 77, Tit. 500, no. 50, Bd. 2, bl. 155, LA Konitz, June 28, 1900.

94. *Im deutschen Reich* 6, nos. 6–7 (1900): 331.

95. *Die jüdische Presse* 31, 19 (1900): 189.

96. *Im deutschen Reich* 6, nos. 6–7 (1900): 331. On the importance of denunciation to the spectacle, see Lichtblau, "Die Debatten," 291.

This gallery of stories shows that the idea of ritual murder had taken hold of the people of Konitz. Some stories were born of half-baked theories of how the murder must have happened, others came from conversations people imagined themselves to have overheard, and still others betrayed real fears and anxieties. Finally, some were simply malicious.

An example of the first genre was the story of a fifty-seven-year-old bricklayer, Christian Lübke, who insisted that there were underground vaults and tunnels beneath the synagogue, and that within these vaults and tunnels—so he claimed to have overheard some Jews saying—was where the murder had occurred.[97] Partly through the agitation of the local press, this theory assumed a certain popularity, forcing Mayor Deditius to inspect the temple and to make inquiries of the masons who had worked on the foundations a few years back.[98] But most people did not go to the trouble of imagining whole scenarios. A number of the stories concerned conversations relating directly to the supposed importance of blood for the Jewish community. One man, Anton Hellwig from the village of Görsdorf, a farmer known for his superstitious ways, claimed that a Jewish grain dealer, Alexander Camminer, had told him that "this year blood is so expensive, it costs half a million marks."[99] In other stories, witnesses recreated conversations having to do with ritual slaughter. August Steinke, a raft inspector in Prechlau, claimed that just before the murder, he had had the following conversation with Siegfried Eisenstadt, a Jewish cattle trader from Schlochau.

> STEINKE: The Winter family is a respectable family with a nice son.
> EISENSTADT: The son is fit for slaughter.
> STEINKE: He is too thin.
> EISENSTADT: He has a lot of blood.[100]

Naturally, none of the Jews implicated in these conversations admitted to saying anything of the sort. But for the local rumor mill, nothing was too farfetched, not even the alleged statements of Alex Prinz. He was a twenty-three-year-old Jewish man known to everyone in Konitz as Dumb Alex, a man who traded in rags, bones, and iron nails. Alex (who claimed he was drunk at the time) allegedly said to Auguste Schiller, the wife of an innkeeper and a reader of cards, that the Jewish cantor in Schlochau had

97. *Der Prozeß gegen Moritz Lewy (Konitz, 13–16.2.1901) nach stenographische Aufnahme* (Berlin, 1901), 118. On Lübke, see *Der Prozeß gegen Masloff und Genossen*, 416–17.
98. *Der Prozeß gegen Masloff und Genossen*, 423.
99. Ibid., 646, 861. Hellwig had supposedly believed in witches when he was younger.
100. Ibid., 548–49.

killed Ernst Winter with a slit to the neck. When Frau Schiller asked if the cantor had done it alone, Alex replied "no, three Jewish cantors," adding that it had been done at Lewy's house and that "yes, blood is very expensive now." Frau Schiller did not go to the police with the news; instead, she went to the butcher Gustav Hoffmann, and from there it landed in the press, circulated throughout the town, and was then brought before the court.[101]

The third line of stories and denunciations came mainly from the world of female servants. Two cases were especially spectacular. The first involved Mathilde Rutz, who claimed that Adolf Lewy had tried to rape her as she was carrying winter potatoes into his cellar. When she dumped out the potatoes, the lantern flickered off, at which point she screamed, "I can't find my way out." Lewy then relit the lantern, and, as she was running out, they came to each other—so Rutz maintained—and Lewy began to press against her. She screamed again. And he allegedly said, "Don't say anything, I'd like to cut you off a piece of meat." She then tried to get out. He grabbed her breasts and pulled her into the straw. Struggling, she brushed him aside with a sweep of her arm, and then her son—who had been there the whole time—took her by the hand, and together they ran out of the cellar.[102] True? Good evidence speaks against it: by all accounts, Lewy was a shy and reticent man, while Mathilde Rutz was a woman who liked to drink and tell tall tales.[103] The second story involved seventeen-year-old Rosine Simonowski, who developed such persecution anxiety that she left Konitz and moved to Berlin, all the while believing that the Jews were "following" her and were trying to stab her with knives.[104] She had a gift for inventing conversations in her mind, which, of course, reached the public via the courts and the press. She reported, for example, the following conversation with Heinrich Friedländer, a Jewish merchant, in his store in Konitz.

FRIEDLÄNDER: The Jews need blood.
SIMONOWSKI: Why?
FRIEDLÄNDER: They just need it.
SIMONOWSKI: That's why you slaughtered Ernst Winter.
FRIEDLÄNDER: I don't know about that.

She was about to go, the door to the store half open, when Friedländer allegedly said, "You don't have to go talking about this" and then

---

101. Ibid., 669.
102. The story is recounted in *Der Prozeß gegen Masloff und Genossen,* 933.
103. Ibid., 933.
104. Ibid., 372, 383.

repeated, "Don't say anything, I'll buy you a nice present."[105] Simonowski had more stories, so many that they ceased to be credible, even to the people of Konitz. Moreover—and this reveals something about the mixed realm of motivation that generated such stories to begin with—it turned out that Simonowski and Friedländer had once been lovers, or at least sex partners, and that Friedländer had spurned her.[106]

The torrent of stories and denunciations, especially from servant girls, was a stream without dam. The source of this torrent was sometimes fear, sometimes malice, sometimes avarice. In Kamin, a village to the south of Konitz, Josef Rosenthal's servant, Margarete Radtke, claimed that she had overheard Rosenthal saying to his wife that "he could not live on after his deed." Soon after saying this, Rosenthal allegedly tried to hang himself on a nail, but was pulled down by his brother.[107] Not a word of this held up in court, but, as Rosenthal lacked a good alibi for the night of the murder, he made something up; when caught in contradictions, he was tried for perjury. Radtke, for her part, had accused a previous master of rape. Was the accusation against Rosenthal a matter of fear, or did it form part of a different pattern?

Then there was the yarn of half-truths and outright lies spun by Anna Roß—the mother-in-law of Bernhard Masloff, the man who claimed to have seen Lewy and two other men carrying a package presumably containing the murder victim's torso. She too focused her accusations on the Lewy family: Adolf's face, allegedly white with fear after the killing; the son Moritz, who allegedly said to Roß, "Don't say anything about the murder"; Lewy's wife, Helene, who after the murder supposedly cried out, "God protect my husband and my son"; the missing handkerchief with bloodstains and the red-stitched initials "E. W." on it, which Roß and her daughter had seen in Lewy's laundry (three weeks after the murder, and a week before Winter's head was discovered near the shooting lodge); the photograph of Ernst Winter in Lewy's house; and so on.[108]

Despite their mendacity, these stories impress by their specificity. They suggest a population working to piece together a story of Jewish culpability, of Jewish ritual murder, and of a Jewish cabal to cover up the crime. Historians are often tempted to see in antisemitic utterances and acts a cloak hiding more profound grievances, such as economic disadvantage, or to see in them a "cultural code" that stands for a range of neg-

---

105. Ibid., 370–71, 382.

106. GStAPK, Rep I/84a Nr. 16776, bl. 48–51, Oeffentliche Sitzung des Schwurgerichts zu Konitz, October 30, 1900.

107. *Der Prozeß gegen Masloff und Genossen,* 238; *Im deutschen Reich* 7, no. 4 (1901): 230.

108. *Der Prozeß gegen Masloff und Genossen,* 67, 71, 107–8.

ative images associated with an out-group, in this case the Jews.[109] But in Konitz, something different was going on. People were piecing together precise stories, using not diffuse symbols but specific ones, symbols that had less to do with economics than with purported religious ritual, symbols that were evocative of the unknown. The stories also resonated with emotion. That Mathilde Rutz imagined that Lewy tried to rape her, that Rosine Simonowski worried that the Jews were chasing her with knives, speaks to the emotional charge of these stories, and to the ability of antisemitism to provision them with form and content. For its part, the investigation created an open space for people to reflect on and to articulate how they imagined the story. And the press, eager for material, rendered all the rumors, all the denunciations, and every story public: a script the people of Konitz both wrote and read. And as it became increasingly their script, they reacted like seismographs to official actions—especially on the part of the police from Berlin—that contradicted what they believed. Thus the importance of the citizen's committee. Thus the crucial impact of the arrest of Hoffmann. Thus the willingness to do battle with the authorities, even with the Prussian military. Thus the focus on Hoffmann's "other": Adolf Lewy.

IV

In his book *Postmodernity and Its Discontents,* Zygmunt Bauman writes, "All societies produce strangers; but each kind of society produces its own kind of strangers, and produces them in its own inimitable way."[110] The murder of Ernst Winter was an event that unleashed a process whose consequence was to render the Jews of Konitz strangers in their own hometown. This is not to say that they were something other than strangers before. Indeed, the summer of 1900 was not the first time that the area had been the site of severe antisemitic riots. In 1881, nineteen years earlier and still in the memories of many residents, there had been a similar outburst, structured, as in 1900, by a dynamic between a new political antisemitism and long-standing tensions between Christians and Jews. And, like the uprisings in 1900, the riots in 1881 left a considerable degree of property damage in their wake, including to area synagogues.[111] Nor would the events of the summer of 1900 constitute the last outbreak of violence here.

---

109. For the first position, see Nonn, "Zwischenfall in Konitz." For the second position, see Shulamit Volkov, "Antisemitism as Cultural Code: Reflections on the History and Historiography of Antisemitism in Imperial Germany," *Leo Baeck Institute Year Book* 33 (1978): 25–46.

110. Zygmunt Bauman, *Postmodernity and Its Discontents* (New York, 1997), 17.

111. See Hoffmann, "Political Culture and Violence against Minorities."

In September 1939, the homegrown German National Self-Protection (Volksdeutsche Selbstschutz) societies initiated a series of killings of Jews, Poles, and people in psychiatric wards. According to the research of Christian Jansen and Arno Weckbecker, nearly fourteen hundred people were killed in the county of Konitz alone. And these killings, it should be emphasized, were not related to the prosecution of the war.[112]

The violence of Konitz was an event that sharpened differences, that shored up the line dividing "we" from "they." There was nothing natural about this, and the differences cannot easily be reduced to the "rational responses" of social groups—whether defined ethnically, religiously, or in terms of class—to some sense of disadvantage. Structure brings us only so far. There is also event, process, and contingency.[113] In Konitz, this process started with the murder, which led to an investigation that dragged on. But because the police did not find the killer, the investigation opened a space for people to fill with their fears and their projections. In this process, the people of Konitz were not alone. An important element came from the outside—from the antisemitic journalists and politicians who pushed the process, further sharpening differences, polarizing the town, marking and persecuting the Jewish population. Here it is the dynamic that mattered: the way that the antisemites sought out rumors and innuendos, then dignified them by virtue of fixing them in print; the way they intervened in the course of events (insisting, for example, that Hoffmann's arrest was still pending when it was not); and the way they helped set up a parallel structure, the unofficial citizen's committee, in order to create a forum for the people of Konitz to piece together and publicly tell their own story of how the Jews murdered Ernst Winter.

But all of this could happen only because the antisemites could draw from a rich mine of popular beliefs about Jews: that they needed Christian blood for their Passover rituals, that they committed secret acts behind the walls of their holy places, that they paid off the police and controlled the press, and that they came together in cabals to cover for one another. These were volatile beliefs—and they provided a warrant for "exclusionary violence."

---

112. Christian Jansen and Arno Weckbecker, *Der "Volksdeutsche Selbstschutz" in Polen, 1939/40* (Oldenburg, 1992). The statistics for Konitz are on p. 214.

113. See, for more general reflections, William H. Sewell Jr., "Three Temporalities: Toward an Eventful Sociology," in *The Historic Turn in the Human Sciences,* edited by Terrence J. McDonald (Ann Arbor, 1996), 245–80.

"Out with the Ostjuden": The Scheunenviertel Riots in Berlin, November 1923

David Clay Large

In his *Ein Kerl muß eine Meinung haben,* Alfred Döblin offered the following observations regarding an outbreak of rioting and looting he had witnessed in the so-called Scheunenviertel, Berlin's chief Jewish "ghetto," on November 5, 1923.

> At noon I was in the Alexanderplatz, just a few minutes' walk from the center of the action, and I noticed—nothing. All was quite peaceful. As in every great city, in Berlin everything is localized, and events in one quarter may not have much impact elsewhere. But when I ventured into the [Scheunenviertel] that night, I encountered sights that seemed weird even to a Berliner. Grenadierstraße and Dragonerstraße, chief refuge of Berlin's Ostjuden, were sealed off by the police; the streets were completely dark. Crowds of people congregated on the corners; there were smashed windows and wrecked shops. . . . Police, the "Greens," ran around with unsheathed sabers dispersing the crowds. . . . Among the Jews there was great anxiety about what might happen next; many contemplated another exile. What transpired in the Scheunenviertel was in some ways reminiscent of old Russia: social tensions unloaded on the Jews. However, I don't see a true pogrom mentality in Berlin. Agitators stir things up, the unthinking masses allow themselves to be pulled hither and yon, but with a solider currency and more food, peace could easily be restored.[1]

---

1. Alfred Döblin, *Ein Kerl muß eine Meinung haben* (Munich, 1976), 217–20.

The events that Döblin had witnessed turned out to be the most extensive outbreak of civilian rioting in the short history of the Weimar Republic. Over the course of two days, thousands of rioters, mostly young men, looted shops, ransacked private homes, and attacked people in the streets of Berlin, beating them bloody, robbing them, and sometimes even stripping them of their clothes. The worst of the rioting took place in the Scheunenviertel, and the majority of the assault victims were Jews, especially the easily identifiable Galician Jews. Cries of "Beat the Jews to death" and "Raus mit den Ostjuden" (out with the eastern Jews) rang through the narrow streets of the quarter.

Some contemporary chroniclers underscored the seriousness of these riots and highlighted their antisemitic character. Others, like Döblin, acknowledged an antisemitic side to the event but downplayed the importance of this dimension.

Historians have also been divided over the nature and implications of the so-called Scheunenviertelkrawallen of November 1923. Robert Scholz, in his study of popular riots in Berlin between 1914 and 1923, sees this upheaval as a product of growing frustration among Berlin's unemployed workers over escalating prices, especially for food. "This kind of thing belonged to the *Alltag* of the great inflation," he writes.[2] Trude Maurer, in her lengthy work on the Ostjuden in Germany between 1918 and 1933, views the riots as the fruit of systematic agitation by *völkisch* elements, abetted by willful incompetence on the part of the Berlin police. In her perspective, the Scheunenviertel rioting points up a telling breakdown in political justice in the Weimar state.[3] In his study of rightist radicalism in Weimar Berlin, Bernd Kruppa describes the November 1923 rioting as Berlin's "first Jewish pogrom," the work of "mobs incited by rightist radicals."[4] A similar verdict is offered by Rainer Zilkenat in a short essay devoted to the rioting, which the author attributes to "planned activities by antisemitic agitators."[5] Dirk Walter, by contrast, characterizes the rioting as "pogrom-like," while disputing the contemporary (and later) assertion that the affair had been planned or orchestrated by "professional agi-

---

2. Robert Scholz, "Ein unruhiges Jahrzehnt: Lebensmittelunruhen, Massenstreiks und Arbeitslosenkrawalle in Berlin, 1914–1923," in *Pöbelexzesse und Volkstumulte in Berlin: Zur Sozialgeschichte der Straße,* edited by Manfred Gailus (Berlin, 1984), 17.

3. Trude Maurer, *Ostjuden in Deutschland, 1918–1933* (Hamburg, 1986), 329–44. See also Gerald D. Feldman, *The Great Disorder: Politics, Economics, and Society in the German Inflation, 1914–1924* (New York, 1993), 780–81.

4. Bernd Kruppa, *Rechtsradikalismus in Berlin, 1918–1928* (Berlin, 1988), 242.

5. Rainer Zilkenat, "Der Pogrom am 5. und 6. November 1923," in *Das Scheunenviertel: Spuren eines verlorenen Berlins,* edited by Verein Stiftung Scheunenviertel (Berlin, 1994), 96.

tators" of the radical right. He proposes, too, that the Berlin and Prussian authorities, by pointing their fingers at professional agitators, sought to distract attention from their own failures in the realms of domestic security and social welfare.[6]

A judicious assessment of the Berlin rioting in November 1923 demands, in addition to a detailed narration of the events based on a critical evaluation of the contemporary sources, that we place this affair within the broader framework of anti-Jewish agitation during the late nineteenth and early twentieth centuries, as well as against the backdrop of the severe domestic unrest in Germany that developed during the First World War and the early years of the Weimar Republic. Taking issue with much of the commentary on the Scheunenviertel rioting, I wish to argue here that this affair was neither just another expression of socioeconomic frustration nor, at the other end of the interpretive spectrum, a deliberately orchestrated attack on Berlin's Jewish community. There is no credible evidence to support contemporary claims—later reasserted by many historians—that the riots were primarily the work of right-wing agitators. The absence of extensive planning or coordination, however, does not minimize the event's importance. On the contrary, precisely because the rioting was essentially spontaneous, and because the majority of the participants belonged to the traditional constituency of the left rather than to that of the radical right, this case was particularly ominous. It showed how easily and quickly socioeconomic frustrations could boil over into anti-Jewish violence and how broad the antisemitic currents ran in postwar German society.

If the Germany of the *Kaiserreich* and the Weimar Republic did not experience waves of large-scale and vicious pogroms, as in Russia, or a national trauma centered on an antisemitic affair, as in France, the country nevertheless experienced a number of violent outbreaks directed against Jews. In Germany, several factors combined to translate the idiom of political antisemitism, which was rooted in the mainstream conservative parties as well as in smaller racist parties and lobby groups, into open violence. These factors included the steady drumbeat of antisemitic agitation; the brutalization of the national psyche in the First World War and the 1918–19 revolutions; the shock and humiliation occasioned by the loss of the war; the growing acceptance of violence and assassination as legitimate modes of political behavior; and, above all, the extreme socioeconomic distress brought on by material deprivation and the Great Inflation of the early 1920s. As we shall see below, this combustible mix had begun

---

6. Dirk Walter, *Antisemitische Kriminalität und Gewalt: Judenfeindschaft in der Weimarer Republik* (Bonn, 1999), 151–52.

to generate a few physical attacks on Jews even before the explosion of concentrated racist violence in the Scheunenviertel in 1923. Moreover, the postwar era brought a proliferation of rightist organizations such as the Deutschvölkische Freiheitspartei, the Deutschvölkische Schutz- und Trutzbund, and, of course, the Nazis, who demanded the elimination of Jewish influences in German life. At the same time, various state-sponsored measures directed specifically against the Ostjuden helped to make this marginalized group more vulnerable and exposed than ever.

Thus, when the mobs took to the streets of the Berlin ghetto in November 1923 shouting "Out with the Ostjuden!" they could harbor the belief that their goal, if not their vigilante-style tactics, harmonized to some degree with official policy. It is this aspect of the Scheunenviertel events that recapitulates the classic pogrom model, in which the assailants believe that they are acting in tacit complicity with or even on behalf of the state. On the other hand, because the Scheunenviertel rioters were also motivated by a desire to strike out against an unjust "system" and sought to relieve their material distress through wholesale looting and pillaging, they could hardly expect carte blanche approval on the part of the authorities. The rioters' willingness to violate traditional norms of civic behavior in the name of redressing social grievances places their action in the tradition of the disruptive street demonstrations, wildcat strikes, and attacks on police that had been endemic on the Berlin scene in the decade or so before the war. Summarized perhaps too crudely, the Scheunenviertel riots of November 1923 were part pogrom, part "Straßenpolitik."

If violent mob assaults on Jews were relatively rare in Germany, riots over food shortages and high prices, the other prime ingredient in the Scheunenviertel upheaval, had become increasingly frequent since the middle years of the First World War, especially in Berlin. Starting in 1915, Berliners, mainly working-class women and teenagers, expressed their outrage over the food crisis by pillaging shops and municipal warehouses. In one such instance, a group of proletarian women descended on a butter store whose owner had recently jacked up his prices. When he responded to their complaints by telling them that they would soon be paying six marks for a pound of butter and "eating shit for dessert," they beat him up and smashed his shop.[7] A little later a mob stormed a meeting of the Social Democratic leadership to protest the party's inaction in the food crisis. As the Socialist politician Otto Braun recalled, the protesters hurled stink bombs, cursed the SPD leaders as "feige Lumpen," and suggested that they be sent to the trenches. "The comrades from other parts of the Reich

---

7. Scholz, "Ein unruhiges Jahrzehnt," 83.

got a very graphic demonstration of the unspeakably low level of political discourse in Berlin," commented Braun in his diary.[8] Significantly, by early 1916 radical rightist organizations in the city were attributing the food crisis to the machinations of the Jews, who were said to be waging "economic war" on the German people. Such assertions had broad resonance in the city because wartime Berlin witnessed an influx of refugees from the east, many of them Jewish, who competed with the native population for scarce resources.[9]

The end of the war brought no respite from the shortages and spiraling prices. Inflation, of course, became much worse in the early years of the Weimar Republic, when the mark actually became worth less than the paper it was printed on. Accordingly, civilian disturbances remained a frequent occurrence across the Reich, and often they assumed an antisemitic character. There were food riots (*Lebensmittelkrawalle*) with a racist taint in a number of cities and towns in the summer of 1919 and in the spring and summer of 1920. For example, during food riots in Karlsruhe in July 1920, rioters hurled insults against the Jews, whom they blamed for all their economic difficulties.[10] In early 1923 food riots in the eastern German towns of Neidenburg and Beuthen similarly segued into attacks against local Jews.[11] In Berlin, where looting of food shops had been especially extensive, a rumor went around that the wurst being sold in the local markets contained human flesh, which, being cheaper than pig, allowed for greater profits. Jewish butchers were said to be behind this outrage.

Citing alleged widespread criminality among local Ostjuden, in March 1920 Berlin's Social Democratic police chief, Eugen Fuchs, ordered a raid on the Scheunenviertel, which resulted in the arrests of over seven hundred people. These individuals were soon released, but new raids in 1921 led to the internment of hundreds of Ostjuden in special camps (harbingers of the future!) at Stargard and Cottbus, where the inmates were systematically mistreated.[12] During the Kapp Putsch in March 1920, civilian backers of the putschists called for a pogrom against the Jews of Berlin. There were in fact some attacks against Ostjuden in the Scheunenviertel during the putsch, though a full-scale pogrom was averted, largely

---

8. Braun quoted in Scholz, "Ein unruhiges Jahrzehnt," 85.

9. See Belinda J. Davis, *Home Fires Burning: Food, Politics, and Everyday Life in World War I Berlin* (Chapel Hill, 2000), 132.

10. Manfred Koch, "Die Weimarer Republik: Juden zwischen Integration und Ausgrenzung," in *Juden in Karlsruhe: Beiträge zu ihrer Geschichte bis zur nationalsozialistischen Machtergreifung,* edited by Heinz Schmitt (Karlsruhe, 1990), 158.

11. Walter, *Antisemitische Kriminalität,* 151.

12. Steven E. Aschheim, *Brothers and Strangers: The East European Jew in German and German Jewish Consciousness* (Madison, Wis., 1983), 240–42.

because Jewish self-defense forces managed to keep most of the Jews off the streets for the duration of the abortive coup. Even after the coup had failed, police and military forces in Berlin refused to take action against a mob of women in the Kurfürstendamm who were spreading antisemitic propaganda. Meanwhile, a Berlin-based working-class group calling itself the Association of the Poorest of the Poor warned eastern Jews to leave Germany immediately or face "thorough eradication through killing."[13] Down in Munich, the leader of the Bavarian People's Party, Dr. Heim, demanded the expulsion of "the 80,000 louse-ridden Ostjuden" in exchange for food deliveries by peasants to the cities.[14] Responding to such threats and appeals, Prussia's interior minister, Wolfgang Heine (SPD), rejected a wholesale expulsion of the eastern Jews to their former homelands on grounds that if they returned, they faced "danger to life and limb."[15]

As for Berlin itself, the majority of food rioters in this era came from the ranks of the unemployed, which had swollen dramatically with the return of soldiers from the front, an influx of refugees from the east, and the dismissal of females from wartime jobs. In January 1919 the capital had 164,000 registered unemployed, and that figure was expected to climb.[16] Concern over what this might mean in terms of security and order was one of the factors prompting the decision to hold the constitutional assembly in Weimar rather than in Berlin.

Over the course of the next three years, the rates of unemployment and inflation reached crisis proportions. By November 1923 the number of unemployed in the capital had reached 210,536, of which only 145,000 could be covered by public assistance. Long lines formed outside the offices of charity organizations and municipal soup kitchens. But even those who received some public help could hardly keep up with the escalating prices, especially for food. On November 5, the day the Scheunenviertel riots began, the price of a loaf of bread was officially pegged at 140 billion marks.[17] At the beginning of that month, some food riots in the city were already targeting Jewish stores; as the rioters went about their looting, *völkisch* agitators cheered them on.[18]

---

13. Quoted in Maurer, *Ostjuden,* 326.

14. Ibid., 327.

15. Quoted in Reiner Pommerin, "Die Ausweisung von 'Ostjuden' aus Bayern 1923: Ein Beitrag zum Krisenjahr der Weimarer Republik," *Vierteljahrshefte für Zeitgeschichte* 34 (1986): 319.

16. Scholz, "Ein unruhiges Jahrzehnt," 105.

17. On unemployment and the inflationary spiral in this period in Berlin, see Feldman, *The Great Disorder,* 754–80; and Wolfgang Ribbe, ed., *Geschichte Berlins,* vol. 2, *Von der Märzrevolution bis zur Gegenwart* (Munich, 1987), 838–45.

18. Kruppa, *Rechtsradikalismus,* 242.

Until the fall of 1923, the food rioting afflicting Berlin had largely spared the Scheunenviertel, which, as one of the poorest quarters of the capital, was hardly an attractive target. Also thus far, with the exception of the isolated acts of violence in early 1920, the assaults against the Jews in that district had been mainly verbal, coming from racist newspapers and antisemitic tub-thumpers decrying the concentration of "un-German" elements in the quarter who allegedly preyed on the native population.

There was no question that the Jewish presence in the district was large and noticeable. Since the late nineteenth century, the area had been a haven for eastern European Jews fleeing persecution in their homelands. During the First World War, the German military command forced Jews from their homes in German-occupied Poland in order to secure more workers for Berlin's war industries. Many ended up in the Scheunenviertel, now recognized as the chief "ghetto" of Berlin. The postwar era brought a new wave of refugees from Poland and Russia, where national independence and civil war were generating vicious pogroms. The majority of Berliners, including assimilated Jews who lived in wealthier, western parts of the city, rarely visited the Scheunenviertel, and when they did they found a world that struck them as quite foreign, and possibly dangerous. Venturing into the district in 1920, the writer Joseph Roth described a "strange sad ghetto world," devoid of the racing autos and glittering lights typical of western Berlin. The streets were filled with "grotesque eastern figures" holding "a thousand years of pain in their eyes" and wearing clothes that appeared to have been salvaged from a medieval rummage sale. While the men shuffled about in long black caftans, the women carried their children on their backs "like sacks of dirty laundry." Altogether, they seemed like "an avalanche of disaster and dirt, growing in volume and rolling irresistibly from the east over Germany."[19]

As Roth's comments suggest, and as Steven Aschheim has thoroughly documented in his classic study of the Ostjuden, *Brothers and Strangers,* the notion that the eastern European Jews constituted a foreign and unassimilable element was indeed pervasive in German society. These alien-looking creatures were widely decried as "dirty, loud, and coarse."[20] Significantly, this caricature image was propagated not only by gentile antisemites, but also by western European and (above all) German Jews, who were anxious to distinguish themselves from their less fortunate and less "emancipated" eastern brothers. Vilification of the Ostjuden accelerated during the war and in the immediate postwar period, with rightist

19. Michael Bienert, ed., *Joseph Roth in Berlin: Ein Lesebuch für Spaziergänger* (Cologne, 1996), 73–79.

20. Aschheim, *Brothers and Strangers,* 3.

groups such as the Alldeutscher Verband calling for the closing of Germany's borders to eastern Jews, or even for their expulsion from the country. The onset of the Great Inflation intensified this agitation, since Jews, having long been caricatured as scheming money manipulators, now were accused of milking the crisis for their own gain. This image found expression in some of the *Notgeld* (emergency currency) notes printed by German cities and other political entities during the inflation. Bills were emblazoned with caricatures of Jews busily pulling wires behind the scenes. One notable example showed a cabal of shifty-looking Jews identified as "the Wise Men of Zion"—a reference, of course, to "The Protocols of the Elders of Zion," a supposed blueprint for Jewish world domination that in reality was hatched in the fertile minds of the czarist secret police.[21] Although these caricatures embraced all Jews, they especially targeted the Ostjuden, who were thought to be the most adept at sharp financial practices.

In November 1923 the growing hysteria over "die Gefahr aus dem Osten" (the danger from the East), along with accumulated bitterness stemming from the socioeconomic dislocations of the Great Inflation, combined to produce the flash of violence in the Jewish ghetto that many had long anticipated. The trouble began at 11:00 A.M. on November 5 when a crowd of unemployed workers outside an employment office in the Alexanderstraße learned that they would receive no relief money that day. A rumor quickly spread through the ranks that eastern Jews from the neighboring Scheunenviertel had bought up all the relief money in order to loan it at exorbitant rates later on. Another rumor had it that Galician Jews were offering paper currency in exchange for any gold loan certificates the workers might possess. According to later accounts in the Social Democratic press, as well as reports by the Berlin police, the rumors were planted by "professional agitators" who worked the crowd at the behest of the Deutsche Herold, a *völkisch* organization.[22] If this was so, however, the police never brought charges against anyone for inciting a riot. Nor were any such characters specifically identified. There may certainly have been some provocateurs among the crowd, but it is likely that most of the "agitation" came from the workers themselves, who, of course, were amply familiar with the widely disseminated, racially based "explanations" for their economic woes.

Within less than an hour of the "no more money" announcement,

---

21. Liliane Weissberg, "Notenverkehr: Antisemitische Motive auf dem Notgeld der 20er Jahre," in *Abgestempelt: Judenfeindliche Postkarten,* edited by Helmut Gold and Georg Heuberger (Frankfurt, 1999), 276–83.

22. *Vorwärts,* November 6, 1923.

thousands of unemployed workers—as noted above, mainly young men— set off for the Scheunenviertel and began to loot shops up and down Grenadierstraße, Münzstraße, and Dragonerstraße. Proprietors who tried to defend their property were pulled into the streets and beaten. The owner of a kosher butcher shop was knocked about so badly that he died two days later from his injuries.[23] The son-in-law of another butcher was knifed repeatedly while trying to give shelter to a man who had crawled naked into the shop. The rioters also entered private homes and destroyed or pillaged their contents. They singled out Jews—or anyone who "looked Jewish"—beating them and sometimes stealing their clothes, which were thought to contain precious foreign currency sewn inside.[24]

The police did not arrive in any significant numbers until midafternoon. They closed off parts of the quarter but did not immediately expel the rioters. In fact, the first arrests they made were of Jews, supposedly for their "protection." About two hundred Jews were transported in trucks to the police barracks in the Alexanderplatz, where, according to later testimony, they were made to stand for hours with their hands over their heads. Those who protested were beaten. A Jewish doctor who had won the Iron Cross on the western front suffered a broken finger in his right hand. As he later noted, "The treatment accorded us Jews by the police did not leave me with the impression that I was living in a state of law."[25]

Faster on the scene were "self-defense" units from the Reichsbund jüdischer Frontsoldaten, which, alerted by a prearranged signal, arrived with rubber truncheons and pistols. It bears noting that the Reichsbund was a mainstream, deeply patriotic organization made up of assimilated Jews who traditionally had little use for the Ostjuden. However, the intensification of antisemitic sentiment during the war and the immediate postwar period, culminating in the Scheunenviertel attacks, caused these men to recognize a "Schicksalsgemeinschaft" (community of fate) with their eastern brothers, despite ongoing cultural differences.[26] The Reichsbund cadres immediately began to fight with the rioters, trying to drive them from the scene. During the melee a shot rang out, mortally wounding one of the rioters. It was assumed at the time that the shot was fired by a member of the Reichsbund (this assumption has also found its way into the historical literature), but later investigations revealed that the fatal shot came from a man firing out his window, probably to warn off the rioters.[27] In any event, after the shooting, the defense units holstered their pis-

23. Maurer, *Ostjuden,* 331.

24. *Vossische Zeitung,* November 6, 1923.

25. Ibid.

26. Aschheim, *Brothers and Strangers,* 244.

27. See, for example, Zilkenat, "Der Pogrom," 99; and Walter, *Antisemitische Kriminalität,* 153.

Fig. 1.   Berlin police, November 1923, at the corner of Münzstrasse. Note that a storekeeper tries to protect his store with a sign that says "Christian store" (Christliches Geschäft). (© Bilderdienst Süddeutscher Verlag, Munich.)

Fig. 2. Riots in the Scheunenviertel, November 1923. (Courtesy Bundesarchiv. Bild 183/1998/1201/500N.)

tols and did less fighting, but their continued presence in the streets probably intimidated some of the rioters.[28]

By midafternoon the situation had calmed somewhat in the quarter. But the calm lasted only until the onset of darkness, when rioting resumed afresh. Now some of the vandals carried a list of worthy targets, all of which were Jewish. (Here one can speak more assuredly of *völkisch* skullduggery, for this information was undoubtedly supplied by elements of the radical right.) Only after they had thoroughly plundered these shops did the police intervene, closing off the entire area and finally expelling the rioters by pushing them to the north. In the process they arrested about three hundred people, almost all of them unemployed workers. By midnight the district was again calm, though full of signs that it had just been a war zone: discarded booty littered the streets, glass from shop windows lay in shards on the sidewalks, bonfires smoldered here and there, and many stores sported signs saying "Christian-owned."[29]

---

28. Maurer, *Ostjuden,* 332–34.
29. *Vossische Zeitung,* November 6, 1923.

While the Scheunenviertel was being (belatedly) pacified, rioting spread to other parts of the city, including the relatively wealthy district of Charlottenburg. In the Invalidenstraße rioters gutted a shoe store and a canned-food emporium; in the Grolmanstraße they emptied a bakery; and in Kantstraße they pulled drivers from their cars and relieved them of their wallets. Rushing to the scene, police made quick use of their weapons, shooting and wounding two young men who were looting a bicycle store. The Prussian government threatened to call the Reichswehr into the streets if the violence continued.[30]

This proved unnecessary, for the wave of mass rioting ebbed during the course of the following day. A combination of tougher police measures and a reduction of the bread price to eighty billion marks no doubt helped to calm the situation. There were still, however, isolated acts of looting and vandalism. For example, a roving band plundered a cigar store and a jewelry shop in the Friedrichstraße. In Moabit a number of bakeries and a clothing store were hit. There was nothing particularly antisemitic about these actions, nor, in fact, about many of the other cases of looting and robbery that took place across the city during the rioting. When the final totals came in for the entire city, it turned out that 61 of the looted shops were Jewish-owned, while 146 belonged to Christians.[31]

The fact remains, however, that the most extensive damage by far was concentrated in the heavily Jewish Scheunenviertel, and the vast majority of individual assaults had been directed against Jews. This reality moved the local press to try to explain what liberal and socialist commentators were calling a "disgrace" in a city that considered itself worldly and progressive.[32] The spin that the various interpreters put on these events is as revealing as the events themselves—and in fact probably tells us more about the interpreters than about the actions they were trying to interpret.

Vorwärts, the SPD's main organ, argued that the riots were the culmination of "a calculated agitation by Deutschvölkisch elements against the Ostjuden" that had been going on since the war. The ugly events had the undeniable character of "an orchestrated pogrom," insisted the paper. Interestingly enough, however, the paper also accused the Communists, the Socialists' main rival on the left, of exploiting the misery of the unemployed for their own political purposes. *Völkisch* and Communist agitators had worked together to fan the flames of discontent, said *Vorwärts,* and their mutual goal was nothing less than the destruction of the Weimar Republic. As for the Berlin police (whose chief was a member of

---

30. Ibid.
31. Maurer, *Ostjuden,* 336.
32. *Berliner Tageblatt,* November 6, 1923; *Vossische Zeitung,* November 6, 1923; *Vorwärts,* November 6, 1923.

the SPD), the paper insisted that the authorities had performed as well as could have been expected under the circumstances. It noted that the police chief had explicitly instructed his men to protect all citizens "regardless of their religious confession." *Vorwärts* proposed, however, that the Berlin police might become more reliable protectors of public order if, as the chief himself had proposed, more members of the Socialist party became policemen.[33]

The liberal *Vossische Zeitung,* in an article entitled "Die Schuldigen" (the guilty), placed the blame for the riots squarely on the shoulders of the nationalist right. It noted that the *National Zeitung,* a mouthpiece of heavy industry, had for years been urging its readers to employ "propaganda of the deed" against the Ostjuden in the Scheunenviertel. While it was undeniably true, said the paper, that some of the Ostjuden were "exploiting the current disorder for private gain," the true wire-pullers behind the economic crisis were the barons of heavy industry, who had profited immensely from the collapse of the mark. Through papers like the *National Zeitung,* these men were fanning antisemitism in order to distract people from their own nefarious deeds. But if right-wing industrialists bore primary responsibility for the crisis, said "Auntie Voss" (as the *Vossische Zeitung* was called), the Social Democratic authorities in Berlin deserved censure for responding inadequately to its ugliest manifestations. The Berlin police had been too slow to intervene in the recent riots, and in some instances they had apparently mistreated Jewish victims of the violence. The paper reported that it had questioned the police chief on this matter, only to be brushed off with the blanket assurance that there were no antisemitic tendencies whatsoever in the police force. In order that "outrages" like the Scheunenviertel riots might never happen again, the *Vossische Zeitung* urged that the Berlin police become more vigilant and that "decent elements" in the nationalist camp condemn the violence.[34]

Not surprisingly, the *National Zeitung* disputed the charges that its articles about the "Jewish menace" had provoked the attacks in the Scheunenviertel. These actions had not resulted from any concerted agitation, contended the paper, but were the spontaneous outgrowth of popular rage over the "unscrupulous profiteering of the Jews in a time of widespread misery." The riots should be understood as a salutary lesson for all the Jews, as well as for all those Germans who allowed "alien elements" from the east to exploit the national crisis.[35]

Actually, the political faction that believed it had the most to learn from the Scheunenviertel riots was the young Nazi party, which was not

---

33. *Vorwärts,* November 7, 1923.
34. *Vossische Zeitung,* November 7, 1923.
35. *National Zeitung,* November 7, 1923.

yet much of a presence in Berlin but was about to embark on an abortive grab for national power from its base in Munich. Appraising the recent events in the capital, the *Völkische Beobachter* reported on November 8 that "the tumult in Berlin shows how all the signs today point clearly to a coming storm." Far from disputing the riots' antisemitic character, the Nazi paper said that they proved that Berlin was coming around to the wisdom of Munich, where Jews were kept properly in their place. The newspaper acknowledged that on one level the Berlin upheaval was odd, since the capital was "governed by Marxists." But it made sense when one appreciated how brazenly the Jews behaved there, how they had been allowed to plunder the native people for years. The paper further insisted that the chief responsibility for this sad state of affairs rested with the same forces that had produced the "crime" of November 9, 1918, whose fifth anniversary was now approaching. The criminals of November 1918 had allowed Jewish "parasitism" (*Schmarotzertum*) to run roughshod over Germany by holding down the only forces willing to eliminate this evil. Germany's current rulers should take good note of what had just happened in Berlin, insisted the paper, for this showed that the times were about to change.[36]

Berlin's large Jewish population, the group that had the most immediate reasons to be fearful about what had transpired in the capital, was deeply split over the riots' meaning and implications. Most Jewish commentators saw the November 1923 upheaval as a confirmation of warnings they had been making since the war about the likely outcome of unrelenting agitation against the Jews. They were also unanimous in condemning the political factions that sought to channel people's economic misery into racist attacks. But there were significant differences in their definition of the riots' nature and the lessons that ought to be drawn from them.

Before charting these divergences, we should note that they reflected broader differences within the Jewish community with respect to the nature of antisemitism and the threat it posed. While all Berlin's Jews were certainly cognizant of anti-Jewish sentiment in their city and nation, they had experienced it in different ways and to different degrees in their daily lives—and some were hardly troubled by it at all.[37] Ideological differences among German Jews also generated divergent perspectives on and reactions to antisemitism. Depending on which ideological camp they adhered to—say, Zionist or liberal-assimilationist—Jews could blame all Germans

---

36. *Völkische Beobachter,* November 8, 1923.

37. For the experiences of a highly assimilated young Jew, see Peter Gay, *My German Question: Growing Up in Nazi Berlin* (New Haven, 1998).

for antisemitism and find it fundamental to the national psyche, or they could consider it an aberration propagated by a misguided minority.[38]

Turning now to the responses to the Scheunenviertel rioting in the Jewish press, we see that the *Jüdische Rundschau,* chief organ of the German Zionist movement, summed up the meaning of the Scheunenviertel riots as "die Schicksalsstunde des deutschen Judentums" (the hour of fate for German Jewry)[39] The attacks proved that Jews were no longer safe in Germany, said the paper. Equality of treatment under the law, invariably held up as the basis for Jewish existence in the Diaspora, had been shaken. Indeed, the possible reintroduction of exceptional laws for Jews lay on the horizon. All the fruits of Jewish emancipation were vulnerable. The politics of assimilation, involving the systematic destruction of Jewish identity by the Jews themselves, had suffered (one hoped) a fatal mishap. German Jewry now had to face the fact that the accommodationist policy of the past century was completely bankrupt. All Jews must now realize that only the Jews could help themselves. Vulnerable and marginalized as they were, Jews must resist all tendencies likely to yield internal divisions. Above all, they must reject the supposed cultural line dividing Ostjuden and native Jews, along with efforts to "localize" the recent pogrom as an assault exclusively on eastern Jews. "This was not an *Ostjudenpogrom,*" said the paper, "it was a *Judenpogrom.*" Native Jews who hoped to save themselves by turning their backs on their eastern coreligionists would harvest only contempt and derision from their oppressors, to be added to the hatred already accorded all Jews in Germany.

This warning was, of course, aimed especially at the large Jewish assimilationist camp in Berlin, whose most extreme wing, the nationalist-German-Jewish faction, was quick to take up the challenge. Its organ, *Der nationaldeutsche Jude,* argued that the Ostjuden in the Scheunenviertel had partly brought on the trouble themselves by pursuing unethical currency transactions. It contended that the racist attacks, initially directed only at eastern Jews, had spread to the whole community because of the irresponsible actions of a few agitators. The events showed the need for native Jews to proclaim more passionately their Germanness and their identification with the fatherland, argued the journal. The paper even endorsed a comment from a Bavarian Jew who, concerned about separatist tendencies in

---

38. See, among others, Jehuda Reinharz, "The Zionist Response to Antisemitism in Germany," in *Year Book XXX of the Leo Baeck Institute* (London, 1985); and Werner Bergmann and Juliane Wetzel, "'Der Miterlebende weiß nichts': Alltagsantisemitismus als zeitgenössische Erfahrung und spätere Erinnerung (1919–1933)," in *Jüdisches Leben in der Weimarer Republik: Jews in the Weimar Republic,* edited by Wolfgang Benz, Arnold Paucker, and Peter Pulzer (Tübingen, 1998), 176–79.

39. *Jüdische Rundschau,* November 9, 1923.

his state, insisted that he would rather live as a "German under Hitler than as a Bavarian under France." Such words, insisted the *Nationaldeutsche Jude,* indicated the proper road for all German Jews, for it served to remind them that today was a *Schicksalsstunde* for all of Germany, not just for its Jewish citizens.[40]

Taking a more centralist position, the *Israelit,* the organ of Orthodox German Jewry, criticized the extremes within the Jewish community, rejecting both the *Nationaldeutsche Jude's* slurs against eastern Jews and the Zionists' wholesale condemnation of assimilation. It argued that the *Jüdische Rundschau's* call for a combative united front was unwise, for this would be grist for the mills of the antisemites. Nor was the *Israelit* willing to call the riots in the Scheunenviertel a "Judenpogrom," since, as the paper put it, these events "had not engaged the German soul in any intensity." Germany's Jews would be best advised to respond to the challenge of antisemitism by looking to their own souls and rekindling their religious faith, rather than by plunging into the political fray.[41]

Finally, the Centralverein deutscher Staatsbürger jüdischen Glaubens, the main organization of the assimilationists, also advised a spiritual look inward, but one that would not involve any turning away from a basic identification with the German fatherland. The Jews' salvation would not come from the outside, and certainly not from violent activism, said the group, but from the power of the Jews' own character and example. "If we exercise self-control, do not come across as too ostentatious (*nicht zu protzig auftreten*) but nonetheless bare our Jewishness with pride, we have no reason to fear the future," declared a representative for the group.[42]

We of course know what the future held for Europe's Jews, while contemporaries did not. But how, with that hindsight, are we to assess the significance of the Scheunenviertel riots of 1923?

The first point to note is a fact that impressed some contemporaries: namely, that the antisemitic actions in Berlin in the fall of 1923 were hardly confined to the capital. We have already mentioned the racist-tinged food riots in Karlsruhe and eastern Germany. Smaller attacks against Jews also took place in Erfurt, Nuremberg, Coburg, Bremen, Oldenburg, and Breslau.[43] Like the riots in Berlin, these actions were exploited by right-wing agitators who were pleased to see popular frustration over the chaotic economic situation spill over into physical assaults on local Jewish populations. In Bavaria, meanwhile, the archconservative regime of Gustav von

40. *Der Nationaldeutsche Jude,* October/November/December 1923, 1–5.
41. *Der Israelit,* November 15, 1923.
42. Maurer, *Ostjuden,* 344.
43. Feldman, *The Great Disorder,* 781.

Kahr won popular favor by summarily expelling from the state over one hundred so-called *ostjüdische* families, many of which turned out to be long-established residents. They were given just fourteen days to leave, and the property they left behind was confiscated. Kahr justified this action on the grounds that "the Jewish element [was] responsible for much of the German misfortune and economic distress since the war."[44]

Adolf Hitler, convinced that he, not Gustav von Kahr, was the right man to solve the "Jewish problem" on the national level, sought to seize power in Munich just a couple of days after the antisemitic rioting in Berlin. As is well known, on November 8–9, 1923, he launched his ill-fated Beer Hall Putsch. Although the Munich putsch and the rioting in Berlin were not directly connected, and there was no central direction behind the antisemitic disturbances elsewhere in the Reich, all these developments taken together revealed the breadth and depth of the political crisis gripping Germany at the height of the Great Inflation. We know now that the malaise was so damaging that the forthcoming currency stabilization and partial economic recovery after 1925 would not relieve people's sense of vulnerability nor end their distrust of a political system associated with economic chaos.

As some contemporary commentators pointed out, the Scheunenviertel riots exposed a readiness on the part of many Germans to blame Jews for their economic troubles. Of course there was nothing new in this, but it was ominous that the tendency had taken hold among the ranks of the unemployed working classes—many of whom were apparently losing faith in the SPD, their traditional focus of loyalty, and becoming vulnerable to the siren call of *völkisch* nostrums. It was also significant that the attacks were most pronounced in Berlin, which, in contrast to postwar Munich, was no *völkisch Hochburg*. The city was obviously, however, a highly volatile and unruly place, a happy hunting ground for extremist groups of all stripes. This volatility would help make it possible for the Nazis to establish a significant base in "Red Berlin" after Josef Goebbels became *Gauleiter* there in 1926.[45]

The riots also pointed up a problem in the way the authorities reacted to the challenge of violent antisemitism. Although the Berlin police eventually subdued the rioters, there can be no doubt that the forces of order did not respond as quickly or effectively as the citizens of Berlin, especially its Jewish citizens, had a right to expect. Although the chief of the Schutzpolizei denied it, his forces were in fact rife with antisemitism, as some members

44. Pommerin, "Ausweisung von 'Ostjuden,'" 323.

45. For Goebbels's own account of this process, see his *Kampf um Berlin* (Munich, 1934).

admitted.[46] We know that this would not change significantly over the course of the Weimar Republic, even though the Berlin and Prussian police forces were regarded as relatively pro-Republican.[47]

Finally, the divisions within the Jewish community exposed by the Scheunenviertel riots would resurface with a vengeance when the community faced the more far-reaching challenge of Nazism. Once again, Berlin's (and Germany's) Jews would respond in very different ways, some making distinctions between the probable fate of "eastern Jews" and native citizens, some finding Zionism the only possible answer, some trying actively to cooperate with their persecutors, and most—at least among the ranks of the deeply assimilated—simply hoping that their long record of patriotism and loyalty to the fatherland would see them through, especially if they kept a low profile. Tragically, this illusion meant that thousands of Germany's Jews remained in the Reich until it was too late to leave.[48]

Without building the Scheunenviertel rioting of 1923 into a full-scale dress rehearsal for the catastrophic drama to come—there were, for example, important differences between the 1923 event and the infamous "Reichskristallnacht" pogrom of November 1938—we cannot ignore the danger that this action represented. The attacks in 1923 may have focused on the Ostjuden, which was reprehensible in itself, but the hatred behind them, as some commentators recognized at the time, certainly encompassed all Jews. Summarizing this fatal conjuncture, Steven Aschheim could justly write, "The Ostjuden were clearly a metaphor for all Jews well before the undiscriminating devastation of the Holocaust."[49] Thus we can conclude that the *Völkische Beobachter* was not entirely off the mark when it claimed that the events in Berlin pointed toward a "coming storm," even if that storm came somewhat later than the paper predicted.

---

46. Maurer, *Ostjuden,* 347–54.

47. See HsiHuey Liang, *The Berlin Police Force in the Weimar Republic* (Berkeley, 1970).

48. For a discussion of this issue, see John V. H. Dippel, *Bound on a Wheel of Fire: Why So Many Jews Made the Tragic Decision to Remain in Nazi Germany* (New York, 1996).

49. Aschheim, *Brothers and Strangers,* 245.

The November Pogrom of 1938: Participation, Applause, Disapproval

Wolfgang Benz
Translated by Miriamne Fields

The events of November 9–10, 1938, along with the prelude and after-math, constitute one of the most thoroughly researched chapters in the history of Jewish persecution under the Nazi regime.[1] Not only are there numerous reports by witnesses from this period, particularly by people who fled into exile immediately following "Kristallnacht," but the pogrom also plays a central role in local history, a field that has received growing attention since the 1980s.[2] This is partly because the burned-down syna-gogues, the demolished Jewish shops, and the violent harassment and killings of local Jews marked the end of Jewish life in many German-Jew-ish communities.

Research initially focused on establishing the course and direction of events, and later on identifying the triggers and goals of the pogroms. The prevailing assumption was that a minority of fanatics engaged in violent acts amid the silent disapproval of the majority. In the 1980s, a large num-ber of local studies offered a detailed and differentiated picture, which in

---

Translated from the German.

1. The first study was Hermann Graml's oft-reprinted text *Der 9. November 1938: Reichkristallnacht* (Bonn, 1953).

2. See the relevant collections at the Leo Baeck Institute in New York, the Wiener Library in London (on microfilm), the Institut für Zeitgeschichte in Munich, and the Zen-trum für Antisemitismusforschung at the Technical University of Berlin.

turn led to the question of how the pogroms in the cities differed from those in the countryside.[3] With a degree of caution, one can say that the brutality of the aggression in the countryside tended to be greater than in urban areas. But to this generalization there are exceptions, such as the pogrom in Düsseldorf.[4] Perhaps a more important question at this point concerns the behavior of the bystanders.

Since the spring of 1933, violent acts against Jews had been perceived as a public display of National Socialist conviction. Following the Reichstag elections on March 5, 1933, an increasing number of violent antisemitic incidents emerged in several areas. Riots against Jews occurred on the Kurfürstendamm in Berlin; in Breslau, where SA men forced their way into the courthouse and mistreated a Jewish lawyer and judge; and in Görlitz, where judges and lawyers were dragged out of a meeting into the streets. There were also violent incidents in Munich, Wiesbaden, and Magdeburg. In Königsberg, the synagogue went up in flames. In a number of areas, deaths were reported.[5] One month after the elections, on the day of the anti-Jewish boycott of April 1, 1933, violence broke out yet again.

Still, until November 9, 1938, the incidents were of a local nature. The violence was neither organized nor centrally directed. The pogrom of November 1938 marks both the final decay of civic behavior in Germany among the majority and, within the state, the turn from legislative and administrative discrimination to brute force against the Jewish minority. Prior to this date, the regime had pursued two kinds of policies against the Jews. On the one hand, individual acts of violence were tolerated. On the other, administrative measures were used to ostracize the Jewish community. But the violence remained spontaneous or, at worst, under the responsibility of local officials. It was not authorized at the highest level. There was also a recognizable change in the reaction of the population, which during the boycott in 1933 had in part shown open solidarity with the Jews. Even in 1938, the pogrom and subsequent unrest never met with the approval of the majority of the population. Although the pogrom was a clear indication of upcoming policies, the further acts of exclusion and persecution were again based on administrative measures. Nevertheless, the day of the state-planned pogrom against the Jews on November 9, 1938, represents a caesura.

---

3. As an important example, see Andreas Heusler and Tobias Weger, *"Kristallnacht": Gewalt gegen die Münchener Juden im November 1938* (Munich, 1998).

4. Max Eschelbacher, *Der zehnte November 1938*, with an introduction, "Rabbiner Max Eschelbacher und der Novemberpogrom in Düsseldorf," by Falk Wiesemann (Essen, 1998).

5. See Michael Wildt, "Gewalt gegen Juden in Deutschland, 1933 bis 1938," *Werkstatt Geschichte* 18 (1997): 59–80.

The pretext was the assassination of a civil servant of the German embassy in Paris by seventeen-year-old Herschel Grynszpan. The young Jew had wanted to protest the German regime's decision to brutally expel Polish Jews from Germany in response to the Polish expatriation of the Jews.[6] The news of the diplomat's death on November 9 reached the major Nazi figures, who were gathered at the Altes Rathaus in Munich for their annual celebration of Hitler's attempted coup of 1923. From the standpoint of Nazi leaders, it was a propitious moment for the pogrom. A press campaign had assured a fervent mood. In Kurhesse and Anhalt, as well as in Kassel, Dessau, and a number of smaller cities, local inhabitants had already destroyed synagogues and Jewish shops, and the press was exploiting these events. In Munich, on the evening of November 9, during the solemn celebration of the "Old Fighters" in the Altes Rathaus, Goebbels, with the agreement of Hitler, preached revenge and retribution for the assassination. The summons was transmitted by telephone to meeting halls throughout Germany, where the putsch of 1923 was also being celebrated.

It was easy to mobilize the SA and activists of the Nazi party (NSDAP). The call from Munich for a pogrom reached the meeting places of the party, the SA, and the National Socialist Motor Transport Corps (Nationalsozialistisches Kraftfahrerkorps, NSKK) between 11 P.M. and midnight. It was then transmitted by SA leaders, district leaders, and local group leaders of the NSDAP, town mayors, and other functionaries.[7] Within a few hours, National Socialists throughout Germany had received their instructions. They began to set synagogues ablaze, to publicly abuse Jews, and to destroy and pillage Jewish property. Dressed mostly in civilian clothing, SA men and members of other party divisions, such as the NSKK and Hitler Youth, displayed "spontaneous seething wrath" in front of the offices of the Jewish community as well as the shops and apartments of well-known Jews. They hooted and smashed windows. They targeted synagogues, smashing down the doors, devastating the interiors, and setting fire to the temples. The fire departments had received clear orders not to save the burning synagogues but to protect neighboring houses should the flames threaten to spread. Throughout the country, the SA and NSDAP leaders—who were often mayors as well—led the mob in barging

---

6. Michael G. Esch, "Die Politik der polnischen Vertretungen im Deutschen Reich, 1935 bis 1939 und der Novemberpogrom 1938," *Jahrbuch für Antisemitismusforschung* 8 (1999): 131–54; Bettina Goldberg, "Die Zwangsausweisung der polnischen Juden aus dem Deutschen Reich im Oktober 1938 und die Folgen," *Zeitschrift für Geschichtswissenschaft* 46 (1998): 971–84.

7. See Dieter Obst, *"Reichskristallnacht": Ursachen und Verlauf des antisemitischen Pogroms vom November 1938* (Frankfurt/Main, 1991).

into apartments, destroying furniture, intimidating Jews, and abusing and humiliating respected businessmen, lawyers, rabbis, and other people of repute, for example, by forcing them out into the streets in their pajamas.

Many party and SA members, who since the "period of struggle" had been eager for action, enthusiastically approved of the NSDAP's call for a pogrom. The major motivation for their frenzy to destroy objects and people was the appeal of partaking in a party demonstration of power, and the memory of the "period of struggle" prior to 1933. The tide of vandalism, carried out by the official actors as part of an organized riot, also swept up onlookers. Some of the outsiders who joined in were motivated by antisemitic propaganda, reacting to Grynszpan's murder of the diplomat. Others were releasing stifled aggression. Because the acts were state-sanctioned, murder and destruction could be carried out in public. A number of examples of this phenomenon also emerge from smaller towns. That the German population took pleasure in the suffering of the Jews is made indisputably clear by the plundering, extortion, and denunciations from which the public benefited at the expense of the Jews, who had been stripped of their rights. Jewish shops were taken over after the pogrom, as were apartments, offices, doctors' practices, and other properties.

The November pogrom occurred under the influence of National Socialist propaganda. The newspapers, controlled by Goebbels's propaganda machine, reported in unison that the "wrath of the people" had erupted.[8] Although everyone knew that the pogrom had been orchestrated and directed by the regime, reports and public statements presented the official image of a German people indignant over the Herschel Grynszpan's assassination of the legal secretary Ernst vom Rath in Paris, spontaneously expressing its emotion throughout the cities and towns.

I

In this study, our interest lies not in the circumstances under which members of the NSDAP and its organizations were ordered to incite a pogrom, nor in how their leaders, through inflammatory speeches, goaded members into committing violence against Jewish places of worship, Jewish prop-

---

8. On the circumstances and course of the events, see primarily Hermann Graml, *Antisemitism in the Third Reich* (Oxford, 1992); Walter H. Pehle, ed., *Der Judenpogrom 1938: Von der "Reichskristallnacht" zum Völkermord* (Frankfurt/Main, 1988); Wolfgang Benz, "Der November-Pogrom 1938," in *Die Juden in Deutschland, 1933–1945: Leben unter nationalsozialistischer Herrschaft,* edited by Wolfgang Benz (Munich, 1993); and Wolf-Arno Kropat, *"Reichskristallnacht": Der Judenpogrom vom 7. bis 10. November 1938—Urheber, Täter, Hintergründe* (Wiesbaden, 1997).

Fig. 1. In Mosbach, furniture and sacred objects from the synagogue are burned in a pile in the marketplace, November 10, 1938. (© Hauptstaatsarchiv Stuttgart. EA 99/001, Bü 305.)

Fig. 2.   Citizens of Mosbach gather around to watch the burning of the furniture and sacred articles of the synagogue. (© Hauptstaatsarchiv Stuttgart. EA 99/001, Bü 305. All rights reserved.)

erty, and Jewish people. Neither does our study concern the provocateurs and external shock troops, who set the pogrom in motion where local representatives of the party, the SA, and other formations failed to react to the central call for action. We are, instead, principally concerned with the participation of ordinary citizens in the events of November 9, 1938. More precisely still, we are concerned with the relative involvement of different groups, and how the pogroms developed in the countryside and in the cities.

From official reports, we learn little about the reactions of neighbors and passersby, witnesses and bystanders, or about how the pogrom was received by the majority of Germans. Victims' reports that were deposited in archives as unpublished witness accounts or that make up part of the autobiographical literature on the persecution of the Jews contain detailed descriptions of the events, as well as references to both resistance and reserve among the spectators. The Sopade Reports of the intelligence service of the Social Democratic Party's government-in-exile, which, as the voice of opposition, spread news from Germany, are another source for assessing the November pogrom. These reports cover a wide range of regions throughout Germany and are thus more representative than individual victims' reports. Yet they paint an overly rosy picture of popular rejection of the pogrom.

Under the headline "Rejection among the People," for example, the Sopade report for November 1938 claims that "the riots were severely criticized by the majority of the German people." Thus in the Rhineland, the brutal measures "evoked great indignation among the population"; in Cologne the pogrom was not met with "a friendly echo"; and in southwest Germany, the "incidents were generally judged negatively." In Bavaria, according to the reports, the general population had no interest in the Nazi activity. The Berliners' clear protest against "the misdeeds against Jewish men, women, and children" ranged "from scornful glances and gestures of disgust to open words of revolt and excessive swearing." Finally, in Silesia, it was becoming ever clearer that the population disapproved of these excesses.[9]

These reports are not transparent windows onto popular motivations. It remains highly questionable whether one can infer from such reports that the popular reaction was one of either general disapproval of the violence against the Jewish population, or sympathy for the victims of the pogrom.

Partly, responses depended upon the milieu from which people came.

---

9. *Deutschland-Berichte der Sozialdemokratischen Partei Deutschlands (Sopade), 1934–1940,* 5 (1938): 1204f. (Reprint, Frankfurt a.M., 1980.)

One can conclude from a report of the National Socialist Teachers Union in the Traunstein district that the mood was positive regarding the peaceful incorporation of the Sudetenland, and that this move "was not, for the most part, spoiled by actions against the Jews." But after the November 1938 pogrom "the peasants and citizens, especially the blacks [i.e., Catholics], and even a party comrade condemned the use of violence against the 'chosen people.' That goes beyond culture and decency." The disapproval of the action was attributed to the influence of the Catholic Church. Similar reports came from the heavily Catholic area of Lower Franconia. The population found it regrettable that in the violence, raw materials that "could have been used for the common good" were being destroyed. The rural population particularly criticized the destruction of food. In the Oberelsbach community, where three and a half quintals of flour was thrown onto manure, and a crate of eggs was tossed onto the street, numerous "national comrades," according to a report from the district office of Bad Neustadt a.d. Saale, refused to donate to the winter relief collection. The president of Upper Bavaria reported criticism of the use of violence in the organized protest against the Jews. In general, state officials were more reserved than party officials in their reports on the pogroms. The NSDAP district propaganda leader in Franconia reported that "during the Jewish action, the people were thoroughly in the hands of the Party," and spirits remained high.[10]

In state and party reports on the popular mood during the November pogrom, there is little evidence of basic criticism, principled reservation, siding with the victims, or even signs of solidarity with the Jews. In these reports, the criticism that does exist refers almost exclusively to the brutality and to the destruction of material goods. Typical in this sense is a monthly report by the president of Lower Bavaria and Upper Palatinate concerning sentiment in the countryside.

> The Jewish act of murder against a German diplomat in Paris caused utter indignation among the population in all the districts. In general, the government was expected to intervene. The legal measures directed against Jewry were therefore met with total understanding. All the more reason why the majority of the population found little to understand in the manner in which the spontaneous actions against the Jews were performed; they were condemned by all, even among the inner circles of the Party. In the destruction of shop windows,

---

10. Martin Broszat, Elke Fröhlich, and Falk Wiesemann, eds., *Bayern in der NS-Zeit: Soziale Lage und politisches Verhalten der Bevölkerung im Spiegel vertraulicher Berichte* (Munich, 1977), 470ff.

store contents, and apartment furniture, one saw the unnecessary ruin of objects of value, which ultimately was a loss of wealth for the German nation and flagrantly contradicted the aims of the Four-Year Plan, especially in regard to the recent collection of used material. The fear was expressed that in this manner, the drive to vandalize could be aroused among the masses. What's more, the incidents evoke sympathy for the Jews.[11]

Descriptions and judgments of collective behavior against the riot victims can also be found in the numerous court files of trials to investigate and punish the crimes of the Kristallnacht. These trials began immediately following the collapse of the Nazi state and continued well into the 1950s. The reports of both victims and sympathetic bystanders often express disapproval of the incidents and mention offers of assistance on the following day by observers or passersby. This suggests that a silent majority in large cities expressed solidarity with the discriminated and humiliated minority. By contrast, legal investigations in the smaller cities and towns show plainly that a clear division did not exist between activists who served as ringleaders—the functionaries of the NSDAP and its organizations—and bystanders. Evidence about behavior during the pogrom also emerged independently of the criminal proceedings' determinations of "disturbance of the peace" or "severe disturbance of the peace" through the unlawful assembly of people (who, as individuals, may not have participated actively in the events). At first, bystanders were caught in the whirlwind of the vandalistic avant-garde: curious onlookers mixed with raving fanatics, forming a marauding, hooting, violent mob charging through the streets. A desire for excitement drove people out into the streets, where it seemed that neighbors had turned into plundering intruders, and individual citizens had become part of a collective frenzy. This impression is supported by numerous examples.

Perpetrators included fanatic National Socialists as well as people who were lured into the action and those who just happened to be at the site. Such was the case in the small Hessian town of Assenheim, which at the time had 1,216 inhabitants, including twenty-one Jews. In Assenheim, a seventeen-year-old bricklayer's assistant who was not a Nazi and was otherwise of good character returned home on vacation from duty at the Siegfried Line (the fortification under construction along the western boundaries of the Reich). In his hometown, he quickly fell in with the mob that had formed in broad daylight and joined it in wreaking havoc, forcing his way into the house of a Jewish citizen, abusing him, kicking him, and

---

11. Ibid.

then forcing him outside, where the man collapsed. The boy continued to hit him as he lay on the ground, until finally another man came to the victim's aid.[12] In the Hessian town of Büdingen, a similar case occurred. There, an eighteen-year-old butcher's apprentice who was considered to be a hardworking and capable young man and who belonged neither to the Hitler Youth nor to the NSDAP beat a sixty-year-old Jewish woman who had never done anything to him. He hit her and kicked her for more than three hundred meters through the town, all the while threatening to throw her into the water.[13]

One of the most closely documented cases concerns the town of Treuchtlingen in Middle Franconia. In 1946 and 1947, fifty-six citizens from Treuchtlingen, which had a total population in 1933 of 4,227, were tried in court for their participation in the local pogrom.[14] Eight of the accused were women. In contrast to other pogroms, the women's participation in Treuchtlingen allows for general conclusions to be drawn concerning women's roles in the pogroms. In general, the participation of women was noted as consisting of scornful laughter, staring curiosity, or plundering. In Treuchtlingen, however, women were charged with disturbing the peace, and there is no doubt that they were not only agitators, but also actively engaged in violence and destruction. Sofie O., for example, not only shouted, "The Jewish swine hasn't had enough," she also shattered the windows of a Jewish doctor's home. Nora A. was responsible for calling SA men back to Jewish premises that had already been demolished and for shouting, "At Guttmann's there is more to be smashed." She also slashed the beds and upholstery at another house, carried gasoline to the synagogue that was to be set on fire, trampled on merchandise in the window of a Jewish shop, and called to a Jew who was crying for help, "You'd better get out of here, you Jewish swine, otherwise we're gonna beat you to death." Other women also stood out in the pogrom. Hannchen B. expressed her satisfaction at seeing the burning synagogue, and Amalie B., upon seeing the SA withdraw from the property of a Jew, shouted reproachfully, "Look, the Jewish swine hasn't had enough. We have to call the SA back!" Thus another troop of SA men continued the devastation. Ottilie H. participated in the vandalism by slashing beds and upholstery, calling back the pogrom troops, and destroying the dis-

---

12. Giessen regional court verdict, September 17, 1938, in Klaus Moritz and Ernst Noam, *NS-Verbrechen vor Gericht 1945–1955: Dokumente aus hessischen Justizakten* (Wiesbaden, 1978), 132, Archiv Institut für Zeitgeschichte München (IfZ), Gg 01.47.

13. Giessen regional court verdict, January 6, 1949, ibid., 185f., IfZ, Gg 01.08.

14. The legal proceedings of the Nürnberg-Fürth regional court began on December 12, 1945; the verdict is dated November 14, 1947. IfZ, Gn 02.10. Wildt's case study ("Gewalt gegen Juden") examines in detail the occurrences in Treuchtlingen.

played merchandise of a Jewish shop. Leni K., who had large debts at a Jewish shop, forced her way into the building along with the crowd and participated in the destruction of the business records.

Pogroms offer an opportunity to indulge in sadistic, infantile, sexist, aggressive behavior. This was true for the Kristallnacht as well. It is striking that the release of this energy did not require the shield of anonymity offered by a foreign town or a large city. These excesses occurred instead in hometowns and local neighborhoods, where victims and perpetrators knew each other as neighbors and fellow citizens.[15]

The events in Rimbach (Odenwald) may serve as an example. On the evening of November 9, NSDAP members gathered in the local tavern with the local group leader, who called for the mistreatment of the Jews and the destruction of their property. At midnight, the participants gathered at the schoolyard and were split into groups by the group leader. One of these groups was made up of six men between the ages of twenty-four and forty-one. A thirty-seven-year-old took on the role of ringleader, and they set off for the home of the Weichsel family. They circled the house for a while, then smashed open the front and back doors and dragged the married couple out of bed. While the husband, after being severely beaten, fled from the house, his wife, wearing only a nightgown, was sprayed with water; three men flipped her on her head, then "beat her between the legs with a broom and poured water there." Afterward one of the perpetrators boasted at having "grasped Frau Weichsel's breasts." This group then banded together with other men during the night and roamed the streets of the town, devastating the homes of all the Jewish families and afterward meeting again at the tavern. It did not stop there, however. After they had drunk for a while, one of them suggested that they put Leo Wetterhahn "on ice." A group of six set off again and entered the damaged property of the Jewish man. The two youngest perpetrators (twenty-four and twenty-six years old) brought ice blocks from a nearby business belonging to the father of one of the men. They forced the victim to sit naked for ten minutes on the ice and to hold another block of ice on his head. The man suffered second-degree frostbite. After returning to the tavern for a while, the offenders set off to the house that they had first attacked, destroyed more furniture, and again abused the Weichsels.[16]

Had the pogrom organizers feared that locals would be too reluctant to act violently against their own neighbors, strangers would have com-

---

15. Christhard Hoffmann, "Verfolgung und Alltagsleben der Landjuden im national-sozialistischen Deutschland," in *Jüdisches Leben auf dem Lande: Studien zur deutsch-jüdischen Geschichte,* edited by Monika Richarz and Reinhard Rürup (Tübingen, 1997), 373–98.

16. Case before the Darmstadt regional court, indictment, September 24, 1946, IfZ, Gd 01.47.

mitted the crimes instead. This was not the case in Rimbach, but "pogrom tourism" did nonetheless exist. Locals encouraged eager strangers to pass by and vandalize Jewish property, all the while assuring them of approval for their actions. The inhibition against using violence on the stigmatized minority was so low, and the latent willingness to ostracize them through excessive abuse was already present to such a degree, that the mere call for violence by the local party functionaries sufficed to set in motion the pogrom mechanism in rural areas.

The fact that adults encouraged children and young people to participate in the pogrom suggests the enthusiasm with which the aims of the regime were, for the most part, shared by the inhabitants of rural areas. In the villages of Grossen-Linden and Leihgestern in the district of Giessen, on the morning of November 10, an ever-growing crowd roamed the streets, inflicting violence on the Jews under the direction of the NSDAP local group leader and the mayor. The school principal, following the wishes of the mayor, ordered some two hundred schoolchildren, under the supervision of their teachers, to attend the demonstration. They wandered through the community, obeying the demand to smash the windows of Jewish shops, until they were completely out of control.[17]

Such incidents also show an alarming degree of consensus and cooperation among local inhabitants. The development of the pogrom in Wachenbuchen in the Hanau district offers illuminating details in this respect. The local group leader and mayor of the town had organized a public rally at the local tavern on the evening of November 8, one day prior to the centrally organized violence against the Jews. Two hundred people attended the rally, including fifteen to twenty SA men. The crowd was called upon to tear down the Jewish schoolhouse and to give the Jewish teacher a "rubdown." The mayor was well aware that such activities were unlawful, for when the designated participants arrived at eleven o'clock at night to begin the destruction, he cautioned them to be careful, so as not to "become acquainted with the state prosecutors." Guards were assigned so that the police would not surprise them. A crowd of three hundred gathered to watch, and between thirty-five and forty people entered the schoolhouse. There the teacher was attacked with an axe, and the rioters began to dismantle the roof, throw furniture out the windows, and tear the walls down. They had brought the necessary tools with them. At around one o'clock in the morning, the chairman of the rural district council arrived with the NSDAP district leader and the district propaganda leader. They had been called in by the mayor, who, struck with fear, now denied his role in the events. He also claimed that the action had been set

---

17. Verdict, Giessen regional court, March 2, 1949, IfZ, Gg 01.23.

in motion without his approval and that he had already gone to bed. The council chairman forbade further destruction and assigned guards, this time to prevent further rioting. He also declared the schoolhouse to be in a state of decay and ready for demolition. The sole motivation for these measures was that on this evening a ban still existed on individual acts of violence against Jews. On the following evening—November 9—the pogromists and crowds gathered again, this time with the consent and encouragement of the authorities, to complete the demolition of the schoolhouse. The chairman of the council had not wanted to limit the damage or prevent escalation when he had prohibited further action on the first night; instead, he had merely feared the consequences. On the first pogrom night, he had told the crowd they should have beaten the Jewish teacher to death instead of letting him get away.[18]

II

The recorded memories of victims often note demonstrations of solidarity among non-Jews who were critical of the regime and who expressed noticeable disapproval of the organized violence as well as shame over the violation of civil norms of decency. These examples do not diminish the abundant evidence of collective barbarism. However, they must be taken into consideration in what is otherwise a much less optimistic picture.

Ruth Andreas-Friedrich, who was riding in a bus along the Kurfürstendamm on November 10, makes an observation that illuminates one facet of the majority's conduct. The complicated mixture of shame and inaction also seems more typical of testimonies concerning the reaction of ordinary people in a large city such as Berlin.

> The bus conductor looks at me as if he wanted to tell me something important. But then he just shakes his head and looks guiltily to the side. The other passengers don't look up at all. Each face bore an expression as if wanting somehow to ask forgiveness. The Kurfürstendamm is an ocean of shattered glass. At the corner of Fasanenstrasse, the people are gathering. A silent mass moving in the direction of the synagogue stares at the dome which is shrouded in clouds of smoke. "A damned disgrace" whispers a man next to me. I look at him warmly. It occurs to me, that this would be the right time to say "brother" to those nearby. But I don't. That is the kind of thing you never do. You only think it. And when you finally muster up the

---

18. Verdict, Hanau regional court, March 17, 1947, IfZ, Gh 04.06, published in Moritz and Noam, *NS-Verbrechen vor Gericht,* 142.

courage and make a start, then you end up merely asking "ah, excuse me, could you tell me what time it is?" and are ashamed to no end of your cowardliness. But we all do feel like brothers. We, the people sitting here in the bus, are dying of shame. Brothers of shame, we are comrades of the same remorse. If everyone is ashamed, then who smashed the windows?[19]

There is evidence that many Germans were ashamed of the events of November 1938 and shocked by what they considered a relapse into barbarism: the public scenes of humiliation, the pillaging of property, and the abuse of a minority that in the fall of 1935 had been stripped of their rights as full citizens. Some Germans even responded beyond merely feeling shame. Some became active by showing solidarity with the persecuted minority or by engaging in resistance against the regime. The following examples of civil courage, decency, and protest against the ruling powers suggest what was possible.

In the central district of Berlin, SA men arrived at the New Synagogue at Oranienburger Strasse 30 and set fire to the entrance hall. The synagogue, whose completion had been celebrated in 1866, contained three thousand seats and a glorious interior; it was one of the most magnificent Jewish places of worship in Germany. The lavishly designed façade and the golden cupola that could be seen from afar demonstrated outwardly the claim and rank of the building. This did not trouble the arsonists, however. Yet a man named Wilhelm Krützfeld, the chief of police precinct 16 at Hackescher Markt, prevented them from destroying more of the building. Armed with a document certifying that the building was protected under historical preservation laws, he rushed to the synagogue with a few other policemen, pushed the SA men aside, and called in the fire department, which actually arrived and extinguished the fire. The precinct chief had to answer to the police director on November 11, but he was not punished. Upon his own request, he retired in 1942. By then he had been a longtime opponent of the regime.[20]

Another case of active resistance involved the regional court director of Landshut, Dr. Ignaz Tischler, a conservative. At the time of the November pogrom, he was sixty-two years old. From 1918 to 1933, he had been a member of the German Nationalist People's Party, and in order to boost his career, he had even joined the NSDAP in 1935. But on the afternoon of November 10, 1938, Dr. Tischler proved that he had not been led

---

19. Ruth Andreas-Friedrich, *Schattenmann: Berlin Underground, 1938–1945* (New York, 1999).

20. See Heinz Knobloch, *Der beherzte Reviervorsteher: Ungewöhnliche Zivilcourage am Hackeschen Markt* (Berlin, 1990).

astray from his conservative thinking. When one of the court employees boasted of having demolished the home of the Jewish businessman Ansbacher together with other SA men during the night, the court director replied that, were he to preside over their case in court, he would charge them with reparations and possibly impose a jail sentence. On the following evening at a rally, Tischler was attacked by NSDAP district leaders. The incident was in the local papers on November 12, and on the same afternoon the judge was dragged through the city by fifty young people, led by a NSKK head troop commander. He was kicked and derided as a "Jew servant" and "swine dog." He also had to carry a poster before the howling crowd that read "Tischler is a national traitor. He belongs in Dachau."[21]

The case is significant in that beyond the public defamation, nothing happened to Tischler. His superior, the Landshuter regional court president, was so skilled in handling the relationship between the official claim of "spontaneous wrath," which had supposedly led to the pogrom, and the NSDAP's actual steering of events that Tischler jumped all of the hurdles set before him, from the threatened legal indictment (for violating the "treachery law") to the party proceedings. His application for retirement was pointless; his rehabilitation in 1947 during the denazification process proved difficult (because he had been a member of the NSDAP), but his second attempt in 1948 was successful.

Julius von Jan, the minister in Oberlenningen (Württemberg), did not get off as lightly. His sermon on the Day of Repentance in November 1938 clearly condemned the pogrom.

> A crime has been committed in Paris. The murderer will receive his due punishment for transgressing the divine law. Together with the entire nation, we mourn the victim of this criminal act. But who would have thought that a crime in Paris could result in so many crimes at home in Germany? We paid with consequences for turning away from God and Christ, for the organized anti-Christianity. Passions are released; God's law disdained; houses of worship, holy to others, have been burned to the ground with impunity; the property of others has been robbed or ruined; men who loyally served our nation, conscientiously fulfilling their duty, have been thrown in concentration camps, merely because they belong to another race! The powers above may not want to admit the injustice—the healthy

---

21. Alfons Beckenbauer, "Das mutige Wort des Dr. Tischler zur Kristallnacht in Landshut," *Verhandlungen des historischen Vereins für Niederbayern* 98 (1972): 21–36; Wolfgang Benz, "Die Entnazifizierung der Richter," in *Justizalltag im Dritten Reich,* edited by B. Diestelkamp and M. Stolleis (Frankfurt/Main, 1988), 126.

national perception feels it clearly, even when no one dares to speak of it.[22]

The sermon was delivered on November 16. Nine days later, a troop of two hundred National Socialists appeared before the Oberlenningen parish, beat up the pastor, and dragged him to the Kirchheim/Teck prison. After four months' incarceration, he was expelled from Württemberg and worked as a parish administrator in Bavaria. The following year he was indicted for violating the "treachery law" and sentenced to sixteen months in prison. He was later released on probation and ultimately conscripted into the army. In September 1945 he returned to his position in the parish in Oberlenningen. Pastor Jan and his family received assistance and words of praise from the ranks of the Confessional Church; the official Protestant church, in contrast, was reserved in its response. A decree from the church leadership in Württemberg, dated December 6, 1938, referred to the Day of Repentance sermon with the comment that it was "a matter of certainty that the servants of the Church . . . should avoid everything that could be equated with an inadmissible criticism of concrete political activity." The church leadership, despite all its reservations about National Socialism, strove for a peaceful relationship with the state authorities.

Yet even those who, like Pastor Jan, were ashamed of the crimes of the Nazi regime, or those who, like precinct chief Krützfeld, showed civil courage, or those who expressed solidarity with the Jews after the pogrom, could not possibly have envisioned that the men in power planned to force the Jews into ghettos or, even worse, drive them out of Germany completely—or, indeed, kill them. How could they have imagined Auschwitz? The total exclusion of Jews, which began with the November pogrom, went beyond even the imagination of those immediately affected by the National Socialist racist mania.

Outside Germany, the violation of basic virtues such as respect for private property, frugality, honoring religious sites, and neighborly conduct (which covers the entire range of behavior from expressing reserve to helpfulness) was registered with amazement. The everyday norms of acceptable civic behavior in a constitutional state seemed to be suspended during the November pogrom. Commentaries noting such changes could be found in the columns of the international press. The German Reich had demonstrated before the entire world that it was no longer a constitutional state. Although civic conventions were still valid, they applied neither to the Jews in Germany nor, if so desired, to other minorities.

---

22. Wording of sermon quoted in Georg Denzler and Volker Fabricius, *Christen und Nationalsozialisten* (Frankfurt/Main, 1933), 340f. See also Wolfgang Gerlach, *Als die Zeugen schwiegen: Bekennende Kirche und die Juden* (Berlin, 1987), 238.

III

The November 1938 pogrom was staged as a ritual of public degradation of the Jewish minority. The destruction of Jewish property and the derision and abuse of people during the night and the following day served this purpose. So, too, did the aftermath of the pogrom. In the following weeks and months, the National Socialists maltreated and incarcerated 26,500 Jewish men (the "Aktionsjuden") in the concentration camps of Dachau, Buchenwald, and Sachsenhausen.[23] No doubt, these men saw better what the future held. Hitler's order to imprison twenty to thirty thousand Jewish men was aimed at putting pressure on the Jews to emigrate. To this end, well-situated Jews were selected for imprisonment, then released when family members produced visas and travel tickets for any destination. The unfortunate men suffered physical and psychological damage from long periods of standing at attention and from beatings, pointless physical labor, mortal terror, and abasement. The latter was achieved in the camps through the de-privatization of every act of personal hygiene, by abject sanitary conditions, and by the guards' sadism. Jewish men experienced the introduction to the camps in the recreation halls, schools, and ceremonial rooms of their hometowns, where they were tormented and insulted for days.

For its victims, the pogrom was a traumatic experience of humiliation, maltreatment, and loss of identity. It also made clear how seriously the National Socialist policies were to be taken. It was an eye-opener for those who had stayed in Germany and who now desperately sought emigration. Many saw no hope for escape except through suicide.

The end of the derision was often not in sight before the Jewish community was presented with a bill for vandalism against its own property. In Erfurt, the Jewish community was forced to pay not only for the removal of the debris of the burned-down synagogue; the bill also included the cost of the two barrels of gasoline that had been used to ignite the fire. Reinhard Heydrich provided Göring with a summary of the damage, showing that seventy-five hundred Jewish shops had been destroyed and that German windowpanes valued at ten million Reichsmarks had fallen victim to "the wrath of the people" and "just indignation." Vandalism and plunder caused damage estimated at many hundreds of millions of marks. Almost all synagogues and prayer houses were demolished or went up in

---

23. See Heiko Pollmeier, "Inhaftierung und Lagererfahrung deutscher Juden im November 1938," *Jahrbuch für Antisemitismusforschung* 8 (1999): 107–30. A total of 10,911 men were sent to the Dachau concentration camp, 9,845 were sent to Buchenwald, and approximately 6,000 were sent to Sachsenhausen. Ibid., 110.

flames. To this must be added hundreds of deaths: murders, fatal mistreatments, and suicides committed in desperation and horror.

The Reich aviation ministry conferred on November 12, 1938, under the chairmanship of Göring, with representatives of all the Reich ministries and the German insurance industry present. By this time, the decision to expropriate the Jews had already been made; Hitler had resolved to complete the "Aryanization" of the German economy.[24] The ministers and civil servants agreed during the meeting that the Jews should be held responsible for the damages incurred in the pogrom (by confiscating insurance reimbursements, they ensured that the Jews would suffer the financial brunt of the damage). Moreover, the Jews were charged an "atonement tax" of over one billion Reichsmarks. During a brainstorming session, the men discussed how the Jews could finally, and under the most debasing circumstances, be removed from German society. Suggestions included banning them from German forests, requiring them to wear a special costume or identifying marker, forbidding them from using the railways, and excluding them from entire areas of the city. Shortly thereafter, a deluge of decrees and orders deprived the Jews of their rights and property. After the pogrom it was a short step to ghettoization, identification by the wearing of the Star of David (in September 1941), deportation, and murder in the death machinery of the camps in the East. In a speech on the "Jewish question" on December 6, 1938, before district leaders, regional presidents, and Reich governors, Göring made it quite clear that in compliance with an order by Hitler, the exclusion of the Jews should in the future proceed more discreetly than in November 1938. Undisciplined and haphazard riots staged by Nazi party members were to be subordinated to state organization. The "Old Fighters" were to understand that there was no intention of returning to public violence. Hitler had thus decided, for the time being, that "the Jews should not in any way be identified," for if they were, no one would be able to prevent the recurrence of excesses ("since if someone drinks beyond their thirst and goes into the streets, or stands by a lantern and suddenly happens upon a Jew, then he is bound to give him a beating"). In Hitler's proposal, certain districts would exist "in which an identified Jew wouldn't have anything more to eat and wouldn't be able to buy anything."[25]

In a sense, Hitler underestimated the fervor of the Germans' anti-

---

24. Stenographic document by Göring from the meeting on the "Jewish question," November 12, 1938, Nuremberg document PS 1816. In *International Military Tribunal, Trial of the Major War Criminals. Documents in Evidence,* vol. 28 (Nuremberg, 1948), 499–540.

25. Susanne Heim and Götz Aly, "Staatliche Ordnung und 'organische Lösung': Die Rede Hermann Görings 'über die Judenfrage' vom 6. Dezember 1938," in *Jahrbuch für Antisemitismusforschung* 2 (1993): 378–404.

semitism if he thought such special precautions were required. This last slowdown in the tempo of the "Final Solution" to the "Jewish question" can be explained by the fact that the popular mood vis-à-vis the public and excessive form of expulsion and murder of the Jews had not yet been ascertained. But the Germans' silent acceptance and approval of dictated discrimination, from the law prohibiting Jews from having house pets, to the removal of private telephones and radios from their homes, to their wearing of the Star of David, quickly removed any doubt concerning the Germans' attitude.

Conclusion

The November 1938 pogrom was instigated and approved by state and party officials, which distinguishes it from earlier outbursts of violent hostility toward Jews. There are no parallels to the Hep Hep riots and no indications that it was a spontaneous eruption. Even the pogroms in Hessen and Anhalt-Dessau that had occurred the day before were contrived by regional NSDAP authorities. The conclusion should not be drawn from the radicalization of violence, particularly among the rural population, that those who carried out the pogroms were necessarily emotionally driven antisemites.

The events during the days around the ninth of November are not an indication of an inherent German "eliminatory antisemitism," as Daniel J. Goldhagen's thesis claims.[26] The perpetrators among the SA and NSDAP members relapsed into the pre-1933 struggle phase of their movement, when they had eagerly obeyed the calls of their superiors and acted upon their common antisemitic feelings at the expense of the minority. The raging mob, stimulated by propaganda and circumstances, faced the silent majority, which did not approve of the methods and effects of the pogrom but did not make its presence heard. For the course and impact of the pogrom, and its importance for National Socialist politics, it made little difference what motive turned bystanders into perpetrators.

---

26. Daniel Jonah Goldhagen, *Hitler's Willing Executioners: Ordinary Germans and the Holocaust* (New York, 1996).

Exclusionary Riots: Some Theoretical Considerations

Werner Bergmann

I. Introduction

Social historical research on social protest in preindustrial societies has given considerable attention to the causes and dynamics of popular violence. The studies have focused primarily on forms of action such as rebellions, revolts, strikes, boycotts, and riots (food riots and machine-breaking riots) in which the lower classes set themselves against authorities and social elites using collective mobilization to protect their livelihoods, rights, and freedom in the context of modernization, urbanization, proletarianization, state centralization, nation-building, the establishment of the market economy, and social crises. Eric Hobsbawm has written of "collective bargaining by riot," and Manfred Gailus of "participation by riot or threat of riot."[1] Riots should not be understood here as archaic manifestations of "traditional society" or "preindustrial" conditions that in modern society give way to more rational forms of protest. Rather, riots register the "effects of political breakdown and economic hardship more generally," as Geoff Eley, pointing to the years of unrest in Germany from 1916 to 1923, has stressed.[2]

---

1. Eric Hobsbawm, "The Machine Breakers," *Past and Present* 1 (1952): 57–70; Manfred Gailus, "Crowds in History," in *International Encyclopedia of the Social Sciences* (forthcoming).

2. Geoff Eley rejects the assumption that violent forms of protest would disappear in the process of modernization. "Labor History, Social History, *Alltagsgeschichte:* Experience, Culture, and the Politics of Everyday—a New Direction for German Social History?" *Journal of Modern History* 61 (1989): 297–343, esp. 307.

Yet this research has rarely addressed the subject of anti-Jewish riots.[3] This is certainly not a coincidence, because the new history of collective action replaced an older view—much influenced by Gustave LeBon—of evil, psychopathic crowds with an image of "benevolent crowds" playing a primarily emancipatory role. In the newer interpretation, when violence was in play, it usually followed "protocols of riots," whose ritual character served to constrain violence.[4] This emphasis on the progressive function of collective action, even violence, thus obscured other kinds of crowd behavior, such as conservative and nationalistic mass events and ethnic violence, including anti-Jewish riots.[5] Insofar as anti-Jewish riots were addressed, they were interpreted as "displacements of social aggression" and were not analyzed on their own terms. This began to change only in more recent studies beginning in the late 1980s.[6]

The sociological research on the race riots of the mid-1960s in the United States and on the new social movements also emphasized the emancipatory and rational moment of collective violence. Furthermore,

---

3. Important exceptions are Jacob Katz, *Die Hep-Hep-Verfolgungen des Jahres 1819* (Berlin, 1994; first published, in Hebrew, in *Zion* 38 [1973]: 62–115); and Rainer Wirtz, *"Widersetzlichkeiten, Excesse, Crawalle, Tumulte und Skandale": Soziale Bewegung und gewalthafter sozialer Protest in Baden, 1815–1848* (Frankfurt/Main, 1981).

4. The analysis of ethnic conflicts in class-oriented social history is also hindered by the fact that they have been treated as mere epiphenomena of economic interests and contradictions, thereby discarding the reference to cultural differences as "false consciousness." See Theodor Hanf, "The Prospects of Accommodation in Communal Conflicts: A Comparative Study," in *Bildung in sozioökonomischer Sicht,* Festschrift für Hasso von Reccum, edited by Peter A. Döring et al. (Cologne, 1989), 313–32, 314. Countering this position and the opposing position of an ethnic primordialism, in which tribes, peoples, or cultures display central distinguishing social characteristics, a mediating view has asserted itself that supposes that social conflicts arise vertically between different strata as well as horizontally between ethnic groups, thus requiring a two-dimensional approach in analyzing pluralist societies.

5. Gailus, "Crowds in History," 13.

6. See the following studies on violence against Jews in the first half of the nineteenth century in Germany: Katz, *Die Hep-Hep-Verfolgungen;* Rainer Erb and Werner Bergmann, *Die Nachtseite der Judenemanzipation: Der Widerstand gegen die Integration der Juden in Deutschland, 1780–1860* (Berlin, 1989); and Stefan Rohrbacher, *Gewalt im Biedermeier: Antijüdische Ausschreitungen in Vormärz und Revolution, 1815–1848/49* (Frankfurt/Main, 1993). On the waves of pogroms beginning in the 1880s in Russia, see Stephen M. Berk, *Year of Crisis, Year of Hope: Russian Jewry and the Pogroms of 1881–1882* (Westport, Conn., 1985); I. Michael Aronson, *Troubled Waters: The Origins of the 1881 Anti-Jewish Pogroms in Russia* (Pittsburgh, 1990); John D. Klier and Shlomo Lambroza, eds., *Pogroms: Anti-Jewish Violence in Modern Russian History* (Cambridge, 1992); and Stephen Wilson, "The Antisemitic Riots of 1898 in France," *Historical Journal* 16 (1973): 789–806. For case studies on the period following 1945, see Harvey E. Goldberg, "Rites and Riots: The Tripolitanian Pogrom of 1945," *Plural Societies* 8 (1977): 35–56; and Tony Kushner, "Anti-semitism and Austerity: The August 1947 Riots in Britain," in *Racial Violence in Britain, 1840–1950,* edited by Panikos Panayi (Leicester, 1993), 149–68.

they dealt foremost with forms of collective action that as movements of *inclusion* aimed to break down existing social inequalities (the women's movement and the civil rights movement).[7] Exclusionary riots (pogroms), in contrast, are forms of violence that were already considered "medieval" by contemporaries of the nineteenth century and that seemed to run counter to the inclusive trend of broader social developments.

Anti-Jewish riots of the nineteenth and twentieth century do not easily fit into the paradigms of social protest research and the sociology of race riots. Nevertheless, analyzing these riots allows us to develop a theory of exclusionary riots (pogroms). For this reason, I join Heinrich Volkmann and Jürgen Bergmann in their call to give up the collective term *social protest* in favor of a more exact designation of specific protest forms and to investigate the respective "conditions of manifestation."[8]

To distinguish *exclusionary* riots from other forms of collective violence, I propose to combine three theoretical approaches: (1) the power approach to intergroup hostility (also known as the competitive ethnicity model); (2) frame analysis, which stresses the communication processes in defining a social problem or threat; and (3) the theory of social control, developed by Donald Black, which regards crime as a form of self-help against violations of norms or against a grievance.[9] The first theory aims to explain the prerequisites of violence (external threat), while the third explains the resulting reaction. The second concept, framing, serves as the link between the other two, since group competition or structural strains must be publicly debated and thereby transformed into a "menace" that legitimizes collective violent self-help as the last resort.[10]

---

7. James A. Geschwender, "Civil Rights Protest and Riots: A Disappearing Distinction," *Social Science Quarterly* 49 (1968): 475–84.

8. Heinrich Volkmann and Jürgen Bergmann, "Einleitung," in *Sozialer Protest: Studien zu traditioneller Resistenz und kollektiver Gewalt in Deutschland vom Vormärz bis zur Reichsgründung,* edited by Heinrich Volkmann and Jürgen Bergmann (Opladen, 1984), 14.

9. Herbert Blumer, "Race Prejudice as a Sense of Group Position," *Pacific Sociological Review* 1 (1958): 3–7; Hubert M. Blalock, *Toward a Theory of Minority-Group Relations* (New York, 1967); Michael W. Giles and Arthur Evans, "The Power Approach to Intergroup Hostility," *Journal of Conflict Resolution* 30 (1986): 469–86; Donald Black, "Crime as Social Control," *American Sociological Review* 48 (1983): 34–45; idem, ed., *Toward a General Theory of Social Control,* vol. 1 (Orlando, 1984).

10. The framing concept, developed in the social movements research, can be used for the analysis of definition processes. See William Gamson, *Talking Politics* (Cambridge, 1992); and David A. Snow and Richard D. Benford, "Ideology, Frame Resonance, and Participant Mobilization," in *From Structure to Action: Social Movements Research across Cultures,* edited by Bert Klandermans et al. (Greenwich, Conn., 1988). With "injustice frames," problems can be dramatized and defined and the guilty can be accused. "Identity frames" make it possible, in regard to in-group/out-group differences, to mark the contrast between the values and interests of the in-groups and out-groups.

II. The Social Conditions of Collective Violence in Exclusionary Riots

General Crises or Ethnic Conflict?

In the case studies in this volume, questions continually arise concerning the relationship between, on the one hand, general social tensions and crisis factors and, on the other, concrete anti-Jewish acts on the local level, in particular when the riots take a wavelike form and do not remain purely local. Our studies show that there is no simple or uniform answer to this question. In the anti-Jewish riots that took place during the Revolution of 1848 and in the Scheunenviertel pogrom (1923), the importance of the general political and economic crisis situation cannot be missed, whereas the connections for the Hep Hep riots (1819) or the Konitz case (1900), in which religious or ethnic conflicts are of central importance, are very difficult to determine.[11] The answer therefore cannot be determined with a clear "either-or," but rather, in each case, the connection between, say, an economic crisis or a local murder and how the Jews are held responsible for the event has to be investigated by looking at local processes. This problem was pointed out first by Karin Hausen and later by Richard Evans. In their review of the aggregate data used by Charles and Richard Tilly on the level of the nation-state, Hausen and Evans argued for the significance of specific historical contexts of acts of "collective violence" and the importance of "smaller units of investigation."[12]

It is therefore necessary to clarify the process in which the interests (the objective plane) are shifted onto social tensions (the subjective plane) and transferred from tension to action (the action plane).[13] In each of the riots investigated in this volume, the *construction of a Jewish threat* is of central significance, a threat that is often intensified and spread by agitators and interested groups who utilize the available widespread "antisemitic knowledge" about the Jews. In all cases, a "threatening scenario" based on antisemitic prejudices must be constructed to legitimize collective

---

11. In the case of Konitz, we also have (as with the Hep Hep disturbances, analyzed by Eleonore Sterling, Jacob Katz, and Stefan Rohrbacher) two diverging interpretations concerning the role of general crisis factors. Compare Helmut Walser Smith's essay in this volume and Christoph Nonn, "Zwischenfall in Konitz: Antisemitismus und Nationalismus im preußischen Osten um 1900," *Historische Zeitschrift* 266, no. 2 (1998): 387–418.

12. Karin Hausen, "'Schwierigkeiten mit dem sozialen Protest': Kritische Anmerkungen zu einem historischen Forschungsprogramm," *Geschichte und Gesellschaft* 3, no. 2 (1977): 263; Richard Evans, "'Red Wednesday' in Hamburg: Social Democrats, Police, and Lumpenproletariat in the Suffrage Disturbances of January 1906," *Social History* 4, no. 1 (1979): 1–31, 2.

13. Volkmann and Bergmann, "Einleitung," 15.

violence. This is true whether or not an actual conflict of interest between Jews and non-Jews exists (for example, an improvement in the legal status of the Jews or an influx of immigrants); whether a threatening situation develops as a result of general social conditions, as with the inflation crisis of 1923; or when contingent (local) events are regarded as an attack on a group, as was the case in Konitz. Conversely, as we know from prejudice research, perceived threats encourage the production and regeneration of such prejudices.[14]

Preconditions of Collective Violence

An ethnic exclusionary conflict has different preconditions in comparison to other forms of collective violence such as race riots, food riots, revolts, or protest actions of social movements. In the latter examples, violence is structured by the experience of relative deprivation in situations of political breakdown, by economic hardship, or by social dislocation. Moreover, tensions are fought out along class lines and opposing interests. Ethnic minorities and protest movements resort to collective action in order to emphasize their demands for the solution of social problems or for the equitable allocation of public goods. Violence is used against authorities who are strong in resources (with a corresponding risk for the activists). An ethnic intergroup conflict of the exclusionary type is, in contrast, marked by a clear *asymmetry of power* benefiting the instigators of the riot.[15] Under what conditions does this kind of majority–minority conflict arise and escalate?

In analyzing the conditions of emergence, I draw on the power approach to intergroup hostility, which focuses on two processes: the real or imagined threat by an out-group and the identification with an in-group, since without this identification individuals would only react to competition and threats that affect them personally.[16] According to this model, opposing interests and individual conflicts have to be "collectivized" into an ethnic antagonism. This occurs when the dominant ethnic or national group perceives a collective threat to its group position from

14. Lincoln Quillian, "Prejudice as a Response to Perceived Threat: Population Composition and Anti-immigrant and Racial Prejudice in Europe," *American Sociological Review* 60 (1995): 586–611, 586; see also the research cited by Giles and Evans, "The Power Approach," 475.

15. For a definition of exclusionary riots, see the introduction to this volume, section II.

16. Blumer, "Race Prejudice"; Blalock, *Toward a Theory of Minority-Group Relations;* Giles and Evans, "The Power Approach." Studies on antisemitism and xenophobia continually encounter national pride as a significant factor in hostile attitudes toward out-groups. Andrea Herrmann and Peter Schmidt, "Autoritarismus, Anomie und Ethnozentrismus," in *Autoritarismus und Gesellschaft,* edited by Gerda Lederer and Peter Schmidt (Opladen, 1995), 287–319.

an out-group. This model views ethnic groups as being in an ongoing conflict over the control of resources and assumes that a hostile group's antagonism is the result of a perception of *illegitimate* competition. This perception is often a misperception of larger economic, cultural, or political processes, which contemporaries interpret as "unfair competition" (as can be seen in the case of unrest in Pomerania and West Prussia in 1881). A participant in exclusionary violence operates within a friend-foe schema as a victim of an injustice, discrimination, or aggression and reacts, under certain circumstances, with violent forms of social control.[17] In 1923, for instance, the *National Zeitung* of November 7 interpreted the Scheunenviertel riots as a spontaneous reaction to the "unscrupulous profiteering of the Jews in a time of widespread misery," which should teach the "alien elements" a "salutary lesson."

Exclusionary riots are almost always connected to general periods of crisis and social unrest. Historical research has shown that changes in the dominant group's position, caused by the improvement of the rights or the economic status of a minority (for example, the Jewish emancipation of the nineteenth century or the liberation of slaves in the United States), or by rapid urbanization, or by a group's loss of status, prestige, or self-esteem resulting from a lost war (as in postwar Germany in 1923), or by real or imagined attacks on members of the in-group by members of the minority (as was the case with the alleged ritual murder in Konitz in 1900 or in the Rhineland in 1834), can lead to the group's feeling threatened and to a corresponding "defense reaction" by the dominant group.[18] Only under these threatening conditions will class distinctions be dismissed and ethnic membership become the sole differentiating category.[19] The collec-

---

17. On the importance of experiences of (in-)justice and on the function of the rhetoric of injustice in the genesis of social conflicts, see Michael Wenzel et al., "Funktionen von Gerechtigkeitsauffassungen und Gerechtigkeitsrhetoriken für Genese, Verlauf und Management von Konflikten," *Zeitschrift für Sozialpsychologie* 27 (1996): 137–47.

18. Panikos Panayi, "Dominant Societies and Minorities in the Two World Wars," in *Minorities in Wartime: National and Racial Groupings in Europe, North America, and Australia during the Two World Wars,* edited by Panikos Panayi (Oxford, 1993), 3–23; Rohrbacher, *Gewalt im Biedermeier;* Erb and Bergmann, *Die Nachtseite der Judenemanzipation;* Werner Bergmann and Christhard Hoffmann, "'Kalkül oder Massenwahn'? Eine soziologische Interpretation der antijüdischen Unruhen in Alexandria, 38 n. Chr.," in *Antisemitismus und jüdische Geschichte: Studien zu Ehren von Herbert A. Strauss,* edited by Rainer Erb and Michael Schmidt (Berlin, 1987), 15–46.

19. Hanf ("The Prospects of Accomodation") sees group conflicts as tending generally to take the form of a communal conflict rather than a class conflict. He offers three reasons for this. First, communal markers such as ethnic, religious, or linguistic affiliation facilitate mobilization, in contrast to the complexity of economic relationships. Moreover, there is often an overlapping of class and ethnic affiliation. Finally, another form of deprivation exists, namely, the symbolic; the group, regardless of its economic status, reacts with particular bitterness to displays of contempt for its religion and language.

tive self-consciousness is challenged and reacts with fantasies of intimidation and superiority or with actual persecution of groups defined as not-belonging. Thus the eastern Jews of the Scheunenviertel in Berlin were presented as "alien elements" exploiting the national crisis after the First World War (see the essay by David Clay Large in this volume). In this view, the dynamics of conflict arise out of *changes* in the balance of power between groups. Purely objective changes, however, such as a strong increase in immigration or economic competition, will not suffice. The change has to be translated into a threatening scenario. Processes of interpretation, narratives involving preexisting prejudices, memories of past conflicts, and ethnic and national semantics always play an important role.[20]

Against this perceived threat through illegitimate competition, disregard of cultural norms, or feared crime, the majority turns to collective violence as a means to "punish" the minority or to restore the old order. In his theory of social control, Donald Black has addressed this relationship and has put forward hypotheses concerning when certain groups turn to collective violence as a means of social control.[21]

The probability and severity of collective violence increase when there is a large relational and cultural distance between the conflict groups and when both functional independence of the groups and inequality of status are high.[22] The use of violence as the last resort occurs when attempts to avert the external threat by legal means are exhausted or when it is solely the in-group that perceives the "threat" as illegitimate such that there is no possibility of using legal means to remedy the problem. In such cases, violence can be targeted at either the local authorities or the minority, as in 1848, when violent actions "against an assumed cartel of local notables and Jews" were called for (see the essay by Manfred Gailus in this volume).

In this view, collective violence is not a total breakdown of social order or an aberrant behavior but a means of self-help. Ritualized responses to the breaching of a norm, such as charivaris, often entail a high level of controlled collective violence.[23] In Konitz, for instance, the Jews charged with murdering Ernst Winter, who "had the justice system in

---

20. See Janice Gross Stein, "Building Politics into Psychology: The Misperception of Threat," *Political Psychology* 9 (1988): 245–71, on cognitive and affective causes of the misperception of threat—for example, preexisting belief systems, the lack of empathy in contrasting cognitive contexts, the "proportionality bias," the "fundamental attribution error," certain mental fears or needs, and so on.

21. Black identifies a number of typical models but points out that a comprehensive theory of self-help does not exist. Black, "Crime as Social Control."

22. Roberta Senechal de la Roche, "Collective Violence as Social Control," *Sociological Forum* 11 (1996): 97–128, 106, passim.

23. See John Cashmere, "The Social Uses of Violence in Ritual: Charivari or Religious Persecution?" *European History Quarterly* 21 (1991): 291–314, 314.

their hands," were not to go unpunished (see the contribution by Helmut Walser Smith to this volume).

On the Triadic Conflict Relationship

Race or food riots or movements of social protest almost always focus their demands on state authorities—either the state is attacked or the state acts on behalf of a group's interest. In exclusionary riots, we are dealing with a different triadic relationship: the target is another ethnic group, with the state playing the role of an ambivalent third party in the aggressors' mind. On the one hand, the aggressors regard their self-help as legitimate; on the other hand, they "know" that they are infringing on the state's monopoly of power and that their actions are punishable. When the state does not act to ward off the perceived threat against the in-group, violent self-help can assume the character of a loyal compensatory act or an act critical of the government, as in Konitz. In the first case, the aggressors regard themselves as the legitimate representatives of the majority and believe they are cooperating with the state, which for whatever reason remains inactive. Exclusionary riots often are so-called conflicts of loyalty.[24] When interrogated after the fact, a rioter in the West Prussian town of Jastrow claimed that "this action was of course wished 'from above'— Bismarck is Henrici's friend—no one can and will punish us if we drive off the Jews." Similarly, in Schivelbein a witness told the court that rioters were motivated by the "belief that in the end they were doing the state a favor" (see the essay by Christhard Hoffmann in this volume). There are indeed cases in which parts of the political elite and police tolerated—in some cases even participated in—the violent actions, as in 1819, when the police in Heidelberg stood idly by.[25]

Moreover, there are often recognizable differences in the conduct of the central administrations and local state agencies, such as when the police in the Scheunenviertel were slow to take action and initially arrested mostly Jews—which the aggressors in turn interpreted as a legitimization

---

24. Reichskristallnacht is difficult to assess, because the National Socialists used the pogrom form (disguised as the "wrath of the people") in spite of the fact that the conditions of its emergence, namely, the central order from above and the execution of the order by local Nazi organizations, had nothing to do with a pogrom. What makes the case difficult is, on the one hand, the "dual state" structure of the Third Reich, which made no clear distinction between party and state power, and, on the other hand, the fact that parts of the population spontaneously participated as the event was happening. This means that it is possible that in certain localities in November 1938 we are indeed confronted with a pogrom as it is defined here.

25. See Wirtz, *"Widersetzlichkeiten,"* 60–71.

of their actions.[26] On the other extreme, there is rapid and massive state intervention, as, for example, in Würzburg in 1819, in Konitz in 1900, or in Stolp in 1881, where the state's intervention turned bloody. If the state does step in on behalf of the attacked minority or if it acts against members of the majority population, then the conflict can lose its "loyal" character and acquire characteristics of an oppositional movement in which even representatives of the state authority are attacked.[27] The riots in Pomerania and West Prussia in 1900 show that Konitz was "in a state of revolt" against a government protecting the Jews. Troops were attacked and tagged as a "Jewish defense force," and the crowd resisted arrests made by the police. This is not typical of loyalty riots, however. If the control agencies intervene heavily, the riot activists usually do not attack but instead yield, whereas in race riots and actions of protest movements, the involvement of the police often leads to an escalation of the counterviolence.

Thus exclusionary riots require a favorable political structure, in which the behavior of the government, the police, public opinion, and bystanders fulfills key functions in the escalation of violence in intergroup conflicts. This triangular constellation specific to exclusionary riots has retroactive influence on the role of the state control organs, since, unlike in race riots and social movements, representatives of the majority of society are to a certain degree party-affiliated and, moreover, are not the primary focus of the attack. Moreover, crimes that have the character of "collective self-help" are usually treated comparatively mildly, since their goal finds sympathy among parts of the bureaucracy.[28] This was the case, for exam-

---

26. This point must be further delineated. In addition to the various local, regional, and national state agencies, the distinction between state and society can also play a role when the actors in a pogrom regard the state as illegitimate and appeal to "the will of the people," or when the state and minority are seen as being in a close relationship. See the article by Amrita Basu describing the case in Bijnor, India, where riots by Hindus against the Muslim minority were coupled with an attack on the state authorities. Basu, "Why Local Riots Are Not Simply Local: Collective Violence and the State in Bijnor, India, 1988–1993," *Theory and Society* 24 (1995): 35–78, esp. 35.

27. On this displacement of protest, see, for Konitz, Nonn, "Zwischenfall in Konitz," 397. For the lynch actions against individual offenders in Berlin in the early twentieth century, Thomas Lindenberger has suggested a similar ambivalence: on the one side, the public supports the police in that the public itself brought the disturbers of the peace to justice. But in other cases, this direct, popular justice collided with the bureaucratic-minded police, and the police had to prevent excesses. See Lindenberger, *Straßenpolitik: Zur Sozialgeschichte der öffentlichen Ordnung in Berlin, 1900 bis 1914* (Bonn, 1995), 133–36.

28. Black, "Crime as Social Control," 40. The lynchings in the American South of blacks accused of assaulting whites, for example, were seldom prosecuted, although the perpetrators were known and could easily have been arrested. This is also true generally for the prosecution of participants in loyal exclusionary riots. They are usually tried but receive for the most part light sentences.

ple, when the *Oberpräsident* of Pomerania in 1881 held the Jews responsible for the social discontent among the population, or when liberal critics accused the state of tolerating and supporting antisemitic agitation (see the contribution by Hoffmann to this volume). This sympathy helps explain why it is so difficult to extinguish rumors about a state-driven pogrom (for example, in Russia in 1881), why the control organs hesitate to take strong action against the aggressors in an exclusionary riot, and why they sometimes even took the side of the rioters. In Würzburg in the Hep Hep riots, for example, some soldiers supported the rioters. Similarly, in the Scheunenviertel riots of 1923, the police also arrested members of the victim group.[29] On the other hand, the acts of collective violence always represent a challenge to the state's monopoly of power, which it cannot forever tolerate, even when the elite shares in the rejection of the minority. This was the main reason for the Prussian government's policy of intervention in Pomerania and West Prussia in 1881 and 1900.[30]

Based on this triadic relationship, the following changes in the balance of power can lead to violent actions.

1. Real or perceived claims on, or gains of position by, a minority—legally, politically, culturally, or economically—or a quantitative shift that benefits the minority and leads to a reaction of resistance by the group threatened by a loss of political, cultural, or educational status, economic security, and so forth.[31] As Stefan Rohrbacher shows in this volume with respect to the Hep Hep riots of 1819 in Würzburg, the principal motivating factor behind the riots was popular reaction against the perceived change in

---

29. In more recent research on the wave of Russian pogroms from 1881 to 1883, the lack of police resources and incompetence are pointed to as reasons for delayed state intervention. Aronson, *Troubled Waters.* Similarly, Nonn sees in the Konitz case "banal incompetence" and "cowardliness in admitting one's own mistakes" rather than the existence of anti-Jewish attitudes as the cause for the state's inability to provide sufficient protection. "Zwischenfall in Konitz," 395. See also the charge of negligence directed against the Heidelberg *Stadtdirektor* on the occasion of the Heidelberg "Judensturm" in August 1819. Wirtz, *"Widersetzlichkeiten,"* 60–71.

30. See the essay by Hoffmann in this volume; and Nonn, "Zwischenfall in Konitz," 396.

31. The *Oberpräsident* of Pomerania saw the cause of the riots of 1881 in the perceived fact that "Jewish businessmen have increasingly entered into competition with small merchants and tradesmen and have begun to reduce the food source of the aforementioned classes." See the essay by Hoffmann in this volume. Others in Neustettin complained of "Jewish domination." In 1819, the *Untersuchungscommissar* (investigative commissioner) of the Grand Duchy of Baden found that among the Heidelberg population, "mistreatment of the Jews" (*Judenmisshandlung*) was motivated by the "rapid advancement and unjustified enrichment [of the Jews], the supposed advantages they received from the government, and also the competitive envy by craftsmen, since some Jews were permitted to do business in furnishings." Wirtz, *"Widersetzlichkeiten,"* 70.

the legal and social status of the Jews in the process of Jewish emancipation. Similarly, nearly a century later, rioters in Konitz reacted to the perceived guilt of "the Jews" in the murder of a local schoolboy. In both cases, the reaction of the state regulated the pace and intensity of the riots.[32]

2. Situations of power displacement or general power decay on the state level. Two different constellations can be distinguished here: (a) a power vacuum (caused by, for example, a political murder, a system change, a lost war, or a withdrawal of occupying forces); or (b) a power struggle in a revolution or civil war, which as a result of the absence of state protection often leads to violence against minorities, who are regarded as partisan toward the internal or external enemy.[33] In such cases violent "self-help" is an obvious alternative, since the state is regarded as restricted in its ability to act.

3. The power model, however, must be extended to include the scenario in which the minority is seen as causing a threat, a tendency arising from the general constellation of forces within the society. Structural crises that create destabilizing life situations (wars, economic depressions, inflations, loss of social status) and in which the instigators are difficult to pinpoint—and are "framed" within a conspiracy theory—are often explained as intentional damage caused by and benefiting the minority.[34] The external conflict is thus a projected symptom of internal problems. In these cases, we are dealing with what Lewis Coser has called "unreal conflict," in which a conflict situation is created with a substitute object (scapegoat).[35] The choice of target depends on determinants that may or may not be directly connected with the disagreement but that can be found in the existing tradition of prejudice and in the weakness or availability of the attacked group (this is why there are alternatives in the choice of targets—as in 1923, when the Scheunenviertel violence by the unemployed was aimed not only at the eastern Jews, but also against the shops of Chris-

---

32. In other cases, exclusionary violence tries to hinder further immigration. See Panikos Panayi, "Anti-immigrant Riots in Nineteenth and Twentieth Century Britain," in idem, ed., *Racial Violence in Britain,* 1–25.

33. See, on the Russian Revolution, Matthias Vetter, *Antisemiten und Bolschewiki: Zum Verhältnis von Sowjetsystem und Judenfeindschaft, 1917–1939* (Berlin, 1995).

34. Robert A. LeVine and Donald T. Campbell refer to a tendency, typical of ethnocentrism, "to blame the outgroup for the troubles and deprivations of ingroup members." *Ethnocentrism: Theories of Conflict, Ethnic Attitudes, and Group Behavior* (New York, 1972), 19.

35. Lewis A. Coser, *The Functions of Conflict* (Glencoe, Ill., 1956), 55–56. The explanation for why "unreal conflicts," with their hostile perceptions, appear more often in ethnic relations than among interest groups is that the members of ethnic groups do not partake of the conflict partially, as they would in the role of manager or union leader, but with their whole personality.

tians). This form of conflict has the function of letting off aggression and serves to integrate the destabilized community in a struggle against a minority.[36] In such cases, the consideration of using peaceful instead of aggressive means is less likely than in a "real conflict," since satisfaction is sought in the aggressive action itself, not in the outcome. It can be assumed that the level of violence is higher in these cases, since it is not aimed at the elimination of a concrete threat.

Framing: The Sociocultural Definition of the
"Demoralized Other"

Power relations have, as one aspect of their reproduction, symbolic forms in which they are interpreted and understood. A collective assault on an ethnic minority within a community must be legitimized and prepared culturally, since it violates the fundamental norms of communal life and—particularly in pacified societies—violates the state monopoly of power. This means that certain "frames" that the in-group has agreed upon and that define the action of the out-group as "unjust" and "threatening" have to be accepted by the public, as a so-called "injustice frame." In Pomerania, the antisemites and the conservative camp blamed the Jews themselves for having provoked the ire of the people through their "usury," "arrogant behavior," and "interference in the relations of Christians." In addition, appropriate defensive "action frames" must be suggested, such as measures to protect the middle class against "usurious exploitation" or the abolition of the emancipation laws (see the essay by Hoffmann in this volume). Recent research on prejudice has found that the development of prejudices against an out-group depends less on the individual's experience than on a collective process based on the perception of an external threat, which increases one's willingness to unconditionally identify with one's own group.[37] Thus the previously discussed shifts in power induce the development of an extremely negative view of the out-group, a view that has often been pre-formed by traditional beliefs.[38] In order to legit-

---

36. See the hypothesis of the realistic group conflict theory: "False perceptions of threat from outgroups cause increased ingroup solidarity and outgroup hostility." LeVine and Campbell, *Ethnocentrism,* 41.

37. A. Wade Smith, "Racial Tolerance as a Function of Group Position," *American Sociological Review* 46 (1981): 558–73; Quillian, "Prejudice as a Response."

38. Jakob Rösel distinguishes between three forms of radicalization within the friend-foe schema: decontextualization from events, that is, the intention to do damage is projected on the behavior of the other group; reinterpretation, that is, each new incident is interpreted in light of the conflict's historical background; and solidarity and identification with one's own group. "Vom ethnischen Antagonismus zum ethnischen Bürgerkrieg: Antagonismus, Erinnerung und Gewalt in ethnischen Konflikten," in *Soziologie der Gewalt,* edited by Trutz von Trotha, special issue of *Kölner Zeitschrift für Soziologie und Sozialpsychologie,* 37 (1997): 162–82.

imize the use of violence, a dichotomous order made up of incontestable members and outsiders must be established and radicalized into a friend-foe relationship. This suggests that, in contrast to race riots and social movements, which have to justify their demands through appeal to universal values (for example, equal rights or nondiscrimination), exclusionary riots are based on *particularistic* norms ("Germans first!" or " I am a Prussian!"), which deny the out-group equal rights (in work, housing, or religious activity, for example).

For this reason, communities that are based on exclusive values and allegiances justify particularistic exclusion as a necessary measure of self-defense. Rumors or pamphlets about assaults committed by the minority (kidnappings, charges of participation in assassinations, exploiting Christians, social encroachments, and so forth) are a typical form of communication legitimizing and preparing violence as a means of "social control" immediately prior to the outbreak of exclusionary violence. In 1847–48, anonymous pamphlets were distributed against "Jews and crop profiteers" with threats of "death and ruin" (see the essay by Gailus in this volume). These rumors are often spread for long periods of time—sometimes involving mass media, in which prejudices and nationalistic semantics consolidate and radicalize. Case studies show the ground for collective violence is prepared for with flier campaigns, inflammatory articles in newspapers, political debates, and public events (in this sense, the role of the *Norddeutsche Presse* proved exemplary for the antisemitic excesses in Pomerania and West Prussia in 1881).[39] "Ethnic agitators," who in some cases traveled to areas in order to deliberately incite the population to engage in self-help against the Jews (as did the well-known agitator Ernst Henrici in Neustettin) or who joined the local antisemites in order to heat up an already smoldering conflict (as in Konitz), play an important role here in developing a view of reality for the public in which the out-group is presented as a threat and is responsible for the in-group's present disadvantaged situation. In each of the cases presented in this volume, antisemitic communication (rumors, suspicions, threatening letters, pamphlets) plays a key role by putting an anti-Jewish spin on a general structural crisis and presenting local Jews as the target for collective action. This is particularly dangerous when prestigious figures from the administration and the church participate or when antisemitic organizations exist, since they are predestined to propel the campaign and to form the core of the action (on Pomerania, see Hoffmann's contribution to this volume).

The use of violence requires a communication process in which values and norms change and the target group is gradually "excommunicated" so

---

39. On the intensified tension caused by the local press in Bijnor, India, see Basu, "Why Local Riots Are Not Simply Local," 58–59.

that the collective violence represents the final step in a process of delegit-imization and dehumanization. The balance between impulse and inhibi-tion, which regulates the aggression, is lost when one resorts positively to "higher principles" or to authorities interpreting one's own behavior as mere self-defense, for example, as a protection against "exploitative busi-ness practices" of the Jews (blaming the victim).[40]

Even when only a portion of the population participates, such as "restless young men" (apprentices, high school students, workers, and craftsmen; see Smith's essay in this volume), the violent perpetrators can count on a large circle of supporters, among whom many may reject the means but not the aim of the exclusion.[41] Our case studies show that young men (women participated as instigators and looters) often took the lead but acted against the background of a larger crowd. In Konitz in 1900, for example, there were more than a thousand bystanders watching. During Kristallnacht, in 1938, a very similar phenomenon occurred. Members of the upper classes rarely participated in the violence, but they offered "intellectual" support. Indeed, in the German Empire the antisemitic movement was mostly represented by the educated classes. Seen from this point of view, the attack on a group that has been discriminated against for a long time is, in the eyes of the perpetrators' relevant reference group, not deviant but normal behavior, in which the perpetrators are regarded as conformists who have merely gone a little further than their peers. The use of illegal political violence is ultimately guided by social norms and gratification, just as is the use of legal and nonviolent means.[42]

III. The Dynamics of Exclusionary Riots

Parties in conflict usually tend to have only negative expectations of the opponent, believing that the other party will attempt to cause harm. Con-

40. John Bohstedt, "The Dynamics of Riots: Escalation and Diffusion/Contagion," in *The Dynamics of Aggression: Biological and Social Processes in Dyads and Groups,* edited by Michael Potegal and John F. Knutson (Hillsdale, N.J., 1994), 257–306, 266; see also Wolf-gang Benz's essay on the Reichskristallnacht in this volume.

41. It is typical in exclusionary riots that alongside activists, a large audience is present from among which a few individuals engage in plundering and violence, but that the entire group signals approval by watching and, as a large mass of people, prevents the control organ from intervening. In general, one can say that the acts of collective violence consist of very diverse actions of individuals and small groups (not "mob violence"); that not all the people present are involved; and that even the participants do not act continuously. Refer-ring to riots, Clark McPhail speaks of "patchworks and kaleidoscopes of individual and col-lective, nonviolent and violent, alternating and varied actions." "Presidential Address: The Dark Side of Purpose: Individual and Collective Violence in Riots," *Sociological Quarterly* 35 (1994): 1–32, 12.

42. Hans Matthias Kepplinger, "Gesellschaftliche Bedingungen kollektiver Gewalt," *Kölner Zeitschrift für Soziologie und Sozialpsychologie* 33 (1981): 469–503, 472.

sequently, they take steps toward what one might call "self-defense" and act equally destructively. Thus a proclivity for escalation is always embedded in conflict communication. How does a situation of latent tension escalate to an open riot?

1. In situations of ethnic tension, the social networks branching out to the other ethnic group begin to weaken. In contrast to the food riots of the early nineteenth century, in which such networks existed and violence was contained by negotiations and customs ("protocols of riots"), among ethnic groups there are fewer overlapping relationships, and those that do exist are continually reduced during an escalating conflict. In Neustettin, for example, a conflict between the Jews and liberal inhabitants of the state and the antisemites over the cause of a fire in the synagogue in February 1881 led to a deterioration of social relations, resulting in a boycott of Jewish shops and attacks by Christian children on their Jewish classmates (see Hoffmann's essay). When all other communication is cut off, violence continues to function as an unconditional, physical form of communication and offers the more powerful party a strong assurance of success. This constellation explains why violence is mobilized so quickly. The breaking off of communication with the out-group, coupled with the intensive communication within the local in-group, is commonly described as the "pogrom atmosphere," an intense and emotionally laden situation created by previous agitation (threatening letters and posters), ongoing court trials, occasional shouts of "Hep Hep!" or "Schlagt die Juden tot!" (beat the Jews to death), and the spread of rumors that a pogrom is threatening.

2. During this period of tension, the minority is being carefully monitored for evidence of damaging acts against the in-group or to see whether it is overstepping its social borders. Whether or not a riot erupts depends on contingent events: for the U.S. race riots in the 1960s, structural differences between "riot cities" and "nonriot cities" were difficult to pinpoint.[43] Researchers are, however, in agreement that the outbreak of pogrom violence requires a precipitating incident in which the group conflict manifests itself and collective action can begin. Just as race riots are often set off by the arrest of a ghetto dweller (and successful proceedings against the arrested person), an exclusionary riot can be triggered when an event symbolizes a threat to the majority and actions ensue. When Christian children disappear around Passover, the suspicion of ritual murder committed by the Jews is easily sustained and in turn serves as the occasion for the call for collective violence (see Smith's contribution to this volume). A rumor that was circulated, perhaps by *völkisch* agitators,

---

43. Seymour Spilerman, "The Causes of Racial Disturbances: A Comparison of Alternative Explanations," *American Sociological Review* 35 (1970): 627–49; see, more recently, McPhail, "Presidential Address," 4, passim.

"that eastern Jews from the neighboring Scheunenviertel had bought up all the relief money in order to loan it at exorbitant rates later on" (see Large's essay in this volume) made the age-old prejudice of the "Jewish profiteer" more concrete and steered the anger of the unemployed toward the inhabitants of this quarter. As Jakob Rösel has stressed, it is not the business of individuals to interpret the precipitant events, because collective interpretation models—assumptions about the interests and customs of other groups—are already at hand.[44] The "scandalous occasion," such as the bleeding president of the Neustettin "League of Antisemites" rushing around various alehouses, triggered the emotional arousal necessary for collective mobilization, but it served an additional function in reinforcing the communication and triggering the actual gathering of a "critical mass" of people willing to participate in collective action.[45] Leadership plays an important role here by providing the communal action with a direction and a model that can affect the mass by either escalating or deescalating "extremities shifts"—as in the case of Hammerstein (see Hoffmann's essay).[46] In our case studies, there are naturally occasions when an assembly of crowds remains strictly a demonstration and does not end in violence.

3. Unlike long-term social movements, which often mobilize their nationwide network of networks for special operations, exclusionary riots, like race riots, are determined by their local and episodic character and require a mass of people who can be mobilized to a certain location. The presence of such crowds cannot be accepted as a given precondition, and in this sense Thomas Lindenberger has rightly criticized the research tradition of "crowd history" (including the work of, for example, George

---

44. Rösel, "Vom ethnischen Antagonismus," 166.

45. On the importance of feelings such as anger and revenge, see Charles D. Brockett, "A Protest-Cycle Resolution of the Repression/Popular-Protest Paradox," *Social Science History* 17 (1993): 457–84, 464; Pamela Oliver, Gerald Marwell, and Ruy Teixera, "A Theory of Critical Mass I: Interdependence, Group Heterogeneity, and the Production of Collective Action," *American Journal of Sociology* 91 (1985): 522–56; and Pamela Oliver and Gerald Marwell, "The Paradox of Group Size in Collective Action: A Theory of the Critical Mass II," *American Sociological Review* 53 (1988): 1–8.

46. On leadership, see Bohstedt, "The Dynamics of Riots," 263–64. Christian Lüdemann and Christian Erzberger, in their threshold value model of collective violence, make a distinction between the incentives for the initiators to act first and demonstrate their daring and willingness to take risks, and the late "joiners." They assume that for initiators with the threshold value of zero, negative attitudes and sentiments against the attacked group and the desire to express them form the basis for their decision to act. "Fremdenfeindliche Gewalt in Deutschland: Zur zeitlichen Entwicklung und Erklärung von Eskalationsprozessen," *Zeitschrift für Rechtssoziologie* 15 (1994): 169–90, 181–82.

Rudé, E. P. Thompson, and Eric Hobsbawm). The question must be asked as to how such riotous crowds develop in the first place.[47]

Sometimes crowds simply gather at an event to which people have already come, such as a parade, strike, or market, or while waiting in line outside the employment office (as occurred on the Alexanderstrasse in Berlin in 1923). From there, a trigger event or an agitator can direct the group to a new target. It is not a coincidence that as prevention measures, control organs choose to enforce curfews, forbid markets and festivals, and close local pubs. But such restrictions can in turn become the very reason for mob violence (see Hoffmann's essay). In a research summary, Clark McPhail accentuates the importance of *structural conduciveness* for the assembly and mobilization process: the temporal availability of people (after work, on weekends or holidays, in summer); the social density of the people in a public space (for example, milling around the market square in the evening or talking in a pub about upcoming action; see Smith's essay); the frequency of encounters between members of the groups in conflict; and the speed with which the information about a riot spreads.[48] A violent conflict is not necessarily intended from the start. It can be the result of a process of escalation of ordinary conflicts between members of the groups involved—for example, a fistfight between a Jew and a Christian in the heated atmosphere around Neustettin in 1881 or Konitz in 1900; or it can occur as the result of a displacement of another conflict, as a redirection of activity.[49]

Groups on the local level may also exist or come into existence during a wave of riots (as did the "citizens' committee" in Konitz). Workforces, student groups, hooligans, or nationalistic or antisemitic organizations can quickly form ad hoc groups that intend to use violence and to form an

---

47. Lindenberger, *Straßenpolitik,* 26. See also Robert J. Holton, "The Crowd in History: Some Problems and Considerations of Theory and Method," *Social History* 3 (1978): 219–33.

48. McPhail, "Presidential Address," 8, passim. Lüdemann and Erzberger discovered a systematic preference in Germany for the weekend as a time for xenophobic riots: 54 percent of such riots took place between Friday and Sunday. Thus the attacks were connected with situations in which leisure-time cliques could meet to celebrate, visit local restaurants, and so on. "Fremdenfeindliche Gewalt," 171.

49. In reference to the historical analyses of Charles Tilly, see McPhail, "Presidential Address," 22. Charters Wynn, in his examination of czarist Russia, found numerous examples of work riots and strike actions that turned into anti-Jewish pogroms, especially when the workers could not attack their actual target. Wynn speaks of a "mixture of causes" (dissatisfaction with working conditions, hunger, a cholera epidemic, and antisemitism) and a "mixture of targets." *Workers, Strikes, and Pogroms: The Donbass–Dnepr Bend in Late Imperial Russia, 1870–1905* (Princeton, 1992), 117.

effective and organized pogrom mass. This mass of people must also have a spacious, easily identifiable target area. This condition is easily met if the minority is concentrated in an ethnic colony, such as the Scheunenviertel, or if the minority owns well-known synagogues, churches, or mosques and identifiable houses and shops. In some cases, these buildings have been clearly marked so that the property of the attacking group is not struck accidentally. In the Scheunenviertel, lists of Jewish shops were distributed, and Christian shopkeepers wrote "Christian-owned" on their shops to protect themselves from the violence (see Large's essay).

Exclusionary violence in a certain place becomes the single most important trigger event for subsequent acts of violence. This is true for the escalation of violence at the original location; it is also true for large, wave-like outbreaks of violence that occur periodically and in a widening geographical area.[50] All the cases presented in this volume confirm the wave-like character of pogroms, whether one anti-Jewish riot led to others, as in Würzburg, Neustettin, or Konitz, or whether the anti-Jewish riot was part of a larger complex of social or political unrest, as in the revolutionary phase around 1848 or during the inflation crisis of the Weimar Republic. Social density (that is, the possibility of en bloc recruitment of participants) and communication density and routes play an important role for diffusion of the violence. For the Konitz riots, Helmut Walser Smith works out the "tight network of news and information" very clearly. The mass media, at that time primarily the local newspapers, also played an important role (see the essay by Hoffmann). A successful riot, seen as a model of action, changes the cost/benefit relationship to the advantage of potential participants in future violence, since a riot of large size and a lenient reaction by the state lessen the risk of sanctions. The local mob is reinforced mostly by young men from the environs who flock into town, like those in Konitz who were notified and animated by antisemites riding around on their bicycles. Imitation, encouraged by mass media, also plays an important role in the escalation of violence.[51]

Exclusionary riots, like race riots, have an *episodic* character, since the "critical mass"—unlike army units—cannot be mobilized for a long period and is seldom based on enduring networks or organizations. Moreover, the perpetrators of the pogrom usually accomplish their destruction in a short period of time, and the state cannot countenance a lasting disturbance for too long.

---

50. Margaret J. Abudu Stark et al., "Some Empirical Patterns in a Riot Process," *American Sociological Review* 39 (1974): 865–76.

51. See Helmut Willems, *Jugendunruhen und Protestbewegungen: Eine Studie zur Dynamik innergesellschaftlicher Konflikte in vier europäischen Ländern* (Opladen, 1997), 467, passim.

IV. Goals and Impacts of Exclusionary Actions

Protest and movements research, primarily the resource mobilization theory, has attributed a high degree of rationality and cost/benefit calculation to militant operations of social movements, as well as to race riots, which for the most part involve a long course of nonviolent protests.[52] The observed containment of violence can be attributed to the following: (1) nonviolence, or at least limited violence, is intrinsic to the self-definition of the educated stratum supporting the new social movements and to their central values of an "uninjured, autonomous life"; (2) long-term organizational aims exclude a short-term effective interest in violence, because social movements are "repeat players," while participants in exclusionary riots are "one-shotters" without any extended prospects for the future;[53] and (3) in order to achieve their goals, protest movements need the support of public opinion and therefore cannot easily resort to violence.

The violence of exclusionary riots does not, then, fit easily into the categories of purposeful or symbolic action. For such riots also contain moments of extremely violent expression.[54] It is true that in comparison with the level of violence of the Russian pogroms in Odessa in 1905, in which there were 3,302 dead and 5,000 injured, the limited violence in the anti-Jewish riots of nineteenth- and twentieth-century Germany is striking. Kristallnacht remains the exception, since in number of victims and scale of destruction it was comparable to the Russian pogroms. The violence still follows the "contentious repertoires" with marching demonstrators, rock-throwing, chanting of antisemitic catchwords, and in cases of escalation even pillaging, arson, and short-term expulsion. Harsh attacks on people and cases of death remain the exception, occurring primarily when small armed groups form, as was the case in Schivelbein in 1881 (see Hoffmann's essay). It is striking that this limited actual violence was accompanied by unbridled fantasies of violence and verbal threats, in which Jews were threatened with expulsion and death. Indeed, in 1819, 1848, 1900, and 1923, rioters chanted "Beat the Jews to death!" This suggests that at least

---

52. Michael Banton, *Racial and Ethnic Competition* (Cambridge, 1983), constitutes an attempt to apply rational choice theory to the situation of ethnic competition. This attempt earned him criticism from T. S. Chivers for neglecting other forms of rationality, such as value rationality, that are so central to ethnic conflicts. Chivers, "Is Expulsion Rational? Dealing with Unwanted Minorities as Issues of Rationality," *Ethnic and Racial Studies* 8 (1985): 581–89.

53. Senechal de la Roche, "Collective Violence," 119.

54. See Werner Bergmann, "Soziale und kulturelle Bedingungen kollektiver Gewalt in Pogromen," in *Lerntag über Gewalt gegen Juden: Die Novemberpogrome von 1938 in historischer Perspektive,* edited by Herbert A. Strauss et al. (Berlin, 1989), 7–22, esp. 15. For a summary of recent research, see Bohstedt, "The Dynamics of Riots," 271, passim.

on the level of public action, the state's demand for law and order had a restraining effect. In the early Weimar Republic, which was characterized by chaos, unrest, assassinations, attempted coups, and political violence—"the brutalization of the national psyche," as Large called it—this restraint no longer held. Nor did it hold amid the ordered violence of the Nazi state. Apparently, the feeling of state "authorization" in certain situations contributes to the removal of inhibited moral standards of action (see especially Wolfgang Benz's contribution to this volume).

What did the rioters hope to achieve from their limited violent action? On the first level of escalation, one can speak of a concrete violent punishment, which is typically aimed at individual Jews accused of violating a norm—usually "profiteering," as Manfred Gailus has reported particularly for the years 1847–48. In this case, the form of self-help chosen by a group was public banishment of Jews and targeted damage of materials as the means for social control. The attacks were aimed at the places where the incriminating activity occurred—Jewish shops, for example, as was the case in Würzburg, where the signboards were torn down; or crop warehouses, such as the storeroom of a Jewish landowner in Landsberg an der Warthe (see the essays by Rohrbacher and Gailus). These attacks could be interpreted as a public ritual of rebuke (charivari). On a higher level of escalation, the violence was aimed principally at all members of the minority from one area. The aim could vary: either to lower the status of the minority by using violence to drive them from certain places (from the Hamburg coffeehouses and the Frankfurt Wall Promenade, as was the case in the Hep Hep riots of 1819), or to attempt to expel them from the community by destroying their homes and livelihoods, for instance, by creating a threatening climate. In all riots, the prospect of making gains through plundering attracts a large number of "freeloaders." A third level, at which point one can speak of pogroms narrowly defined, entails, in addition to plundering, destruction and arson against property and places of worship and excessive physical damage to persons, going as far as killing. At that point, the collective violence finally loses its more symbolic and ritualized, restrained character, as the rioters attempt to use direct means to realize their goal—the complete exclusion of the minority through exile and extermination. These pogroms are usually highly organized, as can be seen from the role that the SA, SS, and other Nazi formations played during Kristallnacht and from that of other nationalistic organizations, such as the Black Hundreds during the Russian pogroms between 1903 and 1905. Participants in pogroms often come from violent subcultural milieus (the farmworker and migrant worker milieu in Russia, the storm troopers in Nazi Germany, the skinhead milieu today), in which violence is much less exceptional and instrumental, becoming instead an "obsession."

If we compare race riots as a form of ethnic protest with exclusionary riots, there are distinct differences in the purpose of the actors and in the impact of the action. Studies of U.S. race riots have shown that among the main purposes of violent African American protests was to reduce the discrimination that African Americans experienced in housing, work, education, and legal treatment.[55] The main targets of attack were merchants in the ghetto, who were seen as exploiters (mostly white, but also black); white people in general; and the police as a symbol of the discriminatory white state. The African Americans regarded the looting and arson as primarily a symbolic form of social protest necessary to call the attention of whites to blacks' problems and to improve the situation.[56] In the United States, the reaction was indeed to expand federal aid in education, job training, and housing. But it was also to improve the capacity of police control. By aiming to diminish the status of the attacked minority, aggressors in exclusionary riots also expected to indirectly improve or at least secure their group position. But they wanted something else as well: they wanted to degrade the attacked group. Thus a slogan of the anti-Dreyfus riots of 1898 was "A bas les Juifs"; the rioters wanted to literally remove the members of the minority. The Scheunenviertel rioters in 1923 demanded, "Out with the eastern Jews!" In Neustettin in 1881, they yelled "Jews to Palestine!" These rioters wanted, moreover, to rob the attacked group of their material basis (through looting and arson attacks on their homes and workplaces), and sometimes they even wanted to kill them.

Exclusionary violence also *indirectly* calls for protective measures by the state against the minority for the benefit of the in-group. These demands, such as limits on immigration, the passing of discriminatory laws, and delays in establishing equal standing, have often been achieved. Taking all these actions and demands together, we are talking about a redefinition of the balance of power to the advantage of the majority. The (intended) effect is to make the minority feel insecure and fearful and to worsen their social situation to the point of destroying their economic livelihood.

On the first escalation level, which entails concrete complaints and demands, the attacked persons or group still have a wide range of possible actions they can take to secure their status and divert the danger. The victims often respond by moving away from the community. Many Jews, for

---

55. T. David Mason, "Individual Participation in Collective Violent Action: A Rational Choice Synthesis," *American Political Science Review* 78 (1984): 1040–56, 1048.

56. David O. Sears and T. M. Tomlinson, "Riot Ideology in Los Angeles: A Study of Negro Attitudes," *Social Science Quarterly* 49 (1968): 485–503, 495. The race riots should be regarded as a form of social control from below, in which people in a higher social position are punished or a compensatory balance is achieved (for example, by plundering). On rebellions in general, see M. P. Baumgartner, "Social Control from Below," in Black, *Toward a General Theory of Social Control,* 303–45, 305, passim.

example, left Pomerania for Berlin or the Ruhr region after the 1881 riots. In the case of Kristallnacht and the Russian pogroms, there were waves of outright emigration. The threatening atmosphere usually remained after the riots, and Christian-Jewish relations hardly improved. For example, in the region of Konitz, antisemitic candidates were successful in the elections of the year following the riots, and a number of liberal figures who had acted on behalf of the Jews left the city (see the essay by Smith). In Neustettin, new riots occurred in 1884, and the anti-Jewish wave of violence around 1900 again struck Pomerania and West Prussia. Consequently, we can refer to this area as a "pogrom region," as we do for the Rhineland and Franconia.

V. Conclusions

Exclusionary riots (together with lynchings and massacres) present a specific phenomenon of collective violence, whose analysis could redress the imbalance in the research, in particular the one-sidedness of resource mobilization approaches. What makes exclusionary riots a specific phenomenon is, for one thing, the form of ethnic majority–minority conflicts, in which the state's involvement is, or rather should be, different than in race riots, terrorism, and social movements. They are also specific because their ethical and political values run counter to those of the emancipation movements. Exclusionary violence also raises issues concerning the role of expressiveness, emotion, and violence.

For a theoretical analysis, I propose combining three theories. The power approach to intergroup hostility can explain the conditions that give rise to a situation of tension, but it has nothing to say about when this hostility takes on the form of pogromlike violence, and it does not explain "unreal" ethnic conflicts. The power approach assumes that the hostility between ethnic groups is caused by competition over limited resources and that this increases in-group identification and communication and the tendency toward closing group boundaries. The likelihood that a manifest conflict will occur increases when the inequality of power resources decreases.[57] The increased tension can be caused by

(1) the quantitative increase of a minority group (through immigration or migration);

---

57. I assume, together with Walter Korpi, that the likelihood that a manifest conflict will occur is low if the resources are quite unevenly distributed; the likelihood increases with decreasing inequality and decreases again when the resources are more or less equally distributed. "Conflict, Power, and Relative Deprivation," *American Political Science Review* 38 (1974): 1569–78, 1574.

(2) an increase in economic competition (improved relative economic status of a minority);

(3) an increase in the minority's political power (for example, by achieving legal equality);

(4) a (perceived) violation of a group's cultural values (symbolic deprivation); or

(5) an increased level of identification with the in-group (ethnocentrism).[58]

This theory regards the competition as *real,* but it has to be translated into a perceived threat that is valid for the entire group.[59] The power approach has so far paid scarcely any attention to this process of the transformation of real competition into a perceived threat. I make the assumption that two factors influence this process of definition: first, the estimate of one's own resources (for example, political influence) in controlling the situation and advantageous environmental conditions; and second, the cognitive-cultural transmission through frames that define the situation as a threatening social problem for the group as a whole.[60] The framing concept, developed in social movements research, can be used for the analysis of this definition process.[61] This framing process, in resorting to existing biases and evaluations, can also wrongly attribute real threats for which the actual responsible party is difficult to identify to a group that is not responsible (unreal conflicts).

If a threat is transformed into a perceived threat, then, according to Donald Black's theory of social control, it can result in collective violent self-help when

(1) a recourse to law (state monopoly) is not possible or proved unsuccessful;

(2) a status or power imbalance exists to the advantage of the "threatened" group;

(3) the relational and cultural distance between the groups is large;

(4) the functional independence between the groups is high (on all levels); and

---

58. See LeVine and Campbell, *Ethnocentrism,* 40; and Giles and Evans, "The Power Approach."

59. Micheal W. Giles and Arthur Evans, "External Threat, Perceived Threat, and Group Identity," *Social Science Quarterly* 66 (1985): 50–66, 63.

60. The professional advancement of blacks in the 1970s was not perceived by the white population as threatening because the expanding job market eliminated any sense of increased competition. Ibid., 52.

61. Gamson, *Talking Politics;* Snow and Benford, "Ideology, Frame Resonance, and Participant Mobilization."

(5) the authorities do not apply preventive negative sanctions against the self-help.

The collective self-help takes on the form of exclusionary violence when the group possesses a low degree of organization and when the attacked group is accused collectively. Whether an attack that has begun with violence grows into a pogrom and how violent it becomes depend on other determinants: a contingent triggering event, the existence of organized groups, the speed and size of the involvement of the police and military, and the effect of diffusion.

Continuities and Discontinuities of Anti-Jewish Violence in Modern Germany, 1819–1938

Richard S. Levy

> The practice of violence, like all action, changes the world, but the most probable change is to a more violent world.
>
> Hannah Arendt, On Violence

Histories of antisemitism record innumerable earlier instances, but this volume of interpretive and descriptive essays is the first to take the long view of anti-Jewish violence in modern German history. Why hasn't this been done before now?

Before the Holocaust, it appeared reasonable to dismiss the German examples of anti-Jewish violence in the nineteenth and twentieth centuries as of minor importance. In loss of life and property damage, these episodes paled before the pogroms of eastern Europe. The 250 riots in Imperial Russia in 1881 and the nightmarish eruptions of rape, murder, and arson in 1903–5 and during the civil war of 1919–20, when many thousands of Jews were killed, had no parallel in German-speaking Europe. Indeed, to Jews fleeing for their lives, Germany seemed a safe haven, vastly preferable to the chronic insecurities of the East. Moreover, German Jews themselves had reassuring ways of explaining the few such aberrations that took place on German soil. They were minor detours on the road to better times, lamentably atavistic, to be sure, but no cause for undue alarm. These last flickerings of medieval prejudice posed no threat to a steadily brightening future. Even the surprising recrudescence of violence at the beginning of this century failed to shake the Jews' confidence. After all, the state stood committed to protect its own authority and the lives and goods of its citizens. Public condemnations of violent behavior were swift and sincere. Thus heartened, Jews took every new outburst in stride; their leaders and organizations urged patience, good will, and better communications, hoping thereby to surmount the lingering vestiges of an unhappy past.

The victims' tendency to minimize this part of their history, some going so far as to transform it into a "growth experience," may have carried over into the larger society. Or Jews may have been assimilating the already well established attitudes of non-Jews on this subject. "Senseless and fanatic persecution of the Jews" was the dismissive judgment of those isolated liberal writers and historians of the mid-nineteenth century who had anything at all to say about the rioting.[1] Such judgments went well beyond relativizing the pogrom; they approached the point of denying the need for historical investigation. Categorizing anti-Jewish violence as indubitably "medieval" also helped convince many that the problem had no bearing on current relations between Jews and non-Jews. No one seemed anxious to study this particular past.

Even after 1945, when historians might have been expected to seek causal connections between mass murder and prior acts of collective violence, few serious students explored these avenues. The scale and duration of the Holocaust, the vital participation of state power on the side of murder, and the international scope of the Final Solution argued against seeing this cataclysm as significantly related to a paltry riot or two in the German hinterlands. The Holocaust was so large a moment in human history that it eclipsed lesser ones, even when they possessed some obvious common traits. Only in the most general way, and with scant attention to the modern era, did past violence against Jews enter into interpretations of the Holocaust. Raul Hilberg's monumental *The Destruction of the European Jews* (1961; rev. 1985) begins with a discussion of precedents for the Final Solution but focuses on ideology and law (canon and secular), giving only passing mention to a riotous episode in Vienna in 1406. Hilberg's more sustained attention to the assault on the Jews of ancient Alexandria intends to establish what he sees as Diaspora Jewry's habitual pattern of compliance in the face of physical force. He does not consider whether or how historical violence may also have acted as a precedent for the Nazis.[2]

---

1. A slightly more ambivalent view can be found in Johann Gustav Gallois, *Geschichte der Stadt Hamburg,* 3 vols. (Hamburg, 1853–56), 3:280ff. The former radical derided intolerance toward Reform Jews—"real ornaments" of Hamburg's civic and social life—as wholly misplaced. Jewish peddlers and the "tasteless, spirit-deadening" Orthodox, on the other hand, had provoked the riots of 1819 and 1830 in Hamburg, and they remained a liability.

2. See Raul Hilberg, *The Destruction of the European Jews* (Chicago, 1961), 1–17. Lucy Dawidowicz, *The War against the Jews, 1933–1945* (New York, 1975), 30, is only slightly more interested in the subject. In her chapter on antisemitism in modern Germany, she

The contributors to this anthology think it is time to remedy this neglect. Their premise is not that historical anti-Jewish violence holds the key to understanding the Holocaust, only that it is an important element of explanation, because it forms one of the ways in which Germans and Jews interacted. Over time, the potential for violence became part of the calculus of that relationship, affecting both sides of the equation, but in profoundly different ways. The Third Reich's solution to the Jewish question, although neither spontaneous nor "popular," nonetheless employed violence of a kind that was not foreign to the German past. It is therefore reasonable for historians to ask what influence earlier cases of exclusionary violence against Jews may have had on their ultimate brutalization by the Nazi state.

Accept anti-Jewish violence as a worthy subject of investigation and it becomes immediately apparent that its history in Germany is a long and full one. The six discrete episodes examined in depth in this volume might well stand in for many others. From the Hep Hep riots of 1819 through the Reichskristallnacht of 1938, incidents of anti-Jewish violence occurred in nearly every decade, in large cities and small towns, in the rural east and west, among Protestants and Catholics. Rioting broke out in coffeehouses in Hamburg (1830, 1835) and Berlin (1880); anti-Jewish tumult was endemic in the Rhineland through the 1830s; university students led the mayhem in Breslau in 1844 and Vienna in 1925; physical attacks on Jews took place in ninety-three locales during the Revolution of 1848–49, mostly in Baden and surrounding territories; mobs assaulted Jews and their property in Vienna in 1885, 1925, and 1931. There is, alas, no dearth of material for study.[3]

By design, the present collection of essays spans a lengthy period of time, making it possible to raise—if not fully to answer—some worthwhile questions about the phenomenon of anti-Jewish violence. Are there commonalities in the separate occurrences, or is each unique? What long-term patterns of development can be discerned? Is there a difference between

---

devotes a paragraph to the Hep Hep riots of 1819 as a major first stage "in the history of German nationalism in which the Jews were marked as the enemy." She, too, puts greater emphasis on ideology and state policies than on collective violence against Jews.

3. It is well to remember that physical attacks on Jews were not confined to Germany during this period. Helmut Berding, *Moderner Antisemitismus in Deutschland* (Frankfurt/Main, 1988), 74, counts 180 outbreaks ranging from Alsace to Bohemia and Moravia in 1848–49. When Pius IX abolished the ghetto in 1847–48, elements of the Roman populace, especially workers and small shopkeepers, committed acts of violence against Jews that remained part of the Roman scene until the early 1900s. See Andrew M. Canepa, "Emancipation and Jewish Response in Mid-Nineteenth-Century Italy," *European History Quarterly* 16 (1986): 410–11. See also Heinz Holeczek, "The Jews and the German Liberals," *Leo Baeck Institute Year Book* 28 (1983): 77–91.

modern and premodern episodes of violence? What is the relationship between antisemitic ideology and anti-Jewish action? Does public memory of historical pogroms have a role in later outbreaks? Finally, what lessons were drawn from collective anti-Jewish violence? Who learned them? Who failed to learn them?

How best to set about answering these and other questions is open to debate. Werner Bergmann presents the case for applying social science techniques to the historical problem of anti-Jewish violence and attempts to construct a paradigm that allows the general shape of the pogrom to emerge without fading away into local variants and exceptional circumstances. The difficulties of doing this he makes clear. The strong presentist thrust of the social sciences hampers their ability to deal with phenomena that belong, we hope, to the receding past. Even the most assiduous historian is unlikely to turn up the kind and quantity of evidence that has been collected to explain recent outbreaks of antiforeign violence in Germany and elsewhere. The sophisticated tools developed for analyzing the views and motives of victims, perpetrators, and bystanders in race riots cannot easily be utilized on historical subjects. Nevertheless, Bergmann shows the need to treat the pogrom as a separate subcategory of collective violence, differentiated sufficiently from the race riot, other forms of social protest violence, and general ethnic conflicts in order to make this a legitimate project. He extracts several techniques from the modern study of these phenomena and applies them to the pogrom, showing that much can be learned from the types of questions being asked about current events, even if the evidence to answer them is lacking for the historical cases. Particularly suggestive in this regard are his sketch of pogrom dynamics, the description of a "pogrom atmosphere," and analysis of the factors that contribute to an escalation of violence. The six occurrences discussed here conform to this general scheme, and the theoretical framework itself may well facilitate further historical analysis.

Historians, of course, have developed their own interpretive models, which in some respects are more suitable for the kinds of questions they ask. But as Christhard Hoffmann's analysis of the Neustettin riots demonstrates, Bergmann's sociological insights can also inform historical studies. Hoffmann posits three crucial factors present to some degree in all the instances of anti-Jewish violence: social-economic distress associated with Jews, organized antisemitic agitation, and the opaque attitude of the official forces of order. All the contributors acknowledge these elements, but their interplay and importance vary widely in the accounts of the individual pogroms. This has been so since the "invention" of our subject by the two notable scholars Eleonore Sterling and Jacob Katz, already discussed at several points in this volume. So significant is their influence, so important is it for those who work in the field to come to terms with the two approaches represented by these two, that perhaps some further comments are in order.

Sterling, born Elli Oppenheimer in Heidelberg (1925), came to America in 1938. She began studying the anti-Jewish excesses of 1819 even before her return to Germany in 1953. Her Frankfurt doctoral dissertation eventually appeared in 1956 as the pathbreaking book *Er ist wie du.* She died in 1968. These biographical details, especially Sterling's return to the land where her parents perished, may help explain her central conception concerning anti-Jewish violence in the *Vormärz:* that it was first and foremost "displaced social protest," almost fortuitously worked out on the bodies and property of Jews.[4] Writing in the 1950s and trying to salvage her identification with *Deutschtum,* she may have drawn needed solace from the idea that Jew-hatred was not authentically characteristic of the *Volk* but was, rather, the handiwork of Nazi fanatics and their predecessors in demagogy who had manipulated desperate Germans into violence and ultimate disaster. Sterling exemplified the mainstream German Jewish experience, one committed to a dignified assimilation to the positive values of German history and culture. She resisted the temptation to condemn the *Volk* and therefore had to find less harsh explanations for its periodic descent into violence. The original title of the book conveys a little of the wistfulness, the pathos, of this outlook: *Er ist wie du*—"He is like you." The *you* is pointedly in the familiar, the form used with children, menials, and the lower classes. Her mission was to express a truth simple enough to be grasped by ordinary people left to their own experiences and impressions.

Others find the Sterling thesis appealing for far different reasons. "Antisemitism as a symptom of crisis" is still an accepted tool of explanation among students of the phenomenon. In most cases the perpetrators of violence were hard-pressed peasants, small-scale merchants, and artisans, social groupings that can almost always be portrayed as "in crisis" in the nineteenth and twentieth centuries. Sterling, to be fair, talks about the role of anti-Jewish prejudice in producing the disturbances, although she dismisses it as a primary cause of the outbursts and confines her attention to the views of educated demagogues.[5] But for many who accept the explana-

---

4. Sterling's conceptualization of anti-Jewish violence as displaced social protest is most clearly advanced in "Anti-Jewish Riots in Germany in 1819: A Displacement of Social Protest," *Historia Judaica* 12 (October 1950): 105–42. It also molds her larger study of the *Vormärz.* See Eleonore Sterling, *Er ist wie du: Aus der Frühgeschichte des Antisemitismus in Deutschland, 1815–1850* (Munich, 1956), and the second posthumous edition, published under the title *Judenhaß* (Frankfurt, 1969).

5. The most dangerous enemies of the Jews came from the educated rather than from the uneducated classes, from urban populations rather than from the superstitious peasantry, she claimed. See Sterling, "Anti-Jewish Riots," 107.

tory power of the *soziale Krisenmodelle,* it is not altogether mandatory to confront the prejudices of the perpetrators, or even their ability to act politically. They were, after all, buffeted by socioeconomic and structural forces far beyond their ken. They may have lashed out mindlessly at Jews as traditional and defenseless enemies, but the "real" target was society, the economy, state power, or some other faceless abstraction. One example of this argument has it that in 1819, and again in 1848, the peasant violence directed at Jews in Westphalia was only latently antisemitic, that it must in reality be understood as part of a war against the vestiges of the feudal order.[6]

Jacob Katz (1905–98) countered this line of argumentation, first in a Hebrew-language essay of 1973, then trenchantly in two English works.[7] Katz wrote out of a personal history quite different than Sterling's. A Hungarian rather than a German, he was also a Zionist. Two years after taking his Frankfurt doctorate in 1934, he emigrated to Palestine. As a Zionist, he found it far less difficult than Sterling to acknowledge that there was a reality-based "Jewish problem," that it was not purely the creation of clever demagogues. Obviously no antisemite, he was, of course, unwilling to concede that Jews bore unilateral responsibility for the Jewish question or that it had anything to do with the bogus concept of "race." The trouble with Sterling's interpretation was that it attempted to sever antisemitism from its connection with the Jewish people. Regarding the Hep Hep riots of 1819, Katz insisted that the source of the violence was real Jewish-Gentile antagonisms, that Jews were the conscious, deliberate target of mob action, not merely the convenient lightning rod for some larger crisis.[8] He warned against disconnecting Jews from the history of antisemitism and condemned just as strongly another important error implicit in Sterling's writing: it simply would not do to divorce ordinary Germans from responsibility for antisemitism.

---

6. Among the foremost proponents of this school of interpretation are Arno Herzig, *Unterschichtenprotest in Deutschland, 1790–1870* (Göttingen, 1988), 60ff; and Moshe Zimmermann, "Antijüdischer Sozialprotest? Proteste von Unter- und Mittelschichten, 1819–1835," in *Arbeiter in Hamburg: Unterschichten, Arbeiter und Arbeiterbewegung seit dem ausgehenden 18. Jahrhundert,* edited by Arno Herzig, Dieter Langewiesche, and Arnold Sywottek (Hamburg, 1983), 89–94. For a succinct discussion of the Sterling approach, see Stefan Rohrbacher, *Gewalt im Biedermeier: Antijüdische Ausschreitungen in Vormärz und Revolution, 1815–1848/49* (Frankfurt/Main, 1993), 23–27.

7. Jacob Katz, "The Hep-Hep Riots in Germany of 1819: The Historical Background," *Zion* 38 (1973): 62–115, in Hebrew with English summary; *From Prejudice to Destruction: Anti-semitism, 1700–1933* (Cambridge, Mass., 1980), 92–104; "Misreadings of Anti-semitism," *Commentary* 76 (July 1983): 39–44.

8. Another who makes this argument forcefully is Alex Bein, *Die Judenfrage: Biographie eines Weltproblem,* 2 vols. (Stuttgart, 1980), 2:159–60.

The antithesis of the two views is all but absolute. While Sterling considers the role of anti-Jewish ideology in provoking the outbreaks, and Katz urges that attention to economic and social conditions is necessary for an understanding of the virulence of the "antisemitic bacillus,"[9] there is no easy way to reconcile their viewpoints. For resolution cannot hinge on whether one puts more or less weight on the ideological versus the socioeconomic causes of anti-Jewish violence, however clearly the two motives might be present in any historical instance. It is, after all, nearly impossible to disentangle the economic from the ideological motives of those who attacked Jews. During the First Crusade and sporadically throughout the Middle Ages, Jews were murdered because they were "pagans in our midst." Yet in several locales, massacres took place as records of indebtedness to Jewish moneylenders were being purposefully destroyed. This sort of behavior, evincing the same mix of crass material and broadly ideological motives, can still be seen operating among ordinary participants in the November pogrom of 1938, as described by Wolfgang Benz.

Opinions on the centrality of socioeconomic factors may vary; they certainly do so in this anthology. For example, Stefan Rohrbacher does not see economic distress as a proximate cause of the riots of 1819; the post-Napoleonic disruptions in commerce and industry seemed no worse in 1819 than in the years immediately preceding or following. Benz adduces no obvious economic motivations for the November pogrom of 1938, aside from the lust after plunder evidenced by some of the rioters. But the other essayists all attribute some degree of influence to economic factors. Despite the variations in approach and the highly nuanced interpretations to be found here, there is little difference of opinion on one crucial question that divided Katz and Sterling. In all the examples studied here, Jews are seen to have been the "real" targets of violence. Katz, it would seem, has displaced Sterling.

Antithetical though they may be, the two explanatory models can each contribute to our understanding of anti-Jewish violence, although neither is completely satisfactory. Sterling cannot convincingly explain the leading role of university students in several places throughout the period under consideration. Nor is she able to account for the frequently commented upon presence of "better elements" of society amid the usual urban riffraff. Moreover, the close coupling in the *Vormärz* of debates on Jewish emancipation with acts of collective violence aimed specifically at preventing legal equality for Jews surely supports Katz's views. The struggles for emancipation may have had economic ramifications, but they

---

9. Katz, "Misreadings of Anti-semitism," 43.

occurred, at least in some places, where economic conditions fell far short of "crisis." On the other hand, Katz's emphasis on historical *Judenfeind-schaft,* awakened when it looked as though Jews were poised to move beyond well-defined traditional limits, is not particularly illuminating for some cases of rioting, especially when they do not correlate with a concurrent emancipation debate. Sterling may be more helpful in explaining why violence against Jews frequently spilled over into attacks on the representatives of state power or the social hierarchy or on Christian "persecutors," as in several of the outbreaks in Hamburg in the 1830s, in Konitz and West Prussia around 1900, and during the Berlin pogrom of 1923.

The widespread disturbances in Baden and neighboring Alsace in 1848 argue in favor of keeping all interpretive options open. Jews in both areas worked primarily as middlemen for the largely agricultural population. Bad harvests in the two preceding years, news of the revolutionary events in Paris, and the perceived threat of rising Jewish influence touched off the violence. But in Alsace a number of Catholic priests took the lead, rousing hatred with a particular religious edge to it. Synagogues became the target of choice, following the familiar practice of the region's long tradition of *Judenfeindschaft.* In Baden, on the other hand, neither Catholic nor Protestant clergymen were visible in the popular movement against Jews. Although, as Manfred Gailus mentions, religious justifications appeared after the fact of violence in North Baden, Jews seem to have been attacked primarily as economic oppressors, only secondarily because they were the historic outsiders. Here, and in neighboring Hesse, attacks on the local landowning nobility and non-Jewish exploiters also took place.[10]

An attempt has been made in these essays to move beyond the creative lead provided by Katz and Sterling. Each case is unique; each must be understood on its own terms. Important lessons and valid comparisons should come after such investigations, not in anticipation of them. Certainly, the authors in this anthology attempt to do what the historian is supposed to do. Resisting preconceptions and with no particular theory to vindicate, they investigate the specific episode of collective violence, tell the story, put events in a larger historical context, and then step back to contemplate the meaning of this history. Microhistory, as represented

---

10. See Michael Anthony Riff, "The Anti-Jewish Aspect of the Revolutionary Unrest of 1848 in Baden and Its Impact on Emancipation," *Leo Baeck Institute Year Book* 21 (1976): 21–41. Neither explanatory model places sufficient weight on the extortionate character of many of the pogroms in the Rhineland during this period. See Jonathan Sperber, *Rhineland Radicals: The Democratic Movement and the Revolution of 1848–1849* (Princeton, 1991), 166–67.

here, has the additional advantage of being able to highlight process, giving definition to the complexities so often blurred in larger historical canvases.

Such an approach, combining minute investigation of individual cases with an expanded historical scope, raises questions that may never have occurred to Katz or Sterling, neither of whom pursued the subject of popular anti-Jewish violence out of the *Vormärz* into the *Kaiserreich,* Weimar, and the Third Reich. With a longer view of the subject, the introductory essay to this collection supplies as a necessary organizing principle the three-phase scheme—emancipation, modern antisemitism, state antisemitism. The individual studies suggest, I think, a dramatic break between the first two—the modern and premodern occurrences of anti-Jewish violence—that deserves some further comment.

When viewing the discrete occurrences of anti-Jewish violence serially, their changing political nature becomes evident. Prior to the achievement of legal equality for Jews nationally in 1869–71, the most common political aim to be found in the rioting was the prevention of Jewish emancipation, or any constructive movement in that direction. Rohrbacher's depiction of events in Würzburg in 1819 rejects the notion that the rioters were acting out some dimly recollected and age-old pageant of Jew-hatred. Picking their targets well, and interpreting signals from state authorities and social superiors to convince themselves that they acted on behalf of the majority, they sought to prevent Jews from crossing boundaries that had kept them in an inferior position. The ideology of Jew-hatred undoubtedly encouraged them to transgress the law, but even at the grass roots, the defense of concrete social and economic self-interests is not difficult to discern. Whenever state governments threatened to grant legal equality to Jews in the *Vormärz,* craftsmen and shopkeepers could be depended on to object, sometimes forcefully. Coercing peasant communes to accept Jews as equals with the all-important rights of residence meant the imposition of new tax burdens and legal liabilities. This led frequently to violence, not merely to demonstrate "symbolic" rage, but to accomplish political ends.

The successes of pre-emancipation violence were striking and, one suspects, noticed by the rioters themselves and by others in a position to derive benefits from continued repression of Jews. The riots of 1819 effectively tabled debate on Jewish emancipation in Bavaria until 1848; the subsequent, largely nonviolent anti-emancipation petition drive of 1850 postponed it for another decade. The Hep Hep riots in Hamburg and renewed outbreaks of violence in 1830 and 1835 gave the patrician *Senat* exactly the pretext it wanted to withhold emancipation (until 1849). Violence in

Baden in the 1830s delayed Jewish equality until the 1860s.[11] Physical assault on Jews, or even the threat of it, was a strategy that worked time after time, at least to achieve limited aims. After emancipation, however, the political rewards for violence grew less certain. Indeed, only in Bergmann's sense of violence being used as an attempt to stave off further change in the power relations between groups can the later rioters be seen as conscious political agents. Others stood ready to steer their agency in a political direction, but I, unlike several contributors here, fail to see the same degree of political consciousness among the actual perpetrators of violence as in the pre-1848 events. As a political strategy, collective violence from 1881 onward could no longer be seen as ensuring success.

Two other developments in the nature of collective violence separate the episodes of 1819, the 1830s, and the Revolution of 1848 from what came later. In Neustettin and Konitz, the pogroms bring to mind the media events of our own era; this is difficult to detect in the pogroms of 1848 and before.[12] Christhard Hoffmann and Helmut Walser Smith underline the pivotal role of the newspaper. Journalists, especially antisemitic journalists, gave legitimacy to rumor and authenticated the darkest suspicions of ordinary people. "Evidence" was not merely reported but at times fabricated. Pacification became more difficult because of the inflammatory role of the local press, its capacity to define importance, its unwillingness to let the story die, and its power to gratify the quintessentially modern desire to get one's name in the papers, or, in these cases, to participate anonymously and then read about it the next day. Newspapers and newspapermen became actors in the violent outbreaks.

Another modern development is more significant. Prior to the Hep Hep riots of 1819 and through the 1820s and 1830s, individuals had written and agitated against Jews and Jewish emancipation. In some cases they may have even directly inspired mob action. But they acted in virtual isolation from one another and were motivated by a great variety of interests. Gailus argues that 1848 marks a change in this pattern, that it is the moment at which traditional anti-Jewish feelings, economic protests, and

---

11. Rohrbacher, *Gewalt im Biedermeier,* 154–55, 164; Moshe Zimmermann, *Hamburgischer Patriotismus und deutscher Nationalismus: Die Emanzipation der Juden in Hamburg, 1830–1865* (Hamburg, 1979), 46–100. Frank Felsenstein, *Anti-semitic Stereotypes: A Paradigm of Otherness in English Popular Culture, 1660–1830* (Baltimore, 1995), 187ff., provides an interesting English parallel to the political effectiveness of popularly based Jew-hatred, even in the absence of violence, on the passage and then hasty repeal of the Naturalization Bill of 1753 (the Jew Bill).

12. However, James F. Harris, *The People Speak! Anti-semitism and Emancipation in Nineteenth-Century Bavaria* (Ann Arbor, 1994), 87ff., does grant a leading role to the conservative-Catholic press in the Bavarian anti-emancipation petition drive and assesses this as one of its most modern elements.

anxieties about the future began to be absorbed by Christian-conservative political movements. This may well have diminished the pressure to attack Jews physically as a form of "self-help," because now, "at last, something was finally being done" about them. Certainly, the clusters of pogroms that occurred in 1819 and 1848 do not recur in anything like the same scale as in the later period. But if the adoption of Jew-hatred by socially prestigious circles reduced the perceived "need for violence," it quickly generated conditions that were ultimately more menacing. The Jewish question, debated and discussed in parliaments, pamphlets, and press, penetrated more fully into the German public sphere, becoming a thoroughly legitimate concern of politics.[13]

In the later outbursts of violence, antisemitic political activists were always present. In some cases they may have helped organize the tumults; in others they showed up soon afterward to goad the mob to further action. From Neustettin onward, a nationally organized antisemitic movement with networks of activists, publicists, and roving agitators—no longer solely Christian-conservatives but with a large contingent of lower-middle-class *völkisch* racists—sought to extract every available shred of propaganda value from the occasional anti-Jewish riots. They took local occurrences with complex local causes and transformed them into national happenings of world-historical importance. They gave national publicity to these events and integrated them into their own more grandiose—although not yet widely shared—conceptions of the Jewish peril. The locus of political agency thereby shifted from the mob to those in pursuit of a larger political program.

Most of the contributors to this anthology ascribe great importance to antisemitism in either the fomenting or the unfolding of anti-Jewish riots and see it as a long-range cause as well as an immediate precondition. This may seem like belaboring the obvious. But if antisemitism is conceived of as a coherent ideology and a political movement with its own

---

13. Harris, *The People Speak!* 209–31, would like to push the origins of organized political antisemitism back from the conventional date of 1879 to the aftermath of the Revolution of 1848. He argues persuasively on the basis of a well-organized and successful petition drive against Jewish emancipation in Bavaria that sported many of the mobilizing techniques of the later antisemitic political parties. However, I still think it makes more sense to see the Bavarian events as part of a general period of experimentation for political antisemitism that stretched from 1848 to 1879, years in which various techniques were explored and old and new animosities given trial runs, but before a conscious and multiple-issue agenda was in place. The discontinuous and defensive nature of the Bavarian initiative is what really separates it from later developments. It spawned no lasting institutions—no parties, journals, newspapers, or grassroots clubs devoted to fighting Jewish power, all features of the post-1879 era. Its conception of Jewish evil, the fantasies of Jewry's world power, stood at an early stage of development.

agenda—not merely inherited popular prejudices about Jews—then the matter is not obvious at all, and the precise role of antisemitic *ideology* in the violence becomes problematical. Was it causal or a casual accompaniment? Were antisemites present at pogroms to lead or to learn? Their mere presence ought not decide the issue. Strong feelings about the Jewish question were engendered by the emancipation debates from the late eighteenth century. By 1880 antisemitism was becoming a familiar part of German political culture, and by the 1920s it was ubiquitous and intense. It is not surprising, therefore, to find it associated with violent acts of pillage and vandalism. Yet antisemitic discourse was present in many places where violence never eventuated.

Thomas Scheuring's rhetoric may have moved Würzburgers toward action in 1819; Ernst Henrici's presence in Neustettin before the pogroms and Bismarck's flirtation with the Berlin Movement possibly helped to unleash them; Wilhelm Bruhn may have been more than a spectator in Konitz; and nameless *völkisch* agitators perhaps stirred up the unemployed workers of Berlin in 1923.[14] But it is equally possible that antisemitic activists did no more than play a passive supporting role in the pogroms. Their simple presence may have been a signal to the mob that its social superiors, "educated men" from the big city, sanctioned violent desires. It is hard to believe, however, that agitators planted the seed of Jew-hatred in a populace unfamiliar with that particular plant. As several of the essays show, there is abundant evidence that the rioters could recognize their own interests and were not simply putty in the hands of clever demagogues. The evidence of the professional antisemites' direct influence is almost always circumstantial, admitting of no simple interpretation. Perhaps a more cautious conclusion may be in order: antisemitism and mob violence had a reciprocal relationship. Conceivably, pogroms may have been inspired by antisemites, but antisemites were inspired by them as well.

On the use of violence as a solution to the Jewish question, individual Jew-haters and organized antisemites were at once cautious and calculating. They were ever ready to use any sign of "the wrath of the people" to educate the nation and hector the authorities. Thus, they would insist that popular explosions made it a matter of utmost urgency for the parliament to take immediate action to disenfranchise the Jews and for the government to step in to emancipate the German people from them. Otherwise, they prophesied, violence would surely escalate. This sort of finger-wag-

---

14. These "outside agitators," invoked by the press to explain some unpalatable truths, may well have been imaginary, as they usually are; they seem to have left no traces in police or judicial records as thoroughly evaluated by Dirk Walter, *Antisemitische Kriminalität und Gewalt: Judenfeindschaft in der Weimarer Republik* (Bonn, 1999), esp. 152.

ging political blackmail was common, but it constituted exploitation of a situation, rather than a programmatic invocation of violence by the antisemites.[15] At least until the closing stages of World War I, active promotion of violence such as that by Wilhelm Bruhn in Konitz was atypical of the party-political antisemites. Whatever their inmost desires, they were far too solicitous of their own and their cause's good repute to advocate blatant lawbreaking or to suggest that state functionaries were no better than tools of the Jewish world conspiracy, a libel that quite often resulted in a costly conviction on the charge of "defamation of the entire civil service." This sort of radical, even revolutionary posturing was rare, but not unknown, during the *Kaiserreich.* Bruhn, one of the few to indulge in it and not be expelled from the mainstream antisemitic parties, was nonetheless regarded as a maverick by his fellow antisemites, especially in light of his extremism during the Konitz riots.[16]

Throughout the nineteenth century, German antisemites occasionally clamored for murder, made pointed allusions to the need for a new St. Bartholomew's Night, or spun out other violent fantasies in speech or print. Even though the actual violence never reached the ghastly levels of our century, the threatening letters that often accompanied the riots of 1819 and 1848 were filled with bloodlust and homicidal threats.[17] After

---

15. An early example can be found in Jakob Fries (1773–1843), a student of Fichte's and a leading figure in the *Burschenschaften:* "This scandal [Jewish commercial exploitation] will not come to an end without dreadful acts of violence if our government does not halt the evil quickly." Quoted in Paul Rose, *Revolutionary Antisemitism in Germany from Kant to Wagner* (Princeton, 1990), 125–30. Similar threats in the Antisemites' Petition of 1881 and the writings of Wilhelm Marr can be found in Richard S. Levy, ed., *Antisemitism in the Modern World: An Anthology of Texts* (Lexington, Mass., 1991), 76–93, 125–27.

16. Bruhn (b. 1869), like many of his colleagues in the movement, began as a schoolteacher and went on to a career in publishing shabby newspapers. He succeeded Hermann Ahlwardt, another schoolteacher and the rowdiest antisemite of the era, as a member of the Reichstag for Arnswalde in 1903. Like Ahlwardt, he managed to make antisemitism and its collateral activities into a (poorly) paying career. He narrowly avoided conviction for blackmail; one of his close associates was found guilty of murder. Particularly damaging to the good name of antisemitism was his manipulation of mad Count Pückler, who acted out bloody charades in which Jews fell before his threshing flail and who in the 1907 Reichstag election promised every German man a sword with which to cleanse the streets of Berlin. Bruhn repeatedly scandalized fellow antisemites, who disavowed any connection to him, but in fact he represented a radical new tendency in antisemitic politics that would come to full flower in the Weimar era. On the revolutionary implications of his Konitz exploits and evidence of other new departures in antisemitic political agitation, see Richard S. Levy, *The Downfall of the Anti-Semitic Political Parties in Imperial Germany* (New Haven, 1975), 206–8.

17. For a discussion of imagined acts of violence against Jews, see Rainer Erb and Werner Bergmann, *Die Nachtseite der Judenemanzipation: Der Widerstand gegen die Integration der Juden in Deutschland, 1780–1860* (Berlin, 1989), 174–216. For the reality they became in the 1920s, see Walter, *Antisemitische Kriminalität,* passim.

midcentury, open calls for the use of force abated; they were far more prevalent in France, Austria, and Russia. But even when presented in the form of "jokes" or heavy-handed satire, they presumably bespoke an enduring readiness for violence, certainly an unwillingness to ban it from politics altogether. For example, neither Wilhelm Marr nor Court Chaplain Stoecker could bring themselves to wholly denounce the bloody pogroms in Russia in 1881. Then there was Eugen Dühring, who worried aloud that "enlighteners" and "do-gooders" were successfully alienating the *Volk* from its instinctive and oftentimes violent hatred of Jewry. For Hitler, one of the few virtues to be accorded the German masses was their religious-like enthusiasm and willingness to shed blood for "ideal causes," among which he surely included antisemitism.[18] The violent proclivities of some of the *Volk,* generalized to embrace the totality, instilled confidence in the antisemites, who happily found their own enmities reflected in those of the people.

Comforting though it was to have their prejudices "democratically" confirmed, several important antisemites and others openly hostile to Jews nonetheless spoke out against violence as the solution to the Jewish question. Heinrich von Treitschke, Stoecker, Marr, and many others solemnly warned against recourse to physical violence against Jews.[19] Adolf Hitler's first writing on the Jewish question decried the mob's proneness to the sort of emotional Jew-hatred that led *only* to pogroms, the very opposite of the calm, disciplined, informed antisemitism that he saw himself espousing.[20]

The rejection of the pogrom was in almost all cases tactical rather than moral. There was nothing intrinsically wrong with physical force being applied to Jews. It simply did not work as a solution to the Jewish problem. Its limited successes in delaying emancipation had been ultimately reversed by the scheming Jews and their allies. Antisemites were certain that the attainment of emancipation had altered the power rela-

---

18. Dr. E[ugen] Dühring, *Die Judenfrage als Racen-, Sitten- und Culturfrage: Mit einer weltgeschichtlichen Antwort* (Karlsruhe, 1881), 1–2, 11–12; Adolf Hitler, *Mein Kampf,* translated by Ralph Manheim (Boston, 1943), 101–6. On Stoecker, see Donald L. Niewyk, "Solving the 'Jewish Problem': Continuity and Change in German Antisemitism, 1871–1945," *Leo Baeck Institute Year Book* 35 (1990): 343.

19. See Levy, *Antisemitism in the Modern World,* pt. 2; see also Wilhelm Marr, *Wählet keinen Juden! Der Weg zum Sieg des Germanenthums über das Judenthum: Ein Mahnwort an die Wähler nichtjüdischen Stammes aller Confessionen,* 2d ed. (Berlin, 1879), 43, 49. Their admonitions were so frequent in the early days of the Berlin Movement that one suspects that several acts of violence—below the threshold of a pogrom—may not have made it into the historical record.

20. See Eberhard Jäckel, ed., *Hitler: Sämtliche Aufzeichnungen, 1905–1924* (Stuttgart, 1980), 88–90 (the Gemlich Letter). This train of thought also forms a leitmotif in the "grundlegende Rede" of August 13, 1920, 184–204.

tionship in favor of the Jews. Violence alone could not now solve a problem that had become larger and more menacing than in the good old days. "A cultural and historical phenomenon like this is no soap-bubble to be popped with a cheap 'Hep-Hep!' This people is a demonic phenomenon," wrote Marr.[21] He was referring to the enormous and ill-gotten power that he and other antisemites imagined Jews to have obtained. Such power in the hands of so crafty an enemy could not possibly be undone with a simple riot or two.

Marr, Hitler, and many others who came to place antisemitism at the center of their worldview were absolutely certain that what was most needed to solve the Jewish question were virtues almost never found in the common clay of German society: stamina, discipline, rational understanding of the evil. After an outburst of popular fury, ordinary Germans were too willing to forget and slide back into comfortable habits, such as shopping at Jewish department stores or reading the "Jewish" press. Meanwhile, the enemy recouped and became even stronger. The *Volk* may have possessed the right anti-Jewish instincts and useful violent propensities, but it needed leadership, correct theory, and education in the "science" of antisemitism in order to finally solve the Jewish question. The "answer" to the *ineffectual* pogrom provided by political antisemitism focused on the hard work of overturning emancipation, a long-term goal that could not be achieved by mob action and might actually work against it.

Two final and related questions: What role did public memory play in the successive episodes of collective violence? What lessons did they teach, and who learned or failed to learn them? Repeated targeting of synagogues—even when the alleged offenses of the Jews had more to do with economics than religion—suggests to some historians the strength of medieval memories. So, too, the cry of "Hep Hep!" as the signal for the pogrom. But even as early as 1819, there is much to suggest that these characteristics of collective violence were consciously introduced by educated participants. Anti-Jewish university students, in many locales the leaders of the mob, offered erudite derivations for the catchy phrase "Hep Hep!" It supposedly stood for "Hieroselyma Est Perdita," recalling the destruction of Jerusalem by Titus in 70 A.D. Others have suggested that it was simply an abbreviation of the German word for Hebrew (*Hebräer*). Nazi Storm Troopers revived its usage during the 1920s in an attempt to create the aura of a truly *völkisch* and popular action against Jews. It is far from clear that these typical features actually emanated from the wellsprings of folk memory.

Less dismissible as evidence of historical memory at work is the geo-

---

21. See Levy, *Antisemitism in the Modern World*, 106.

graphic location of antisemitic violence. Repeated outbreaks of anti-Jewish rioting, as well as the flourishing of antisemitic political movements, may have had something to do with a kind of oral tradition as well as immediate experience. The southwest and the northeast show a nearly unbroken receptivity to anti-Jewish movements. Hesse with the adjacent areas of Baden and the Konitz-Neustettin region supported antisemitic violence and political parties through the *Kaiserreich* and into the final phase of the Weimar Republic. Smith cites a most telling example of this continuity: the vigilantes who operated in the Konitz area and who numbered Jews among their murder victims in September 1939. It is not unfair to speculate that anti-Jewish violence, once tasted, rendered certain populations and regions unusually susceptible to repeating the experience.

Concerning lessons learned, David Clay Large argues that it was the Nazis who proved the most apt students of anti-Jewish violence and its meaning. In 1923, they followed closely the events of the Scheunenviertel, welcoming the antisemitic nature of the riots even as many others took pains to deny it. Did this episode and previous pogroms influence the most dramatic pre-Holocaust violence against Jews? As analyzed by Benz and Bergmann, the Kristallnacht appears to be in many ways the antithesis of the riots investigated in this anthology. Hoffmann's and Bergmann's crucial ingredients were indeed present, but in vastly altered circumstances. Socioeconomic motives were not evident to observers, nor were they adduced as the cause of the destruction. At best, they may have provided a rationale for those who unleashed it.[22] Prior antisemitic agitation there certainly had been, but it had become generalized and ubiquitous. The regime had not encouraged the people to go into the streets after January 30, 1933; on the other hand, it did not punish numerous individual acts of terror, usually carried out by its most zealous supporters. In the name of order and discipline, the Nazis preferred to exercise administrative and legal control over antisemitic persecution while vigorously indoctrinating the masses on the Jewish peril. In previous outbreaks, the attitude and behavior of the state may have sent uncertain signals to rioters, but with the Kristallnacht no such doubts could exist. The one-party state instigated the pogrom on November 9, 1938, and decreed its end on November 10. Other deviations from historical pogroms were also apparent that night. The controlled press became overtly menacing only a day before violence broke out. Rather than fomenting mob action, its primary function was to justify it and to situate events in the grand picture of the Jew-

---

22. This is the case argued, largely on the basis of inference, by Uwe Dietrich Adam, "Wie spontan war der Pogrom?" in *Der Judenpogrom 1938: Von der "Reichskristallnacht" zum Völkermord,* edited by Walter H. Pehle (Frankfurt/Main, 1988), 74–93.

ish world conspiracy. And, of course, the most important difference—the *Volk*, with some notable exceptions, stood aside almost everywhere.[23]

Nonetheless, "history" was unmistakably being referenced during the November pogrom. The Nazis staged their murderous drama using what they had learned from previous pogroms and included many of the salient features that have been described and analyzed here. Following the vom Rath murder, open threats appeared in the press instead of in the traditional form of the anonymous *Drohbrief*. The burning of synagogues in 1938, long after they had ceased to serve as the exclusive symbol of Jews for the greater public, was a play for historical "authenticity" and verisimilitude. The lame attempts to disguise SA men as the justly enraged *Volk*, the humiliation rituals, the looting of homes and businesses—all this was meant to legitimize the regime's faux pogrom by placing it within a historical tradition. What was missing from all this theater was the "restraint from within," alluded to in the introduction to these essays. The Nazis' unparalleled ability to erase the "taming capacities of culture" distinguished Kristallnacht from its forebears and announced a dreadful future.

Hoffmann and Gailus allude to lessons learned by another group of Germans, the less-than-neutral bystanders. Neustettin, Konitz, and the earlier rioting associated with the Revolution of 1848 allowed educated, upper-class Germans, who could rarely be found throwing rocks or torching shops, to harbor their own brand of "refined" antisemitism. That the forces of order repeatedly suppressed violence and punished the criminals simply convinced this sort of antisemite that his rejection of Jewry was of a different order, that it was a matter of lofty principle, having nothing whatever to do with looting and vandalism. The rowdy antisemites, so vulgar and mindless, encouraged "educated antisemites" to think of themselves as idealists. Smug and self-satisfied, they never felt compelled to confront the ultimately destructive consequences of their own hatreds.

The memory of the past also conditioned the understanding and the actions of those Jews and Germans who opposed antisemitism. They drew, however, the wrong conclusions. Recalling that the institutions of the state had time and again shown themselves prepared to maintain order and pro-

---

23. Once the initiative had been taken by party activists, however, popular participation in small towns and the countryside was not rare. See Wolfgang Benz, "Der Rückfall in die Barbarei," in Pehle, *Der Judenpogrom 1938*, 17–18, 36–37. In this volume, Benz strikes the right balance when he reminds us that documented displays of collective barbarism, not all of which were confined to the stalwarts of the NSDAP, ought to modify the sometimes too rosy assessments of popular noninvolvement in the Kristallnacht. See also, in this connection, postings to the electronic discussion group Geschichte und Kultur der Juden, July 17–21, 2000, at <http://www.egroups.com/messagesearch/geschichte-juden?query=Kristallnacht>.

tect citizens, they felt secure. Antisemitic violence was deeply disturbing, but as long as it seemed quarantined to the lower orders of society, as long as respectable opinion condemned such behavior, and as long as the authorities did their job, there was no compelling need to rethink defensive strategies. Most Jews, buoyed by an unmerited confidence in the future, felt no pressure to reevaluate their commitments to Germany or to question their future in the fatherland. Even as late as 1923, the Scheunenviertel pogrom left them essentially undismayed, because it targeted *Ostjuden.*

How ironic that Jews and Germans of good will who fought bravely against antisemitism were the ones to misunderstand, even trivialize, the phenomenon of anti-Jewish violence. With what to our eyes seems tragic inevitability, they would become the victims of antisemites, specifically, the Nazis, who took pogroms with deadly seriousness and read their lessons carefully.

Contributors

Wolfgang Benz, Dr. phil. (University of Munich), historian, since 1990 Professor and Head of the Center for Research on Antisemitism, Technical University of Berlin. From 1969 to 1990, staff member of the Institut für Zeitgeschichte (Institute for Contemporary History), Munich; cofounder and editor of the periodicals *Dachauer Hefte* and *Jahrbuch für Antisemitismusforschung;* coeditor of *Zeitschrift für Geschichtswissenschaft;* editor of several series; Geschwister-Scholl-Award 1992. Editor of *Die Juden in Deutschland: Leben unter nationalsozialistischer Herrschaft, 1933–1945* (Munich, 1988); and *Dimension des Völkermords: Die Zahl der jüdischen Opfer des Nationalsozialismus* (Munich, 1991). Author of *Zwischen Hitler und Adenauer: Studien zur deutschen Nachkriegsgesellschaft* (Frankfurt/Main, 1991); *The Holocaust: A German Historian Examines the Genocide* (New York, 1999); and *Geschichte des Dritten Reiches* (Munich, 2000).

Werner Bergmann, Dr. phil. (University of Hamburg, 1981), Habilitation (Free University of Berlin, 1996). Professor at the Center for Research on Antisemitism, Technical University of Berlin. Recent publications: *Antisemitismus in öffentlichen Konflikten: Kollektives Lernen in der politischen Kultur der Bundesrepublik, 1949–1989* (Frankfurt/Main, 1997); (with Rainer Erb) *Antisemitism in Germany: The Post-Nazi Epoch since 1945* (New Brunswick, N.J., 1997); (coeditor) *Antisemitism and Xenophobia in United Germany* (New York, 1997); "Collective Violence as Social Control: Right-Wing Youth in Germany," in *Cross-Cultural Perspectives on Youth and Violence,* edited by Meredith Watts (Stamford, Conn., 1998), 99–115; (with Rainer Erb) "Antisemitismus in der Bundesrepublik Deutschland, 1996," in *Deutsche und Ausländer: Freunde, Fremde oder Feinde? Empirische Befunde und theoretische Erklärungen,* edited by Richard Alba et al. (Opladen, 2000), 401–38.

Manfred Gailus, Dr. phil. habil. (Technical University of Berlin), historian. Privatdozent at the Technical University of Berlin. Major publications: *Straße und Brot: Sozialer Protest in den deutschen Staaten unter besonderer Berücksichtigung Preußens, 1847–1849* (Göttingen, 1990); (coeditor) *Der Kampf um das tägliche Brot: Nahrungsmangel, Versorgungspolitik und Protest, 1770–1990* (Opladen, 1994); "Food Riots in Germany in the late 1840s," *Past and Present* 145 (1994): 157–93; *Protestantismus und Nationalsozialismus. Studien zur nationalsozialistischen des protestantischen sozialmilieu* (Cologne, 2001).

Christhard Hoffmann, Dr. phil. (Technical University of Berlin, 1986); 1994–98, DAAD Visiting Professor at University of California, Berkeley; since 1998, Associate Professor of Modern European History at the University of Bergen (Norway). Publications: *Juden und Judentum im Werk deutscher Althistoriker des 19. und 20. Jahrhunderts* (Leiden, 1988); "Between Integration and Rejection: The Jewish Community in Germany, 1914–1918," in *State, Society, and Mobilisation in Europe during the First World War,* edited by John Horne, 89–104 (Cambridge, 1997); "Verfolgung und Alltagsleben der Landjuden im nationalsozialistischen Deutschland," in *Jüdisches Leben auf dem Lande: Studien zur deutsch-jüdischen Geschichte,* edited by Monika Richarz and Reinhard Rürup, 373–98 (Tübingen, 1997).

David Clay Large, Ph.D. (University of California, Berkeley); Professor of History, Montana State University, Bozeman. Recent major publications: *Germans to the Front: West German Rearmament in the Adenauer Era* (Chapel Hill, 1996); *Where Ghosts Walked: Munich's Road to the Third Reich* (New York, 1997); *Hitlers München* [German edition of *Where Ghosts Walked*] (Munich, 1998); *Germany's Metropolis: A History of Modern Berlin* (New York, 1999).

Richard S. Levy, Ph.D. (Yale University, 1969); Associate Professor of Modern History, University of Illinois at Chicago. Major publications: *The Downfall of the Anti-semitic Political Parties in Imperial Germany* (New Haven, 1975); *Antisemitism in the Modern World: Anthology of Texts* (Lexington, Mass., 1990); Binjamin Segel, *A Lie and a Libel: The History of the Protocols of the Elders of Zion,* translated and edited by Richard S. Levy (Lincoln, Neb., 1995).

Stefan Rohrbacher, Dr. phil. (Technical University of Berlin, 1988); Professor of Jewish Studies at the University of Duisburg. Major publications: *Juden in Neuss* (Neuss, 1986); (with Michael Schmidt) *Judenbilder: Eine Kulturgeschichte antijüdischer Mythen und antisemitischer Vorurteile* (Reinbek, 1991); *Gewalt im Biedermeier: Antijüdische Ausschreitungen in*

Vormärz und Revolution, 1815–1848/49 (Frankfurt/Main, 1993); "Die Drei Gemeinden Altona, Hamburg, Wandsbek zur Zeit der Glikl," *Aschkenas* 8 (1998): 105–24; (coeditor) *Die Wissenschaft vom Judentum: Annäherungen nach dem Holocaust* (Göttingen, 2000).

Helmut Walser Smith, Ph.D. (Yale University, 1992); Associate Professor of History, Vanderbilt University. Major publications: *German Nationalism and Religious Conflict: Culture, Ideology, Politics, 1870–1914* (Princeton, 1995); ed., *Protestants, Catholics and Jews in Germany 1800–1914* (Oxford, 2001); *The Butcher's Tale: Murder and Anti-Semitism in a German Town* (New York, 2002).

Index

Social History, Popular Culture, and Politics in Germany

Geoff Eley, Series Editor